Critical Essays on

ALEXANDER POPE

CRITICAL ESSAYS
ON
BRITISH LITERATURE

Zack Bowen, General Editor
University of Miami

Critical Essays on

ALEXANDER POPE

Edited by

WALLACE JACKSON

and

R. PAUL YODER

G. K. Hall & Co. / New York
Maxwell Macmillan Canada / Toronto
Maxwell Macmillan International / New York Oxford Singapore Sydney

G. K. Hall & Company
Macmillan Publishing Company
866 Third Avenue
New York, New York 10022

Maxwell Macmillan Canada, Inc.
1200 Eglinton Avenue East
Suite 200
Don Mills, Ontario M3C 3N1

Library of Congress Cataloging-in-Publication Data

Critical essays on Alexander Pope / edited by Wallace Jackson and R. Paul Yoder.
    p.   cm.—(Critical essays on British literature)
    Includes bibliographical references and index.
    ISBN 0-8161-8862-9
    1. Pope, Alexander, 1688–1744—Criticism and interpretation.
I. Jackson, Wallace, 1930– . II. Yoder, R. Paul. III. Series.
PR3634.C75   1993
821'.5—dc20   93-7761
                                             CIP

10   9   8   7   6   5   4   3   2   1

Printed in the United States of America

Contents

♦

ESSAYS

General Editor's Note

◆

The Critical Essays on British Literature series provides a variety of approaches to both classical and contemporary writers of Britain and Ireland. The formats of the volumes in the series vary with the thematic designs of individual editors, and with the amount and nature of existing reviews and criticism, augmented where appropriate by original essays by recognized authorities. It is hoped that each volume will be unique in developing a new overall perspective on its particular subject.

Jackson and Yoder have confined their selection of essays to those from the last twenty years and particularly those since 1980. The essays are general in nature rather than confining themselves to a specific work, in an attempt to place Pope in the broader perspective of representing the whole person, as opposed to earlier criticism that depicted him as a skilled craftsman and a poet of eminent good sense. What emerges is a dominant contemporary critical strain that sees Pope as a divided self resisting his own ideologies by perceptions "he cannot help but encode within his poems," an ambiguous writer who defies definition even as he represents an age.

ZACK BOWEN

University of Miami

Publisher's Note

◆

Producing a volume that contains both newly commissioned and reprinted material presents the publisher with the challenge of balancing the desire to achieve stylistic consistency with the need to preserve the integrity of works first published elsewhere. In the Critical Essays series, essays commissioned especially for a particular volume are edited to be consistent with G. K. Hall's house style; reprinted essays appear in the style in which they were first published, with only typographical errors corrected. Consequently, shifts in style from one essay to another are the result of our efforts to be faithful to each text as it was originally published.

Introduction

◆

WALLACE JACKSON

In preparing this volume we were guided by several interests. First, we decided to select essays that would not only provide the reader with some indication of the current contexts of Pope criticism, but also offer insight into the range, scope, and dimensions of Pope's imagination, providing as far as possible the outlines of a writing life. We tended, therefore, to exclude analyses of particular works, though obviously general concerns might be illustrated by inquiries into individual poems. Second, we wanted essays published recently, that is, mainly since 1980, because we felt that the best studies published before 1980 have already been assimilated into more-recent works or have been reprinted in other essay collections. Third, we had no desire to attempt to chart the history of Pope scholarship in the twentieth century, nor did we wish to provide seminal essays in Pope studies, for this would inevitably have violated more than one of our guiding principles.

The history of Pope scholarship has been dominated by one event: Pope's assignment by Joseph Warton to a place "next to Milton, and just above Dryden," with the chilling claim that "the largest portion of [his work] is of the didactic, moral and satyric kind; and consequently, not of the most poetic species of poetry: whence it is manifest that good sense and judgement were his characteristical excellencies, rather than fancy and invention." To write poetry that is not very poetic can never be construed favorably, and "didactic" and "moral" are at best ambivalent poetic virtues. Pope was also, according to Warton, "correct" and "exact"; he polished with "care and assiduity. Whatever poetical enthusiasm he actually possessed, he withheld and stifled."[1] Warton's summary appraisal does everything possible to make us forget that he assigns Pope a place just below Milton. But in its entirety it is an estimation from which Pope's admirers have ever since sought to rescue him, with uncertain and ambiguous results. David Morris, one of Pope's most recent critics, concisely states the modern case: "For Pope the challenge of the new age was to create a language in which good sense could at last find a poetic voice without allowing the infusion of sense to rob poetry of its ancient alliance with the mysteries of inspired genius."[2]

The second part of Morris's remark has proven troubling to readers who commonly find the *Essay on Man* bloodless and *The Dunciad* impenetrable. Many readers will remember fondly *The Rape of the Lock* and *Eloisa to Abelard*, but forget that these works are the product of a young poet and not to be numbered among his most ambitious poems. Even these poems, however, have little in common; each is about a woman, but these women are substantially different from each other, and differently invested in their passions. Since many of Pope's poems are relatively short, composed in a variety of different genres, and more or less modeled on or inspired by preceding works, it adds to the critical uncertainty of how to take him all in all; indeed, these facets of his work raise the issue of whether there is an "all in all" in which to take him. Our specific concern with this question underwrites this volume, for we have been encouraged to seek out the broad view of the poet in his culture and in his career, and to this end we have arranged our collection into two sections. Part 1 offers relatively brief excerpts of discussions that are in various ways resumed and enlarged upon by other critics in the essays comprising part 2.

Felicity Rosslyn calls attention to the "ever-widening circles" that constitute the play of Pope's imagination, whereas Robert Griffin speaks of biblical influences on his poetry and the affinity between the roles of satirist and prophet. The relation described by Griffin complements and gives point to Rosslyn's sense of the progress of Pope's imagination and the assimilative power that characterizes it. Christopher Fox argues for the relevance of Locke's "critique of the substantial self" to the "Epistle to Cobham" and proposes that the principle of permanence within personal identity is what Pope means by the ruling passion, the idea that plays so large a role in the *Essay on Man*. Of even greater importance is Pope's exploration of consciousness itself as the essential component of self-knowledge and self-recognition. The emphasis on self-shaping is sustained in Meg Gertmenian's essay and moves her toward inquiry into the darker view of human nature evident in Pope's later works. James Chandler's contribution is the longest in part 1 and is included because of its historical report on Pope's literary reputation in the early years of the nineteenth century and the explicit opposition between a national, English canon and a classical one. David Fairer's introduction to his own collection of essays comes in neatly here, calling attention to the "standards of literary judgement and their consequences for the canonizing and demoting of specific texts" in the late eighteenth and early nineteenth centuries, and focuses attention on Pope's continuing importance in the articulation of Augustan poetic and cultural values, even when such values are assessed negatively. We shall see Carole Fabricant in part 2 enlarge upon this relation. Finally, G. S. Rousseau's review essay concludes part 1 by celebrating Maynard Mack's recent critical biography while suggesting what yet remains to be accomplished in Pope studies.

Robert Markley begins part 2 by focusing on the bearing of Pope's poetry, and the study of literature, on traditional valuations that make of Pope a "classic" author and thereby an index to the values presumably promoted by literary study, citing Pope as the focal point for "fundamental ideological divisions within eighteenth-century studies and within academe at large." Ultimately, Markley's essay is concentrated on one major subject: the relation between poetry and politics and the extent to which valuation is predicated upon that relation. His argument bears primarily on the debate provoked by books such as Laura Brown's *Alexander Pope* (1985) and Ellen Pollack's *The Poetics of Sexual Myth* (1985).

For example, Brown's book was in large part given to observation and commentary on the social and ideological contradictions that are not only evident in the poems, but, as Markley says, help to constitute them. Her approach, therefore, is significantly different from both Rosslyn's and Jackson's, since in each of these studies it is not the self-contradictory aspects of the canon that define the critical perspective, but the ways in which poem builds on poem to constitute enlarged and enlarging imaginative structures. Markley does not consider this particular conflict, but his essay does have the special utility of effectively demonstrating the breakdown of critical consensus, not in itself surprising given the diversity of views and requirements to which Pope's poetry has become subject. While Pope is the ostensible focus of the essay, what is really at issue are the terms by which a canonical poet is currently assessed by the literary community, a community now skilled in the detection of ideological inconsistencies.

Carole Fabricant promises "sustained reflection on the meaning of political, ideological, and cultural engagement, both for Pope in his time and for us today." She locates herself in the context of Pope's "overriding obsession with self" and tends to deflect moral issues into a concern with the moral character, Pope's own, whose virtue becomes the principal topic of the *Horatian Imitations*. Fabricant's subject is not, therefore, ideological positions judged to be unsatisfactory, but Pope's disguise of the political within the general security afforded by the high moral perspective he appropriates as his own.

The latter part of her inquiry shifts from the political to the cultural, the arena in which Pope today is seen as the master of discriminatory activity that distinguishes the cultural guardian from the subverter of culture. In effect, she returns us to the traditional and familiar portrait of Pope as the creator and defender of values that seem to us essentially Augustan, but with one important addition to the portrait. Pope is also the manipulator of his culture in a manner that both rivals and surpasses Walpole's expertise in the same arena and leads Pope, in Fabricant's argument, to an endorsement of himself so fused with his endorsement of the values he advocates that Pope and eighteenth-century "culture" are inseparable and even unimaginable without each other.

Fabricant brings us to the borders of Ripley Hotch's study, which focuses on Pope's early self-nomination as the next great poet and cultural arbiter following John Dryden. Hotch's topic is *An Essay on Criticism*, but his discussion clearly has implications for Pope's career as a whole, for he reads the *Essay* not as a "disquisition on criticism" but as "proof of the qualifications of the author to assume his place as head of the kingdom of wit he describes." Hotch's point becomes more clear if we recognize that between 1711 and 1715—when Pope was in his early twenties—he completed and published not only *An Essay on Criticism*, but also *Windsor-Forest* and *The Temple of Fame*. These three works are all predicated on preceding discourse, John Dennis's *The Grounds of Criticism in Poetry* (1704), John Denham's *Cooper's Hill* (1642), and Geoffrey Chaucer's *House of Fame* (c. 1374–85). All three of Pope's poems assess critical, political, and cultural history and initiate for the young poet an encounter with public and evaluative verse. *An Essay on Criticism*, *Windsor-Forest*, and *The Temple of Fame* are congruent modes of discourse and as such their purpose within the canon reinforces both Fabricant's observation and Hotch's specific interests: "Pope vindicates his own qualities as law-giver and ruler, and therefore justifies his own qualities as heir-apparent to the crown of poetry."

Ronald Paulson's essay is a revision of his earlier essay "Satire and Poetry and Pope" (in Ronald Paulson and Leland H. Carlson, *English Satire*, 1972). We here include the first and fourth parts of the revised essay because of Paulson's effort to connect the epistles of the 1730s with the earlier work of the younger Pope. Mainly, we were interested in Paulson's treatment of Ovidian metamorphosis as a principle regulating and directing Pope's imagination, transforming traditional poets like Homer or Horace or Chaucer into contemporaries while also transforming contemporary figures into traditional heroes and villains.

Sanford Budick's emphasis on Pope's "mythopoeic transportation" of Milton's vision in *Paradise Lost* as re-created in *Windsor-Forest* obviously correlates to Paulson's concerns. Despite the disillusions of his later years, Pope's poetry, Budick argues, "is the drama of a private man in search of a public authority." He is thus "the authorized herald of England's cultural integrity," to which Fabricant might remark, "self-authored," whereas Laura Brown might comment on the inconsistencies characteristic of this herald, and Wallace Jackson in the following selection could elaborate on the ways of Pope's self-representations and thus his own authorizing of himself in the *Horatian Imitations*. Douglas Lane Patey concludes the subject and the volume by returning us to a more-traditional conception of Pope as Enlightenment humanist.

The power to transmute the Western literary tradition into new modes of authoritative English discourse, not merely suited to a particular culture at a particular time, but definitive of that culture at that time, is central to

Pope's achievement. He represents, therefore, an imperial voice for an imperial civilization, for which the appropriation of the past *and* present is the necessary act, and in which such literary terms of approbation as wit or propriety (meaning moral scrupulousness, among other things) are the weapons of a self-consciously superior discourse.

Yet we must not forget that Pope was also an outsider and that his most confident political discourse was a function of the earlier years. *The Dunciad* was not written by a cultural apologist, and into this context we must also find room for Laura Brown's Pope, the self-divided genius who creates an "elegant fantasy [*The Rape of the Lock*] about modern English culture," thus making "a classical 'past' out of his own present beliefs."[3] These views radically derange traditional valuations of Pope by enlisting him under the rubric of visionary or fantasist, self-divided and darkly complicated by ambivalent perceptions of a culture powerful in its aspirations and equally powerful in its contradictions. This sense of Pope is not Brown's alone; it had been evident at least as early as 1963 in Thomas Edwards's study, *This Dark Estate: A Reading of Pope*. Brown extends the perception into political analysis, thereby providing the complement to David Morris's conception of Pope as the man of good sense and inspired genius.

Pope is now self-divided, or possessed of mysteries with which poetry has had ancient alliance. The strong modern interest in the relation between literature and politics, and the bearing of that relation upon evaluative and representational strategies, extends an earlier perception of Pope's doubleness of vision into the political arena, an arena in which Pope was always perceived as a protagonist who may long for respite (note the *Horatian Imitations*), but who was not otherwise divided against himself. This idea of Pope's work is obviously contingent upon the idea of Pope, and John Aden's view of Brown's study (cited by Markley) misses both the obvious relation between poetry and ideology and the equally important relation between poetry and the idea of the poet. So long as Pope was the wicked wasp of Twickenham he was first and foremost a satirist, but as self-divided genius he becomes a figure of imaginative power capable of taking into his charge poetry's "ancient alliance with the mysteries of inspired genius." Yet as "incisive commentator on the political ambiguities of his day" he is also alert to the deep structure (that is, capitalist and imperialist) of his culture. As Markley notes in his essay, insofar as Pope's poems encode the "signs of their ideology" they betray "the structures of belief by which their systems of value are sustained."

In other words, the poems articulate a political unconscious by involuntarily revealing obsessive associations that they cannot otherwise (that is, consciously) disclose. Note that it is often the poems and not Pope who does this, but the point is that Pope cannot do it, which is what is meant by "self-divided." The poems confess their obsessions at a level of discourse that they cannot admit to themselves. Paradoxically, Pope the master craftsman does not lose by involuntarism, but gains by it, becoming a different agent of cultural criticism, even if unconsciously so, from what he was before. The text is finally more honest, more declarative of vital connections that offer a more-essential criticism of the culture, and the poet less the mere technician and witty manipulator of his instrument. Pope the Enlightenment humanist is more thoroughly humanized by way of the behavioral sciences and, by way of familiar deconstructive strategies, rendered more revelatory of cultural irrationalities than he was previously. He therefore comes forth as more poetic, speaking a more-essential truth now uttered by a more-complex presence (self-divided genius).

Perhaps the most specific virtue of this approach is that it provides access to emergent cultural formulae while simultaneously staging the drama of the poet's resistance as that is registered in inconsistencies, contradictions, and tensions. The poems therefore take on a new life of their own and become the antithesis of the New Critical text, which is all tension in the service of unity, becoming instead the Newer Critical text, in which tensions systematically betray ideological incoherence. To the extent that such incoherence is a function of Pope's vision, it identifies him as a resistance leader or, at the very least, as undermined ideologically by perceptions he cannot help but encode within his poems. His poems are now offered as evidence of the subversive effect of the capitalist/imperialist ideology he purports to rationalize, and whatever incoherence they betray testifies not to Pope's deficiencies as philosopher-poet but to the intellectual inconsistencies of the system.

The selections gathered here contribute to the formation of "a grand mosaic" as that subject is discussed by Markley in his essay in relation to bootstrap theory. There is thus no definitive portrait of Pope, no definitive theory that comprehends in any essentialistic way the scope of his creative activity. Instead, the essays are among the most recent efforts by the scholarly community to add to the complexity of Pope's identity, to complicate and thus to question the sufficiency of what was for more than a century the dominant idea of Pope as the poet of good sense, high skill, reactionary politics, and little visionary power, as well, of course, as interpreter of the European literary tradition and thus the grand arbiter of what in that tradition should be sustained and renewed. We hope therefore to have provided entry into the heart of modern evaluations of Pope and access to earlier views that present ones seek to displace or challenge.

Notes

1. Joseph Warton, *An Essay on the Genius and Writings of Pope*, 2 vols. (London, 1806), 2: 404, 401–2, 403.
2. David Morris, *Alexander Pope: The Genius of Sense* (Cambridge, Mass.: Harvard University Press, 1984), 319.
3. Laura Brown, *Alexander Pope* (Oxford: Basil Blackwell, 1985), 26.

An Essay on Pope Criticism

R. Paul Yoder

This book is the result of our review of recent critical work on Alexander Pope, with particular attention to work done since 1980. As our introduction implies, this review has suggested to us certain parallels between the image of a self-divided Pope—evident in such significant oppositions as light/dark, Horatian/Juvenalian, and representative/marginalized, to name but a few—and the critical institution that has created it. Robert Markley's essay from the tercentenary edition of the *New Orleans Review* describes these critical divisions in the most pointed manner of which we know, and the balance of the essays and excerpts in the present collection offer some good instances in the creation of the vocabulary of the divided Pope.

Historically, readers of Pope—at least those readers who also write about him—have generally found it necessary to try to redeem or unify Pope in some way, and the lines of the modern debates tend to follow those established long ago in Joseph Warton's *An Essay on the Genius and Writings of Pope* (1756; 1782), Samuel Johnson's *Life of Pope* (1781), and Matthew Arnold's "The Study of Poetry" (1880). In Warton's four-tiered system, he grants on the one hand that "in that species of poetry wherein Pope excelled, he is superior to all mankind," but then adds, "I only say, that this species of poetry is not the most excellent one of the art," and he places Pope finally, "*next* to *Milton*, and *just* above *Dryden*" (emphasis Warton's). Whatever one thinks of this assessment, it is instructive to note the grudging nature of the respect granted to Pope and his work, and Warton's withholding from Pope the title of "True Poet." By contrast, Samuel Johnson, who had a similar sort of grudging respect for Milton, sees Pope as a definitive poet, such that when he considers the question of "Whether Pope be not a poet," he can only respond, "If Pope be not a poet, where is poetry to be found?" By the latter part of the next century, Arnold, in a strategy very much like Warton's, reasserts, "Though they may write in verse, though they may in a certain sense be masters of the art of versification, Dryden and Pope are not classics of our poetry, they are classics of our prose."[1] These are the critical pronouncements that have defined Pope scholarship for the twentieth century: the bifurcated, contradictory Pope, a master of versification but void of vision, a high-minded writer who finally descends into name-calling squabbles, and who must somehow be redeemed from his apparent self-divisions.

The easiest way to trace the critical constructions of Pope based on Warton, Johnson, and Arnold is to survey the various bibliographies of Pope studies. The following bibliographies provide a fairly complete guide to the modern history of Pope scholarship: James Edward Tobin's *Alexander Pope: A List of Critical Studies Published from 1895 to 1944* (1945); Cecilia L. Lopez's *Alexander Pope: An Annotated Bibliography, 1945–1967* (1970); Geoffrey Tillotson's "Pope," in *English Poetry: Select Bibliographical Guides*, edited by A. E. Dyson (1971); Wolfgang Kowalk's *Alexander Pope: An Annotated Bibliography of Twentieth-Century Criticism 1900–1979* (1981); "Alexander Pope," in Donald C. Mell, Jr.'s *English Poetry, 1660–1800: A Guide to Information Sources* (1982); *The Eighteenth Century: A Current Bibliography* (*ECCB*; published annually, but necessarily several years behind, for example, the nonannotated *MLA Bibliography*); and the section on Pope in *An Annotated Critical Bibliography of Augustan Poetry*, by David Nokes and Janet Barron (1989). Only two of these bibliographies, *ECCB* and Nokes and Barron, extend their range into the 1980s, but Nokes and Barron is very selective, while the *ECCB* is limited by the time necessary for production. Given the bulk of modern Pope scholarship, the availability of earlier annotated bibliographies, and our desire to provide a handy guide to more-recent criticism, we have chosen to focus our bibliographic discussion primarily on the major works on Pope produced in the 1980s. The definitive text of Pope's poems is *The Twickenham Edition of the Poems of Alexander Pope*, II vols., general editor John Butt (New Haven, Conn.: Yale University Press, 1939–69).

Few would dispute our contention that the most important book on Pope to appear in the 1980s is Maynard Mack's biography, *Alexander Pope: A Life* (1985), reviewed here by G. S. Rousseau. Whatever quibbles one may have with it, Mack's biography is a valuable reference, and has quickly become the standard. For a more-introductory view of Pope's life, Felicity Rosslyn offers *Alexander Pope: A Literary Life* (1990), designed in large part for the "quietly mystified student in the corner" (ix). Several more-specialized biographical accounts also appeared in the 1980s. Brean S. Hammond argues in *Pope and Bolingbroke: A Study of Friendship and Influence* (1984) that the two friends were closely aligned politically, and that they developed a common language in their critique of Walpole's government. In *Pursuing Innocent Pleasures: The Gardening World of Alexander Pope* (1984) Peter Martin focuses on Pope's interest in landscape gardening, considering those gardens that Pope visited or influenced in some way, and their impact on his work. Wendy L. Jones's *Talking on Paper: Alexander Pope's Letters* (1990) examines the border between literature and biography by considering "Pope's decision to treat his letters as literary artifacts rather than as personal, biographical documents" (53). Of the earlier biographical accounts, George Sherburn's *Early Career of Alexander Pope* (1934), Marjorie H. Nicolson and G. S. Rousseau's *"This Long Disease, My Life": Alexander Pope and the Sciences* (1968), and Joseph Spence's more-personal *Observations, Anecdotes, and Characters of Books and Men*, edited by James Osborn (1966), remain the most useful.

If Mack's biography was the most important Pope book of the 1980s, the most important event was the Pope tercentenary in 1988. The tercentenary saw the publication of four separate collections of essays on Pope, plus a special number of the *Yearbook in English Studies* (*YES*) devoted to "Pope, Swift and Their Circle." In this number of *YES* (1988), edited by C. J. Rawson, 8 of the 15 nonreview essays are specifically about Pope, including Douglas Brooks-Davies on *Windsor-Forest*, Robert Cummings on *Windsor-Forest*, Frederick M. Keener on Pope's *Homer*, Patricia Bruckmann on *An Essay on Man*, Ian Donaldson on the *Epistle to Dr. Arbuthnot*, Howard Erskine-Hill on Pope's "Epitaph on Francis Atterbury," and Brean S. Hammond on "Scriblerian Self-Fashioning." At least 12 of the review essays consider books on Pope, including *Alexander Pope* by Laura Brown, *The Poetics of Sexual Myth* by Ellen Pollak, *Pope's Dunciad and the Queen of Night* by Douglas Brooks-Davies, and *Pope's Imagination* by David Fairer.

Two other journals offered collections devoted exclusively to Pope. The special number of the *Eighteenth Century: Theory and Interpretation*, edited by David B. Morris, contains a good essay by Morris on the possibilities available to Pope scholarship, plus essays by James Grantham Turner, Susan Staves, Carole Fabricant, Leo Damrosch, and Carey McIntosh that explore some of those possibilities. Turner considers Pope's often-conflicting attitudes toward women; Staves examines Pope's entrepreneurialism and the development of his audience; Fabricant, whose essay is reprinted in the present volume, takes a skeptical view of Pope's representation of himself as holding the moral high ground; Damrosch examines the tension between narrative and description in Pope's work; and McIntosh discusses Pope's efforts in the Horatian poems "to expand the expressive range of English satire" (221).

A special number of the *New Orleans Review*, edited by Ronald Schleifer, and subtitled *The Poststructural Pope*, uses *The Rape of the Lock* as a barometer by which to measure modern theory's approach to Pope. There are 11 essays in the collection, and the contributors include Schleifer, G. Douglas Atkins, Elizabeth Hinds, Pamela Slate Liggett, David S. Grofs, Kate Beaird Meyers, Grant I. Holly, Tom Bowden, Robert Markley, and Richard Cassetta. Pope's encounters here range from Marx, Bakhtin, and Jakobson to William S. Burroughs. Of particular interest to a reader seeking an overview are Cassetta's annotated bibliography of works on the *Rape* in the 1980s, and Markley's examination (reprinted here) of the polemics of review essays.

Two independent collections of essays were also released in 1988. One is *Alexander Pope: Essays for the Tercentenary*, edited by Colin Nicolson (1988), which contains 15 essays from contributors including H. T. Dickinson, Brean S. Hammond, Martin Malone, John Price, Ian Bell, Colin Nicolson, Roger Savage, Peter France, Geoffrey Carnall, Colin Manlove, Alastair Fowler, Michael Phillips, W. W. Robson, R. D. S. Jack, Don Nichol, and Wendy Jones. The essays are varied and generally celebratory; several present useful summaries of information on Pope, often with an eye toward such recent critical interests as rhetoric, ideology, and economics.

Perhaps the most enduring of the tercentenary volumes will be *The Enduring Legacy: Alexander Pope Tercentenary Essays*, edited by G. S. Rousseau and Pat Rogers (1988), whose contributors include Patricia Bruckmann, Howard D. Weinbrot, Felicity Rosslyn, Penelope Wilson, Howard Erskine-Hill, David B. Morris, John Dixon Hunt, Morris Brownwell, A. D. Nuttall, Wallace Jackson, Pat Rogers, G. S. Rousseau, and Donald Greene. The 13 essays are grouped under six headings which themselves suggest both emergent and traditional Popean interests: *The Rape of the Lock*, Pope and women, *An Essay on Man*, landscape gardening and the villa at Twickenham, Pope and translation and criticism, and Pope and posterity.

Published two years after the tercentenary, *Pope: New Contexts* (1990), edited by David Fairer, brings together 13 essays that in various ways seek to "tackle the issue of appropriation, the awkward question of '*whose* Pope?' which is audible now as ever" (7). The authors in this endeavour include Fairer himself, J. A. Downie, Christine Gerrard, Thomas Woodman, Carolyn D. Williams, Steve Clark, Susan Matthews, Stephen Bygrave, Rebecca Ferguson, John Whale, Nicholas Roe, Stephen Copley, and Brean S. Hammond. The issues raised in these essays include Pope's alleged Tory sympathies (Downie), his relation to the depiction of women in the novel (Matthews), and his relation to the romantics (Whale, Fairer, Roe).

All of these essay collections, as does the present volume, continue the work of earlier collections that provide a valuable guide to the critical history of Pope and Pope studies. The most valuable essay collections published before the tercentenary include *Essential Articles for the Study of Pope*, edited by Maynard Mack (1964, rev. 1968; a second edition in 1980); *Alexander Pope: A Critical Anthology*, edited by F. W. Bateson and N. A. Joukovsky (1971); *Alexander Pope, Writers and Their Background*, edited by Peter Dixon (1972); *Pope: The Critical Heritage*, edited by John Barnard (1973); *The Art of Alexander Pope*, edited by Howard Erskine-Hill and Anne Smith (1979); *Pope: Recent Essays by Several Hands*, edited by Maynard Mack and James A. Winn (1980); and Mack's *Collected in Himself: Essays Critical, Biographical, and Bibliographical on Pope and Some of His Contemporaries* (1982).

The following collections are devoted exclusively to the *Rape*: *The Rape of the Lock: A Casebook* (1968), edited by John Dixon Hunt, and *Twentieth Century Interpretations of The Rape of the Lock: A Collection of Critical Essays* (1969), edited by G. S. Rousseau.

Seven book-length career studies appeared in the 1980s, and together they provide a good insight into the dynamics of Pope criticism since each must offer some sort of over-arching scheme for reading poems as divergent as *An Essay on Criticism*, *Eliosa to Abelard*, and *The Dunciad*. Whether the subject is poetic influence, economics, sense, or mythic vision, these critics all strive to demonstrate a coherence among parts assumed to be widely divergent.

Wallace Jackson, in his *Vision and Re-vision in Alexander Pope* (1983), discerns "a coherence of symbolism" in Pope's work which he sees as the trace of a Popean mythology of the Fall. In *Pope's Imagination* (1984) David Fairer expands our understanding of Pope's idea of the imagination by questioning our assumptions about early-eighteenth-century distinctions between, for example, imagination and fancy. David B. Morris's *Alexander Pope: The Genius of Sense* (1984) focuses on Pope's relationship to the past, especially to Dryden, in an argument that sees Pope's interest in the "Man of Sense" rather than the Man of Wit or the Man of Feeling as the governing principle in his work. Laura Brown's *Alexander Pope* (1985) generated more controversy than any other recent book on Pope (see Markley's essay in this volume); Brown's openly antagonistic, Marxian, revisionist reading of Pope's career finds a consistency of rhetoric and poetic forms complicit with the commodity culture of empire and capitalism, but also suggesting an ambivalence about the "new world" of capitalism. G. Douglas Atkins's *Quests of Difference: Reading Pope's Poems* (1986), the first book-length reading of Pope "in light of deconstruction" (xi), draws mainly from Derrida and de Man to consider the questions of definition and difference that are the focal point of Pope's work. Rebecca Ferguson argues in *The Unbalanced Mind: Pope and the Rule of Passion* (1986) that the development in Pope's thinking from his early notion of passion to his later understanding of the "ruling passion" sponsors the explorations and depictions of the unbalanced mind in his later poetry. In *The Imaginative World of Alexander Pope* (1987) Leopold Damrosch, Jr., focuses on Pope's marginality—sexual, financial, political, artistic—in order to show Pope contending with the arguably modern problems of skepticism and the loss of social values and generic authority.

There were almost as many considerations of Pope's relation to Horace, whom Mack has called Pope's "ideal poetic precedent" (*Life*, 563), as there were general career studies. All of these studies owe debts to Reuben A. Brower's *Alexander Pope: The Poetry of Allusion* (1959) and Maynard Mack's *The Garden and the City: Retirement and Politics in the Later Poetry of Pope, 1731–1743* (1969), both of which hold that Pope's life and work become progressively an imitation of Horace. Howard D. Weinbrot, in *Alexander Pope and the Traditions of Formal Verse Satire* (1982), explicitly addresses their arguments in order to redefine our understanding of the changes in Pope's career. While admitting the Horatian connection, Weinbrot contends that Pope's work develops "from an essentially Horatian ethic epistle . . . to mingled satire with a variety of Horatian, Juvenalian and Persian emphases, to the overwhelming Juvenalian–Perisan elevation and gloom of the *Epilogue to the Satires*" (331). In *Reading Pope's Imitations of Horace* (1989), Jacob Fuchs seeks to establish an alternative to the Horatian Pope of Brower and Mack and the Juvenalian/anti-Augustan Pope of Weinbrot, liberating Pope by questioning the eighteenth-century view of Horace: his "point is that eighteenth-century thinking on Augustus and his age could not have constrained Pope in any significant way" (30).

In other approaches to the Horatian poems, Allen G. Wood's *Literary Satire and Theory: A Study of Horace, Boileau, and Pope* (1985) seeks to add a continental component to the debate. Epistemology is the focus of Fredric V. Bogel's *Acts of Knowledge: Pope's Later Poems* (1981) in which Pope's *Epistles* and *Horatian Imitations* provide evidence of a Popean movement between the extremes of an isolating "schematic" knowledge and a more-worldly "substantial" knowledge. Something like Pope's internal movement is externalized into the reader's experience in Frank Stack's *Pope and Horace: Studies in Imitation* (1985), an examination of the "intertextual field" (xv) created by Pope's decision to publish his Imitations of Horace with parallel, facing-page Horatian originals.

Concerning Pope's relationship to other classical authors, Steven Shankman, in his *Pope's Iliad: Homer in the Age of Passion* (1983), makes it his task to support Samuel Johnson's assessment that Pope's translation of the *Iliad* "is certainly the noblest version of poetry which the world has ever seen." Less-well-known classical sources and their English translations are the focus of G.F.C. Plowden's *Pope on Classic Ground* (1983), a study of Pope's borrowings from such works as Manilius's *Astronomica*, translated by Thomas Creech, and George Sandys's notes to his translation of *Ovid's Metamorphosis*.

Three of Pope's poems received book-length consideration in the 1980s. Robert Halsband's *The Rape of the Lock and Its Illustrations 1714–1896* (1980) provides a look at the interpretive history of the *Rape* as it is expressed in the illustrations accompanying the poem from the first edition of the five-canto version to the 1896 edition illustrated by Aubrey Beardsley. The volume includes 6 color and 68 monochrome plates, and the artists considered in addition to Beardsley include C. R. Leslie, and two friends of William Blake, Thomas Stothard and Henry Fuseli. In *Pope's Essay on Man* (1984) A. D. Nuttall presents a close reading of the poem that according to Nuttall, "tells you more of the thought of the time than any other single literary work" (192). Nuttall sees Pope as "not just a source but a potent, *organizing* source" (1), and his concerns include Augustan versification, the decline of theodicy, and Pope's engagement with Milton. Douglas Brooks-Davies's *Pope's Dunciad and the Queen of Night: A Study in Emotional Jacobitism* (1985) uses Pope's most difficult poem to examine both the question of Pope's Jacobitism and his relationship with women, arguing that images of Isis, Elizabeth I, Queen Anne, and Pope's own mother conspire in a critique of monarchy based on Virgil and Milton. Concerning the textual difficulties of *The Dunciad*, David L. Vander Meulen has produced two useful books: *Where Angels Fear to Tread: Descriptive Bibliography and Alexander Pope* (1988), and *Pope's "Dunciad" of 1728: A History and Facsimile* (1991).

In the past decade two areas of inquiry have emerged as particularly volatile topics: the first area concerns Pope and gender issues, the second his relation to Catholicism, especially as it bears on the question of Jacobite politics. Most of the tercentenary collections include considerations of Pope and gender. Other essays on this topic include Felicity Nussbaum's relatively early "Pope's 'To a Lady' and the Eighteenth-Century Woman" (1975); Ellen Pollak's "Pope and Sexual Difference: Woman as Part and Counterpart in the 'Epistle to a Lady' " (1984); Carol Virginia Pohli's "The Point Where Sense and Dulness Meet: What Pope Knows about Knowing and about Women" (1985); Penelope Wilson's "Feminism and the Augustans: Some Readings and Problems" (1986); Molly Smith's "The Mythical Implications in Pope's 'Epistle to a Lady' " (1987), Taylor Corse's "Heaven's 'Last Best Work': Pope's 'Epistle to a Lady' " (1987); Wolfgang E. H. Rudat's "Sex-Role Reversal and Miltonic Theology in Pope's *Rape of the Lock*" (1987); and Laura Claridge's "Pope's Rape of Excess" (1988). Felicity Nussbaum's *The Brink of All We Hate: English Satires on Women, 1660–1750* (1984) provides an extended consideration of the literary context for Pope's female characters.

Two important book-length considerations of Pope and women are Ellen Pollak's *Poetics of Sexual Myth: Gender and Ideology in the Verse of Swift and Pope* (1985) and Valerie Rumbold's *Women's Place in Pope's World* (1989). Pollak focuses primarily on the *Rape* and *To a Lady*, as well as Swift's *Cadenus and Vanessa* in a deconstructionist feminist reading. Pollak presents a good exploration of the "socioeconomic determinants of what, by the early eighteenth century, had become a culturally dominant sexual mythology" (159), in which the developing middle-class family demanded a more-passive role for women. Rumbold discusses the interrelationship between a somewhat feminized Pope and the women in his life. Her focus on the trope of the "unfortunate lady" broadens our view of Pope's involvement with his mother, Teresa and Martha Blount, Lady Mary Wortley Montagu, Henrietta Howard, and Mary Caesar.

The question of the importance of Pope's Catholicism and the possibility of a related Jacobitism has become a surprisingly hot topic in recent Pope scholarship. Despite Sherburn's early references to Pope as a Jacobite in *The Early Career of Alexander Pope* (1934), it had become widely accepted that Pope had no real Jacobite leanings, nor was he much influenced by his Catholicism. In the last twenty years, however, these questions have been reopened. Among the various arguments, pro and con, are the following: John M. Aden's "Pope and Politics: 'The Farce of State,' " (1972), Pat Rogers's "Pope and the Social Scene" (1972); Chester Chapin's "Alexander Pope: Erasmian Catholic" (1973); Aden's *Pope's Once and Future Kings: Satire and Politics in the Early Career* (1978); Howard Erskine-Hill's "Literature and the Jacobite Cause: Was There a Rhetoric of Jacobitism?" (1982); Chapin's "Pope and the Jacobites" (1986); Brean S. Hammond's *Pope* (1986); Howard Erskine-Hill's "Alexander Pope: The Political Poet in His Time" (1988); and J. A. Downie's "1688: Pope and the Rhetoric of Jacobitism," which opens *Pope: New Contexts* (1990). Previously mentioned are the two most recent book-length studies of Pope's Jacobitism: Brean S. Hammond's biographical *Pope and Bolingbroke: A Study of Friendship and Influence* (1984), and Douglas Brooks-Davies' *Pope's Dunciad and the Queen of Night* (1985).

Finally, several good books have appeared since 1980 that provide valuable discussion of various types of background information. Among these works are Anthony Easthope's *Poetry as Discourse* (1983); Margaret Anne Doody's *The Daring Muse: Augustan Poetry Reconsidered* (1985); Allan Ingram's *Intricate Laughter in the Satire of Swift and Pope* (1986); James Sambrook's *The Eighteenth Century: The Intellectual and Cultural Context of English Literature, 1700–1789* (1986); Reginald Berry's *A Pope Chronology* (1988); Christopher Fox's *Locke and the Scriblerians: Identity and Consciousness in Early Eighteenth-Century Britain* (1988, and excerpted here); Mack's *The Last and Greatest Art: Some Unpublished Poetical Manuscripts of Alexander Pope* (1984) and *The World of Alexander Pope* (1988; a descriptive catalog of the exhibitions in the Beinecke Rare Book and Manuscript Library and the Yale Center for British Art); Gretchen M. Foster's *Pope versus Dryden: A Controversy in Letters to "The Gentlemen's Magazine,"* 1789–1791 (1990); and John E. Sitter's *Argument of Augustan Wit* (1991).

Like most of the English romantics, with the notable exception of Byron, William Blake was apparently no great fan of Alexander Pope. In his "Public Address" Blake remarks that the "unorganized Blots & Blurs of Rubens & Titian are not Art nor can their Method ever express Ideas or Imaginations any more than Popes Metaphysical Jargon of Rhyming." Nevertheless, when Blake began his annotations to *The Works of Sir Joshua Reynolds*, he wrote on the title page the following poem, which he had originally entitled "Advice to the Popes who succeeded the Age of Rafael":

> Degrade first the Arts if you'd Mankind degrade,
> Hire Idiots to Paint with cold light & hot shade:
> Give high Price for the worst, leave the best in disgrace,
> And with Labours of Ignorance fill every place.[2]

This short poem is not usually recognized as an imitation of Pope—there is, after all, another Blake poem entitled "Imitation of Pope"—but these lines seem as if they could have been lifted directly from the *Essay on Criticism*. They combine the magisterial tone of the *Essay* with the criticisms of taste of the *Epistles*, and the bitter irony of *The Dunciad*. As such, the lines suggest an unexpected convergence of Blake's thought with Pope's, and an even-more-unexpected parallel between the careers of the successful Pope and the poverty-stricken Blake. They also demonstrate Blake's willingness to appropriate Pope's "Metaphysical Jargon of Rhyming" in order to turn the poet of the Enlightenment against the painter of the Enlightenment, perhaps even against Pope himself, for this is "Advice to the Popes Who Succeeded the Age of

Rafael." Blake's title for the lines, while glancing at papal support for certain arts, also suggests the stature of Pope as a figure of speech, as a figure who has transcended his personal individuality to become a generic term, a viable member of the lexicon. In many ways, this is the Pope we now have, divided in some way against himself and his age, yet still somehow unified and representative of that age.

Notes

1. All bibliographic information for critical work on Pope has been centralized into a *Works Cited* at the end of this essay. Page numbers are given in the text.
2. William Blake, *The Complete Poetry and Prose of William Blake*, rev. ed. David V. Erdman (New York: Anchor Doubleday, 1988), 576, 635.

Works Cited

Aden, John M. "Pope and Politics: 'The Farce of State.' " In *Alexander Pope: Writers and Their Background*, edited by Peter Dixon, 172–99. Athens: Ohio University Press, 1972.
———. *Pope's Once and Future Kings: Satire and Politics in the Early Career*. Knoxville: University of Tennessee Press, 1978.
Arnold, Matthew. "The Study of Poetry." In *The Works of Matthew Arnold*, vol. 4. London: Macmillan, 1903.
Atkins, G. Douglas. *Quests of Difference: Reading Pope's Poems*. Lexington: University of Kentucky, Press, 1986.
Berry, Reginald. *A Pope Chronology*. Boston: G. K. Hall, 1988.
Bogel, Fredric V. *Acts of Knowledge: Pope's Later Poems*. Lewisburg, Pa. 8 Bucknell University Press, 1981.
Brooks-Davies, Douglas. *Pope's "Dunciad" and the Queen of Night: A Study in Emotional Jacobitism*. Manchester, England: Manchester University Press, 1985.
Brower, Reuben Arthur. *Alexander Pope: The Poetry of Allusion*. Oxford: Clarendon Press, 1959.
Brown, Laura. *Alexander Pope*. Rereading Literature, no. 1. Oxford: Basil Blackwell, 1985.
Chapin, Chester. "Alexander Pope: Erasmian Catholic." *Eighteenth-Century Studies* 6 (1973): 411–30.
———. "Pope and the Jacobites." *Eighteenth-Century Life* 10 (1986): 59–73.
Claridge, Laura. "Pope's Rape of Excess." In *Perspectives on Pornography: Sexuality in Film and Literature*, 129–43. New York: St. Martin's Press, 1988.
Corse, Taylor. "Heaven's 'Last Best Work': Pope's *Epistle to a Lady*." *Studies in English Literature* 27 (1987): 413–25.
Damrosch, Leopold, Jr. *The Imaginative World of Alexander Pope*. Berkeley and Los Angeles: University of California Press, 1987.
Doody, Margaret Anne. *The Daring Muse: Augustan Poetry Reconsidered*. Cambridge: Cambridge University Press, 1985.

Downie, J. A. "1688: Pope and the Rhetoric of Jacobitism." In *Pope: New Contexts*, edited by David Fairer, 9–24 New York: Harvester Wheatsheaf.

Easthope, Anthony. *Poetry as Discourse*. London: Methuen, 1983.

Eighteenth Century: A Current Bibliography. Edited by Jim S. Borck. New York: AMS, 1978–90.

Erskine-Hill, Howard. "Alexander Pope: The Political Poet in His Time." In *Modern Essays on Eighteenth-Century Literature*, edited by Leopold Damrosch, Jr., 123–40. New York: Oxford University Press, 1988.

———. "Literature and the Jacobite Cause." Modern Language Studies 9 (1979): 15–20.

———. "Literature and the Jacobite Cause: Was There a Rhetoric of Jacobitism?" In *Ideology and Conspiracy: Aspects of Jacobitism, 1689–1759*, edited by Eveline Cruickshanks, 49–69. Edinburgh, Scotland: John Donald, 1982.

Fabricant, Carole. "Pope's Moral, Political, and Cultural Combat." *Eighteenth Century: Theory and Interpretation*. 29 (1988): 165–87.

Fairer, David, ed. *Pope: New Contexts*. New York: Harvester Wheatsheaf, 1990.

———. *Pope's Imagination*. Manchester, England: Manchester University Press, 1984.

Ferguson, Rebecca. *The Unbalanced Mind: Pope and the Rule of Passion*. Brighton, England: Harvester Press, 1986.

Foster, Gretchen M. *Pope versus Dryden: A Controversy in Letters to "The Gentleman's Magazine", 1789–1791*. English Literary Studies, Monograph Series 44. Victoria, British Columbia: University of Victoria, 1989.

Fox, Christopher. *Locke and the Scriblerians: Identity and Consciousness in Early Eighteenth-Century Britain*. Berkeley and Los Angeles: University of California Press, 1988.

Fuchs, Jacob. *Reading Pope's "Imitations of Horace."* Lewisburg, Pa.: Bucknell University Press, 1989.

Halsband, Robert. *"The Rape of the Lock" and Its Illustrations 1714–1896*. Oxford: Clarendon, 1980.

Hammond, Brean S. *Pope*. Brighton, England: Harvester, New Readings Series, 1986.

———. *Pope and Bolingbroke: A Study of Friendship and Influence*. Columbia: University of Missouri Press, 1984.

Ingram, Allan. *Intricate Laughter in the Satire of Swift and Pope*. New York: St. Martin's Press, 1986.

Jackson, Wallace. *Vision and Re-vision in Alexander Pope*. Detroit: Wayne State University Press, 1983.

Johnson, Samuel. *Lives of the English Poets*. 3 vols. Edited by George Birkbeck Hill. Oxford: Clarendon Press, 1905; reprint, New York: Octagon Books, 1967.

Jones, Wendy L. *Talking on Paper: Alexander Pope's Letters*. English Literary Studies, Monograph Series 50. Victoria, British Columbia: University of Victoria, 1990.

Kowalk, Wolfgang. *Alexander Pope: An Annotated Bibliography of Twentieth-Century Criticism 1900–1979*. Frankfurt am Main, Germany: Peter D. Lang, 1981.

Lopez, Cecilia L. *Alexander Pope: An Annotated Bibliography, 1945–1967*. Gainesville: University of Florida Press, 1970.

Mack, Maynard. *Alexander Pope: A Life*. New York: Norton, 1985.

———. "Collected in Himself": Essays Critical, Biographical, and Bibliographical on Pope and Some of His Contemporaries. Newark: University of Delaware Press, 1982.

————, ed. *Essential Articles for the Study of Alexander Pope*. Rev. and enlarged. Hamden, Conn.: Archon, 1968.

————. *The Garden and the City: Retirement and Politics in the Later Poetry of Pope, 1731–1743*. Toronto: University of Toronto Press, 1969.

————, ed. *The Last and Greatest Art: Some Unpublished Poetical Manuscripts of Alexander Pope*. Newark: University of Delaware Press/Associated Universities Press, 1984.

————. *The World of Alexander Pope*. New Haven, Conn.: Yale University Press, 1988.

Mack, Maynard, and James A. Winn, eds. *Pope: Recent Essays by Several Hands*. Hamden, Conn.: Archon, 1980.

Martin, Peter. *Pursuing Innocent Pleasures: The Gardening World of Alexander Pope*. Hamden, Conn.: Archon/Shoe String Press, 1984.

Mell, Donald C., Jr. *English Poetry, 1660–1800*. Information Guide Series 40. Detroit, Mi.: Gale, 1982.

Morris, David B. *Alexander Pope: The Genius of Sense*. Cambridge: Harvard University Press, 1984.

————, ed. *The Eighteenth Century: Theory and Interpretation*, 29 1988. Special issue on Pope.

Nicolson, Colin. *Pope: Essays for the Tercentenary*. Aberdeen, Scotland: Aberdeen University Press, 1988.

Nicolson, Marjorie, H., and G. S. Rousseau. *"This Long Disease, My Life": Alexander Pope and the Sciences*. Princeton; N. J.: Princeton University Press, 1968.

Nokes, David, and Janet Barron. *An Annotated Critical Bibliography of Augustan Poetry*. New York: St. Martin's Press, 1989.

Nussbaum, Felicity. *The Brink of All We Hate: English Satires on Women, 1660–1750*. Lexington: University of Kentucky Press, 1984.

————, "Pope's 'To a Lady' and the Eighteenth-Century Woman." *Philological Quarterly* 54 (1975): 444–456.

Nuttall, A. D. *Pope's "Essay on Man."* London: Allen, 1984.

Plowden, G.F.C. *Pope on Classic Ground*. Athens: Ohio University Press, 1983.

Pohli, Carol Virginia. "The Point Where Sense and Dulness Meet: What Pope Knows about Knowing and about Women." *Eighteenth-Century Studies* 19 (Winter 1985–86): 206–34.

Pollak, Ellen. *The Poetics of Sexual Myth: Gender and Ideology in the Verse of Swift and Pope*. Chicago: University of Chicago Press, 1985.

————. "Pope and Sexual Difference: Woman as Part and Counterpart in the 'Epistle to a Lady.'" *Studies in English Literature* 24 (1984): 461–81.

Rawson, C. J., ed. *Pope, Swift, and Their Circle. Yearbook in English Studies* 18 (1988). Special issue.

Rosslyn, Felicity. *Alexander Pope: A Literary Life*. New York: St. Martin's Press, 1990.

Rousseau, G. S., and Pat Rogers, eds. *The Enduring Legacy: Alexander Pope tercentenary Essays*. Cambridge: Cambridge University Press, 1988.

Rudat, Wolfgang E. H. "Sex-Role Reversal and Miltonic Theology in Pope's 'Rape of the Lock.'" *Journal of Evolutionary Psychology* 8 (1987): 48–62.

Rumbold, Valerie. *Women's Place in Pope's World*. Cambridge Studies in Eighteenth-Century English Literature and Thought, no. 2. Cambridge: Cambridge University Press, 1989.

Sambrook, James. *The Eighteenth Century: The Intellectual and Cultural Context of English Literature, 1700–1789*. London: Longman, 1986.

Schleifer, Ronald, ed. *The Poststructuralist Pope. New Orleans Review* 15, no. 4 (Winter 1988): 1–85. Special issue.

Shankman, Steven. *Pope's "Iliad": Homer in the Age of Passion*. Princeton, N. J.: Princeton University Press, 1983.

Sherburn, George. *Early Career of Alexander Pope*. Oxford: Clarendon Press, 1934.

Sitter, John E. *Argument of Augustan Wit*. Cambridge: Cambridge University Press, 1991.

Smith, Molly "The Mythical Implications in Pope's 'Epistle to a Lady.' " *Studies in English Literature* 27 (1987): 427–436.

Spence, Joseph. *Observations, Anecdotes, and Characters of Books and Men*. 2 vols. Edited by James Osborn. Oxford: Clarendon Press, 1966.

Stack, Frank. *Pope and Horace: Studies in Imitation*. Cambridge: Cambridge University Press, 1985.

Tillotson, Geoffrey. "Pope." In *English Poetry: Select Bibliographical Guides*, edited by A. E. Dyson, 128–43. London: Oxford University Press, 1971.

Tobin, James E. *A List of Critical Studies Published from 1895–1944*. New York: Cosmopolitan Science and Art, 1945.

Vander Meulen, David L. *Pope's "Dunciad" of 1728: A History and Facsimile*. Charlottesville: University of Virginia Press, 1991.

———. *Where Angels Fear to Tread: Descriptive Bibliography and Alexander Pope*. Washington: Library of Congress, 1988.

Warton, Joseph. *An Essay on the Genius and Writings of Pope*. 1756; 1782. Facsimile reprint in 2 vols. New York: Garland, 1970.

Weinbrot, Howard D. *Alexander Pope and the Traditions of Formal Verse Satire*. Princeton, N. J.: Princeton University Press, 1982.

Wilson, Penelope. "Feminism and the Augustans: Some Readings and Problems." *Critical Quarterly* 28 (1986): 80–92.

Wood, Allen G. *Literary Satire and Theory: A Study of Horace, Boileau, and Pope*. New York: Garland, 1985.

A CENTO OF EXCERPTS

◆

[from *Alexander Pope: A Literary Life*]

Felicity Rosslyn

One of the most interesting aspects of human development is its tendency to go in circles—always returning to the place it started from, though the journey is made from increasingly distant points on the map. This is supremely true of artists, whose work to the discerning eye is always the same piece of work, in a differing stage of development. It is as if the artist had a template within, which he cannot abandon even if he wants to; and though this sounds like a limitation, it is one of those limitations that makes everything else possible. Having found his template, the artist learns how to make it subsume more meaning, how to condense more implications into his form; and by going in circles, he ends in a place very far from his starting point—though it is also that, as well.

This is particularly true of Pope, whose poems go in ever-widening circles from the juvenilia we have seen, to the last revision of the *Dunciad*. The template is not a commitment to one particular genre, but to the simultaneous exploration of many, which enables him to capture conflicting aspects of reality and to exploit the many facets of his nature. The secret of this variety is an exquisite sense of what belongs in each kind of poetry—what the age called "decorum"—and a rigorous exclusion of all else. The poems, however apparently contradictory in tone and philosophy, are each being played by the rules of the game.

The "second circle" of Pope's development shows the *Pastorals* growing into a topographical celebration of country life, *Windsor Forest*, the early translation of Ovid's love letter, *Sapho to Phaon*, growing into *Eloisa to Abelard*, the mock-epic gifts and inverted metaphors of Pope's Dorset and Rochester imitations developing into the *Rape of the Lock*, and Pope mastering two forms he has not attempted before: the verse essay (*An Essay on Criticism*) and the elegy (*Elegy to the Memory of an Unfortunate Lady*). What lay behind this second round of creativity was not only increasing skill as a poet, but a new mental clarity and organisation. Pope seems to have felt that his happy but haphazard education, in which he found his own way through the classics and picked up languages as he went, needed severe discipline in order to bear fruit; and he

From *Alexander Pope: A Literary Life* (New York: St. Martin's Press, 1990), 31–33. Reprinted by permission of St. Martin's Press, Inc. and The Macmillan Press Limited.

regarded himself in later life as someone who had "done" his education twice over. The friend and co-editor of Pope's old age, Warburton, phrases it like this:

> At twenty, when the impetuosity of his spirits began to suffer his genius to be put under restraint, he went over all the parts of his education a-new, from the very beginning, and in a regular, and more artful manner. He penetrated into the general grounds and reasons of speech; he learnt to distinguish the several species of style; he studied the peculiar genius and character of each language; he reduced his natural talent for poetry to a science, and mastered those parts of philosophy that would most contribute to enrich his vein. And all this, with such continued attention, labour, and severity that he used to say, he had been seven years (that is, from twenty to twenty-seven) in unlearning all he had been acquiring for twice seven.[1]

Notes

1. TE [*Twickenham Edition of the Works of Alexander Pope*], IV, 159.

[from "Pope, the Prophets, and *The Dunciad*"]

ROBERT GRIFFIN

"I really wish myself something more, that is, a Prophet."
—Pope in a letter to Edward Blount, 3 October 1721

"When the enemy shall come in like a flood, the Spirit of the Lord shall lift up a standard against him."
—Isa. 59:19

The inseparability of classical and Christian elements in Pope's poetry is so obvious that it would seem to require no further comment. Yet, with few exceptions, Pope scholarship has focused almost exclusively on the classical heritage and, taking Pope's Christianity as a given, has overlooked the significance of biblical influence on his poetry.[1] In particular, the number and range of allusions to the Old Testament in *The Dunciad* has, I believe, been seriously underestimated by its critics. Hence there is an entire dimension of meaning to the poem which has been recognized only intermittently.[2] The argument which follows hopes to re-orient our sense of Pope by attempting to re-vivify the force of only some of the prophetic allusions in *The Dunciad* and, therefore, hopes to restore the Bible as a significant context of allusion for Pope's poetry.

No reading of *The Dunciad* can proceed without reference to Aubrey Williams's early book on the poem.[3] Williams identified several layers of to the "action" which brings the Smithfield Muses to Court. There is the parody of the Lord Mayor's Day procession, the parody of Aeneas bringing his household gods to Latium, the parody of the *translatio studii*, and the parody of the return-of-the-Golden-Age motif which appeared in the contemporary verses of flatterers of the King. There is also what Williams identified as the "anagogic" sense of the poem, or its theological significance. On that level, Dulness, as non-being, is presented as a blasphemous, satanic version of the Christian God. The network of prophetic allusions discoverable in the poem essentially reinforces the theological significance articulated by Williams, while it offers yet another level of meaning created by Pope's art. On that

Robert Griffin, "Pope, the Prophets, and *The Dunciad*." Reprinted by permission of *SEL: Studies in English Literature, 1500–1900 23*, 3 (Summer 1983).

level the dunces are presented in Old Testament terms as either rebellious Israelites who have forgotten their Lord, or as false prophets who, without vocations, prostitute the Word.[4]

The general approach to the poem I am advocating is one already widely accepted, but, as it has been the object of recent criticism, it requires a few words of defense. Donald T. Siebert has argued that Williams's view of *The Dunciad* (along with that of such distinguished critics as Battestin, Brower, Fussell, Price, Sutherland, and Spacks among others) leads us into "too solemn a reading of the poem."[5] Williams's book, in Siebert's view, "gives authority to the opinion that the dunces are truly evil and threatening," whereas Siebert, not denying "the theological metaphor associating the dunces with the forces of darkness," claims that Pope's vision is "essentially comic, not tragic," and that "the consistent attitude of Pope towards the dunces is one of laughter."[6] The value of Siebert's article is in reminding readers of the lighter side of Pope's irony. However, the conclusion that laughter precludes seriousness seems to me untenable. Irony and serious vision are not by necessity mutually exclusive. There is no compelling reason to choose between comic "dunciad" and tragic "jeremiad" ("the two impulses obviously do not harmonize") when it is precisely the presence of irony which allows for their fusion. Maynard Mack, for one, recognized this possibility when, in a discussion of the complexities of the mock-epic vehicle of *The Dunciad*, he observed "the tension between all these creatures as comic and ridiculous, and their destructive potentiality in being so."[7] Furthermore, the representation of Cibber as an evil man is quite explicit in the section, "*Ricardus Aristarchus of the Hero of the Poem*," which, for all its being a take-off on Bentley's style, juxtaposes in a straightforward manner the qualities of "*Wisdom, Bravery*, and *Love*" requisite in the hero of the "*Greater Epic*" with the qualities of "*Vanity, Impudence*, and *Debauchery*" required in the hero of its opposite, the "*little Epic*" or "*Satyric Tragedy*."[8] Illustrations of Cibber's preeminent qualifications for the latter role are drawn from his own self-characterizations.

Turning for a moment to the poem, the Argument of Book III is a good example of the way mock-epic irony is compatible with the moral indignation of the prophets. In an ironic typology, "A Scheme, of which the present Action of the Dunciad is but a Type or Foretaste" (p. 56), Cibber is cast in a role which conflates Aeneas in Hades, Adam's vision in *Paradise Lost* XI (itself adapted by Milton from Ezekiel), and Moses on Mt. Pisgah. In the underworld Cibber is taken to a "Mount of Vision," from which he will view the past and present of Dulness's Empire, and will be given a "glimpse, or Pisgah-sight of the future Fulness of her Glory, the accomplishment whereof is the subject of the fourth and last book" (p. 319). Rome's future greatness and the growth of its civilization as foreseen by Aeneas, the New Jerusalem as seen by Ezekiel when he is taken up into the visions of God and set upon "a very high mountain" (Ezek. 40:2), the future glory of Israel as seen by Moses, and Adam's vision of history finally redeemed by the Son, are all conflated and subjected to the ironic inversions of a mock-epic in which Cibber, as "Bedlam's Prophet" (Book III.6, p. 320), foresees the triumph of Dulness. The Argument thus sets up this mock-epic structure as an explicit context for Books III and IV. Given this structure, the vision of future glory and salvation, in being subjected to irony, results in a prediction of future shame and damnation. The ironic inversions of a mock-epic are, therefore, actually parallel to the other half of the prophets' vision, the denunciation of evil through the vision of its destruction. By means of allusion, Cibber is set ironically against true prophecy, and is therefore seen within the evoked context of Scripture as a false prophet and usurper of the Word. Through irony Pope can make a joke of Cibber, and yet, without explicitly placing himself in the role of true prophet and poet, can draw upon all of the force of righteous scorn for evil available in his tradition. What transpires in *The Dunciad*, therefore, lends itself to interpretation in terms of the vision in the prophetic song Moses gave to his people *before* ascending Pisgah. Knowing he was to die, Moses depicted a grim future for the Israelites should they forget the Lord, giving them the song as a warning, saying: "For I know that after my death ye will utterly corrupt yourselves" (Deut. 31:29).

The general connection between satire and the prophets' denunciation of evil has not gone unnoticed.[9] With Pope's late poetry in view, however, the affinity between satirist and prophet needs to be stressed. To clarify, the root meaning of prophecy is "speaking forth," or a speaking out of one's mind under the pressure of moral vision. In its biblical sense, prophecy does not primarily mean "clairvoyance," although clear-sightedness into the causes of unwitting destruction abounds in the prophetic books. Essentially, prophecy recalls the past, or depicts a future, as either warning or consolation to the present, for its primary concern is direct moral reformation. The prophetic books of the Bible thus evidence two alternating visions: the vision of an ideal, a New Jerusalem projected into the future; and the vision which responds to the reality of corruption by foretelling widespread destruction, from which only a few, a saving remnant, will survive. Scholars such as Battestin and Paulson have discussed the arc of Pope's career in terms of the ideal of a Golden Age.[10] Paulson, in particular, anticipates my point by identifying a "Pollio" and an "anti-Pollio" vision, drawing his terms from the Virgilian half of *Messiah*. But if, recalling Isaiah as the other half of that early poem, we transpose this structure into a biblical key, then *The Dunciad*, as anti-Pollio nightmare, is seen as presenting a parallel to the prophets' negative vision.

Messiah (1712) reminds us that the prophetic books were a constitutive factor in Pope's verse from an early date. In the Advertisement to that poem we learn of Pope's intention to annotate the poem "since it was written with this particular view, that the reader by comparing the several thoughts might see how far the images and descriptions of the Prophet are superior to those of the Poet."[11] Naturally, *Messiah* offers excellent examples of the way Pope fused classical and biblical elements. Lines 81 and 82, for example, describe how, with the return of the Golden Age, "The smiling Infant in his Hand shall take The crested Basilisk and speckled snake" (p. 120). Pope's footnote cites Isaiah 11:8: "And the sucking child shall play on the hole of the asp, and the weaned child shall put his hand on the cockatrice' den." Pope's image, obviously, is not identical to Isaiah's, nor is there an analogue in Virgil's eclogue. It evokes, for me at least, the baby Hercules holding a strangled snake in either hand, the same image, in fact, Milton had used to portray his Infant at the close of the Nativity Ode.[12] Pope appears to be conflating a classical image of strength and courage with an image of strength of a different order, the Messiah who renders evil harmless. With Milton's procedures in mind, the classical element is transformed as it is subordinated and assimilated to religious ideals.

Notes

1.   An exception is Rebecca Price Parkin's "Alexander Pope's Use of Biblical and Ecclesiastical Allusions," *SVEC* 57 (1967):1183–216.

2.   Two critics have recently pressed the case that the role of prophet is part of Pope's poetic persona. Sanford Budick, in *The Poetry of Civilization* (New Haven: Yale Univ. Press, 1974), argues for the "heraldic" voice in Pope and others. Deborah Knuth, in a recent Yale dissertation, "*The Dunciad* and the Old Testament," makes a convincing case for specific allusions, and especially for viewing the physical appearance of *The Dunciad*, with all its annotations, as a conscious analogue to the Douai Bible of Pope's childhood.

3.   Aubrey Williams, *Pope's "Dunciad": A Study of Its Meaning* (Hamden, Conn.: Archon Books, 1955).

4.   Knuth (p. 60) cites Erskine-Hill's comment on Book II.46 ("senseless, lifeless! idol void and vain!"), that the dunces are a "dim analogy" to Israelites worshipping the Golden Calf, in *Pope: The Dunciad* (London: Edward Arnold, 1972), p. 26. Obviously, I am arguing for a broader extension of this analogy.

5.   Donald T. Siebert, "Cibber and Satan: The *Dunciad* and Civilization," *ECS* 10 (1976–1977):211.

6.   Siebert, pp. 204, 211, and 208–209.

7.   " 'Wit and Poetry and Pope': Some Observations on His Imagery," in *Pope and His Contemporaries. Essays Presented to George Sherburn*, ed. James. L. Clifford and Louis A. Landa (New York: Oxford Univ. Press, 1949), p. 39.

8.   *The Dunciad*, ed. James Sutherland, *The Twickenham Edition of the Poems of Alexander Pope*, gen. ed. John Butt, 11 vols. (New Haven: Yale Univ. Press, 1939–1969), 5:254–65. All book, line, and page references made in the text are to this edition.

9.   See, for example, Louis Bredvold, "A Note in Defense of Satire," in *Studies in the Literature of the Augustan Age*, ed. Richard C. Boys (Ann Arbor: Augustan Reprint Society, 1952), pp. 1–13; Alvin Kernan, *The Cankered Muse* (New Haven: Yale Univ. Press, 1959), pp. 7 and 18; Robert C. Elliot, *The Power of Satire: Magic, Ritual, Art* (Princeton: Princeton Univ. Press, 1960), p. 289, where he cites Old Testament curses as examples of "magical satire."

10.   Martin C. Battestin, *The Providence of Wit* (Oxford: Clarendon Press, 1974), pp. 58ff; Ronald Paulson, "Satire, and Poetry, and Pope," in *English Satire*, The Clark Library Lectures (Los Angeles: Univ. of California, 1972), pp. 59–106.

11.   *Twickenham Edition*, 1:111. James A. Winn has suggested to me an analogue from Addison, *Spectator* no. 160, 3 September 1711: "*Homer* has innumerable Flights that *Virgil* was

not able to reach, and in the Old Testament we find several Passages more elevated and sublime than any in *Homer*." For a full discussion of the implications of similar opinions for style see Vincent Freimarck, "The Bible and Neo-Classical Views of Style," *JEGP* 51 (1952): 507–26.

12.   Cf. "On the Morning of Christ's Nativity," stanza xxv. I am grateful to Leslie Moore for pointing out the Miltonic precedent.

[from *Locke and the Scriblerians*]

CHRISTOPHER FOX

. . .

In closing it might help, then, to look briefly at several uses Pope makes of the contemporary discussion of identity and consciousness. Take, for instance, the *Epistle to Cobham* (1734), which addresses at least two themes we have examined: Locke's critique of the substantial self, and his attempt to locate identity instead in consciousness. Georges Poulet has said that it "is the greatness of the eighteenth century to have conceived the prime moment of consciousness as a generative moment . . . not only of other moments but also of a self which takes shape by and through the means of these very moments."[1] As I have tried to suggest, however, this view was not accepted immediately. Pope's *Cobham* in 1734 stands in an interesting historical relation to the movement between the older vision of the self as a substantial and the newer vision of the self-in-consciousness; between the earliest, hostile responses to Locke's new criterion of consciousness—say, Stillingfleet's puzzles "How comes *Person* to stand for *this*?" in 1698—and Hume's pronouncement in 1740 that "Most philosophers" now seem "inclin'd to think, that personal identity *arises* from consciousness."[2] For in this work Pope attempts to recon-cile, in his own eclectic manner, the two visions of the self. This attempt at reconciling the two visions accounts, I believe, for a central problem in the poem: that is, the relation between Pope's opening section (1–173), with its emphasis on the transience, fluidity, and inscrutability of the human personal-ity, and his closing section (174–265), which introduces the ruling passion to argue that beneath these fluctuations there is an observable consistency at the core.

Locke recognized that the problem of identity could not be separated from the problem of knowledge. As we noted in Part II, it was in all likelihood the problem of finding the substantial soul that led Locke to search for a new criterion of identity, another way of saying that we are the same persons. In a chapter that provides the analogue for Pope's lines on the "microscopic eye" in *An Essay on Man*,"[3] Locke emphasizes our inability to glimpse empirically (much less know) the substantial self, an entity that remains a "supposed *something*" of which "we have no clear distinct *Idea* at all" (*Essay Concerning Human Understanding* 2.23.37).* Elsewhere he remarks that it is "past controversy, that we have in us something that thinks, our very Doubts about what it is, confirm the certainty of its being, though we must content our selves in the Ignorance of what kind of *Being* it is" (4.3.6). In 1697, he would tell Stillingfleet that all we know of this underlying substance is "the obscure, indistinct, vague Idea . . . of *something*,"[4] and this word, referring to the substantial self, would recur throughout the controversy.

Thirty years later, for example, in the second edition of his *Procedure, Extent, and Limits of the Human Understanding* (1729), Peter Browne would complain that Locke has "confounded the received way of thinking and speaking" about such subjects. Soon afterward, Browne himself nevertheless tells us that "in this Life" we have no clear idea of the soul. For this reason,

> we are naturally led to express it by a *Negative*, and call it an Immaterial Substance; that is, something which hath a *Being* but is not Matter; something that *Is*, but is not any thing we directly know; and for want of any direct and positive Idea of it, we conceive and express it after the best manner we can; saying it is *Something*.[5]

A decade after that, while discussing his own problematic attempts to "catch *myself*," Hume would argue that someone else "may, perhaps, perceive *something* simple and continu'd, which he calls *himself*; tho' [and a big "tho' " this is] I am certain there is no such principle in me."[6]

Like his contemporaries, Pope connects the problem of identity with the problem of knowledge. At an early point in the *Epistle to Cobham*, subtitled *Of Knowledge and the Characters of Men*, the poet remarks:

> *Something* as dim to our internal view,
> Is thus, perhaps, the cause of most we do.[7]

In positing that our personality does inhere in "something" simple and individual, Pope here, unlike Hume, supports the substantial vision of the self. But like Locke before him, the poet is also aware of the dimness of that "something," of our inability to glimpse that unique core of selfhood and "our Ignorance of what kind of *Being* it is." This problem of knowledge and character—that is, the difficulty of finding an inherent "sameness" in the apparent chaos of individual thought and action—is a central theme of the poem.

In presenting that theme in his opening section (1–173), Pope works out

*Locke references are to book, chapter, and paragraph.

his own poetic version of the self-in-consciousness, which was just beginning in the 1730s to gain some acceptance. Attempting to find language to describe the Lockean self and its implications, writers turned to the image of the river. In its Heraclitean sense, this image had of course long been used to depict the outer flux of the world-in-time. But with Locke's theory and the subsequent controversy over it, the river becomes an apt metaphor for the incessant fluctuations in the *inner* world of consciousness, a world in which successive ideas are always "passing in train, one going, and another coming, without intermission" (*Essay* 2.7.9). Our "consciousness," Thomas Reid writes in his critique of Locke, is "still flowing like the water of a river, or like time itself. The consciousness I have this moment, can no more be the same consciousness I had the last moment, than this moment can be the last moment."[8] Earlier in the century, Berkeley speaks of the "floating ideas" of what he sees as an ever-changing consciousness;[9] and Clarke evokes the same image in cataloguing the ramifications of Collins's Lockean vision. By arguing that consciousness is a "fleeting" activity and that "the person may be the same by a continual Superaddition of the *like Consciousness*," Collins had made "individual Personality" a "mere *external imaginary Denomination*," just as, Clarke adds, "a *River* is called the *same River*, though the Water of it be every Day new."[10] Pope employs the same image in his own evocation of the new vision of the self:

> Our depths who fathoms, or our shallows finds,
> Quick whirls, and shifting eddies, of our minds?
> Life's stream for Observation will not stay,
> It hurries all too fast to mark their way.
> In vain sedate reflections we would make,
> When half our knowledge we must snatch, not take.
>
> (29–34)

Pope here posits the dual nature of experience in consciousness, of the self looking outward on the ever-fleeting stream of human experience and, simultaneously, reflecting on its own operations. And what we observe on both levels, Pope intimates, is a state of incessant change and successive motion, the continual hurrying of "Life's stream" both within and without the self. Any attempt at a "sedate" reflection in this ever-changing human world is "vain," for both the observer and what he observes—be it another or himself—simply will not "stay." The poet's emphasis here is the emphasis of the rest of the opening section: the "Quick whirls, and shifting eddies, of our minds" and the near-impossibility of charting these currents in others, much less in ourselves, with any accuracy. Here, too, Pope develops an attendant implication some critics saw in Locke's theory, that the personality is a transient thing. This seems to be a central motif of Pope's opening, as he repeatedly portrays the puzzling ways the "same man" is, ironically, *not* the same any two moments of his life:

> See the same man, in vigour, in the gout;
> Alone, in company; in place, or out;
> Early at Bus'ness, and at Hazard late;
> Mad at a Fox-chace, wise at a Debate;
> Drunk at a Borough, civil at a Ball,
> Friendly at Hackney, faithless at Whitehall.
>
> (130–35)

Although Pope raises the question of "sameness" prominently, he does not, finally, take the self-in-consciousness to the conclusion of a Collins or a Hume. There is, after all, "something" underlying our experience, even though this substantial self remains ever "dim to our internal view." In his closing section (174–265), Pope still does not admit our ability to find that "something" with any certainty. But he does advance a modified version of the older vision by offering us another way of assuring ourselves that beneath the fluctuations of a seemingly transient self there is an observable permanence at the core. And observing this principle of permanence, which is perhaps most apparent at death, we will have a way of perceiving some real connection between the changes.[11] This principle of permanence—and, perhaps, Pope's direct response to the problem of personal identity—is the ruling passion, a knowable manifestation of that unknowable "something."

Though F. W. Bateson and others have found this doctrine in *Cobham* to be theoretically silly, a young contemporary of Pope's. David Hume, apparently did not. In Book 1 of his *Treatise*, Hume speaks of a "prevailing passion" to which persons are "naturally inclined." Later on in the same book, in his chapter on personal identity, Hume argues that "personal identity" may be considered two ways: as it pertains to the understanding or imagination, "*and* as it regards our passions." Though the passions are not the subject of this chapter, they are the subject of Hume's second book, where he talks at one point about a ruling passion becoming a "settled principle of action" and, at another, about how a "predominant passion swallows up" an inferior one "and converts it [to] itself." And "hence one master Passion in the breast," Pope had written, "Like Aaron's serpent, swallows up the rest."[12] Whether Hume works out the implications of the prevailing passion vis à vis personal identity is unimportant here. Of interest is his willingness, like that of Pope before him, to consider the passions in that context.

Despite Pope's attempt to find a principle of permanence, the *Epistle to Cobham* seems to reflect a larger stress in his poetry of the 1730s on the fluidity of the self and the difficulties of "fixing" it for more than a moment at a time. Melinda Alliker Rabb has noted a related emphasis, in the *Horatian Poems* of the same decade, on "fractured images" of the self.[13] Consider, for instance, the lines to Bolingbroke in *The First Epistle of the First Book of Horace* (1738), where Pope tells his interlocutor and friend:

> You laugh, if Coat and Breeches strangely vary,
> White Gloves, and Linnen worthy Lady Mary!
> But when no Prelate's Lawn with Hair-shirt lin'd,
> Is half so incoherent as my Mind,
> When (each Opinion with the next at strife,
> One ebb and flow of follies all my Life)
> I plant, root up, I build, and then confound,
> Turn round to square, and square again to round.
>
> . . . .
>
> [You] hang your lip, to see a Seam awry!
> Careless how ill I with myself agree;
> Kind to my dress, my figure, not to Me.[14]

The emphasis here is on the lack of coherence Pope senses in himself, on the gaps or (to extend his clothes metaphor) seams in experience. A year later, Hume would notice a similar discontinuity in his experience and point to difficulties of catching *"myself"* from one moment to another or of finding something continued that he could call *"himself"*[15] Both the poet and the philosopher are responding, at least in part, to problems that result from a new way of looking at the self and from the gradual displacement by consciousness of what we used to call our souls.

Notes

1. Georges Poulet, *Studies in Human Time*, trans. Elliot Coleman (Baltimore: Johns Hopkins University Press, 1956), p. 23.

2. Edward Stillingfleet, *The Bishop of Worcester's Answer to Mr. Locke's Second Letter, Wherein his Notion of Ideas Is prov'd to be Inconsistent with it self And with the Articles of the Christian Faith* (London, 1698), p. 59; and David Hume, *A Treatise of Human Nature*, ed. L. A. Selby-Bigge, rev. P. H. Nidditch (2d ed., Oxford: Clarendon Press, 1978), p. 635.

3. Compare Locke's chapter *"Of our Complex Ideas of Substances"* (*Essay* 2.23.12) with Epistle 1, lines 189–204, of *An Essay on Man*, which includes the couplet: "Why has not Man a microscopic eye? / For this plain reason, Man is not a Fly." See *The Twickenham Edition of the Works of Alexander Pope*, ed. John Butt, 11 vols. (New Haven: Yale University Press, 1939–1969), vol. 3, part 1, *An Essay on Man*, ed. Maynard Mack (1950), pp. 38–40.

4. John Locke, *A Letter to the Right Reverend Edward Ld Bishop of Worcester concerning some Passages relating to Mr. Locke's Essay of Humane Understanding: In a late Discourse of his Lordships, in Vindication of the Trinity* (London, 1697), p. 40. In the same pamphlet (p. 58), Locke goes on to tell Stillingfleet that "by the Existence of *Thought* in me, to which *something* that thinks is evidently and necessarily connected in my Mind, I come to be certain that there exists in me *something* that thinks, though of that *something* which I call *Substance* also, I have but a very obscure, confused Idea."

5. Peter Browne, *The Procedure, Extent, and Limits of the Human Understanding* (2d ed., London, 1729), pp. 73, 78–79.

6. Hume, *Treatise*, p. 252. For some other occurrences see, for example, Edward Stillingfleet, *Discourse in Vindication of the Doctrine of the Trinity* (London, 1696), p. 259; Samuel Clarke, *The Works of Samuel Clarke*, 4 vols. (London, 1738), 3:790–91; Anthony, Earl of Shaftesbury, *Characteristics of Men, Manners, Opinions, Times*, ed. J. M. Robertson, 2 vols. (1900; reprint ed., Gloucester, Mass.: Peter Smith, 1963), 2:275; and [Andrew Baxter], *An Enquiry into the Nature of the Human Soul; Wherein the Immateriality of the Soul is evinced from the Principles of Reason and Philosophy* (London, ca. 1733), p. 144n.

7. Pope, *The Twickenham Edition*, vol. 3, part 2, *Epistles to Several Persons*, ed. F. W. Bateson (2d ed., 1961), p. 18, lines 49–50 (my italics). All further *Cobham* citations are to this edition, cited in the text by line numbers alone.

8. Thomas Reid, *Essays on the Intellectual Powers of Man* (1785; reprint ed., New York: Garland Publishing, 1971), p. 336.

9. George Berkeley, *The Works of George Berkeley, Bishop of Cloyne*, ed. A. A. Luce and T. E. Jessop, 9 vols. (London: Nelson, 1948–1957), 2:233.

10. *Works of Clarke*, 3:844.

11. On this point, see Christopher Fox, " 'Gone as soon as Found': Pope's *Epistle to Cobham* and the Death-day as Moment of Truth," *Studies in English Literature* 20 (1980): 431–48.

12. Hume, *Treatise*, pp. 120, 253, 419–20; and Pope, *The Twickenham Edition*, vol. 3, part 1, *An Essay on Man*, Epistle 2, p. 71, line 132. "As a peg for hanging anecdotes on no doubt Pope's hypothesis" of a ruling passion "was adequate," writes Bateson, in the standard edition. See Pope, *Twickenham*, vol. 3, part 2, *Epistles*, ed. Bateson, p. xxxv.

13. Melinda Alliker Rabb, "Lost in a House of Mirrors: Pope's *Imitations of Horace*," *Papers on Language and Literature* 18 (1982): 302.

14. *The Twickenham Edition*, vol. 4, *Imitations of Horace*, ed. John Butt (2d ed., 1953), pp. 291–93, lines 163–70, 174–75.

15. Hume, *Treatise*, p. 252.

[from "Strangeness and Temper: Pope in the Act of Judgment"]

Meg Gertmenian

In Pope's work there is a recurrent note of wonder, an evocation of genuine strangeness in spectacles of human folly and perversity. He is the great satirist of "Imitating Fools":[1] his Timon, his dunces, coquettes, and dowagers all shape themselves, with depraved but intensely aspiring energy, toward some version of an ideal. Their aspirations and failures take deformed shapes, which can invite deflating scorn from a satirist who honors "Temper," but in the act of judging them Pope often registers intelligent awe, or fascination. Passages of sensuous imagery, verging on the phantasmagoric, and of a spoken style like rapt chanting, move beyond ironic deflation in poems throughout his career. Pope's faculty for wonder saves his satire from dismissiveness—potential for unobservant smugness is strong when satire is written from the vantage-point of success in shaping life toward an ideal. The living, sociable reality of Pope's success is present in the urbane conversational style of his poems, often addressed to figures who embody social and moral substance, and who are his friends. His appreciation for the strange energy in failed imitations of an ideal is a healthy complement to his temperate moralizing: it keeps him vividly attentive to the spectacles he satirizes, and makes him a more moving, because moved, voice for the ideals he honors and imitates.

This argument for the healthy moral effect of wondering passages in Pope's work is intended to offer a pertinent objection to the work of two related groups of recent critics. Pope's imitation of the temperate Horatian model for living and writing has lately received much attention from critics and biographers, who have shown the vitality of his commitment to it.[2] The triple correspondence between the persuasive *persona* of the "plain good man," Pope's habitual style in epistolary satire, and Pope's chosen style of private life as we can gather it from his letters or his house, is truly satisfying. Perhaps because of this correspondence, Pope's stability and happiness as a moralist have become linked to the temperate Horatian tone. His departures from that tone are associated mainly with trouble for his ideals.

Meg Gertmenian, "Strangeness and Temper: Pope in the Act of Judgment." Reprinted by permission of *SEL: Studies in English Literature 1500–1900, 22,* 3 (Summer 1982).

Recent critics interested in strains of Pope's style that diverge from Horatian conversation tend to emphasize anxiety, or conflict, or despair for the satirist perceiving too much disparity between a civilized ideal and the debased actualities of his society. Pope excited vocally over long stretches, Pope expanding phantasmagoric images, appears in recent criticism as a "darker" Pope, driven from temperate amusement to outspoken condemnation, or alienated, visionary moralizing.[3] The "un-Horatian" tones are seen to come into Pope's poetry late, as Pope grows older: the later imitations of Horace, and the last version of *The Dunciad*, tend to be the focus for attention to such tones. Thus the note of wonder is linked mainly to Pope's increasingly turbulent and lonely satiric stance toward the close of his career.[4]

A darker view of human nature does seem to me a felt development in Pope's later work. And the moral health and complexity of the civilized Horatian talker is an undeniable source of Pope's persuasive power in satire: his ideal comes alive in his voice, dramatizing Horatian virtues that he consistently honors, "Sense," "Good Humour," "Temper." But excited, wondering depictions of folly and perversity appear in Pope's work as early as his development of an urbane talking style—examples of both may be found in the "Epistle to Miss Blount, with the Works of Voiture," or in *The Rape of the Lock*. Departures from a conversational style into exclaiming witness to the strange cannot, then, simply be taken to signal increasing isolation and anxiety for a sensible moralist. They do indicate that Pope characteristically, early and late, departs from one rule associated with Horatian "Temper," the rule that opens the *Sixth Epistle*:

> "Not to Admire, is all the Art I know,
> To make men happy, and to keep them so."
> —*Sixth Epistle of the First Book of Horace, Imitated*, 1–2[5]

Judicious withholding of excitement, scorn for vulgar or prideful extremes, is a sensible stance urged by the Horatian model. Of course Pope mocks indiscriminate gaping at false splendor. The rapture of fools at "momentary monsters"[6] depends on their taking the monsters for sublime creations; Pope sees the monsters. But that is the point: what he often sees, when he sees through failed imitations of ideals, is still a marvel, fabulous, truly strange, worthy of excited attention. What Pope sees at Timon's villa, for example, carries him beyond mock-wonder.

Pope begins the *Epistle to Burlington* in a somewhat dismissive vein. His use of the word "strange," at first, signals mock-wonder at that which is too stupid or pathetic to merit excitement:

> 'Tis strange, the Miser should his Cares employ,
> To gain those Riches he can ne'er enjoy:
> Is it less strange, the Prodigal should waste

His wealth, to purchase what he ne'er can taste?
    —*Epistle to Richard Boyle, Earl of Burlington*, 1–4

Pope proceeds to mock the "Imitating Fools" who will botch a noble ideal of architecture, "And of one beauty many blunders make" (25–28). The passage on Timon's villa opens with deflating scorn for big blunders, and for visitors awed by empty bigness: "At Timon's Villa let us pass a day, / Where all cry out, 'What sums are thrown away!' " (99–100). Here is the Horatian scorn for indiscriminate gaping; pretending to wonder, Pope teaches not to admire.

But Pope's depiction of Timon's villa is not ruled by ironic deflation. By the end of the passage, a prodigal's perversions of value come alive and take marvelous shapes. Pope invites his reader to let the place happen to the "suff'ring eye" (119) as an immediate, evolving, surrounding adventure. Everything seen and felt, everything created by the prodigal's effort to imitate greatness and civilization in his home, is wrong, backwards, frustrated, sterile. Yet the place is a nightmare funhouse. One cannot dismiss only as "empty" the miracles Pope finds there, the sea-statue that revives the world of myth, then runs it aground, as she sails into dry myrtle, the "gaping Tritons" that regurgitate that world into the buffet, even the quieter metamorphosis when "To rest, the Cushion and soft Dean invite." One is indeed glad, as the bedevilled satirist is, to go home to sane talk with Richard Boyle, but Timon's villa is a wonder.

Some shifting or doubling of focus, between an actual social setting and a more dreamlike realm, assists the tone of wonder Pope evoked for human perversity. Timon's villa is a physical place, but being a made place it is a natural metaphor for its maker's spirit, and Pope makes that spirit move in its animated objects. A similar shift into fantasia lends magic to his "Cave of Poverty and Poetry" (*The Dunciad*, book I, 29–78). The passage is a fine and characteristic revision of Dryden's picture of the "Nursery," the training-school for child-actors, in *MacFlecknoe* (lines 64–93).[7] Dryden's satiric scene remains in the actual social world, relying heavily on local references. The result is assured mock-heroic deflation: all "wonders" are really blunders. Foolish aspiration to greatness in play-writing is cut down to size: the right place for Shadwell's throne is the children's school, where boys squeak a hero's lines, "Where little *Maximins* the gods defy."

By contrast, Pope's satiric scene develops quickly, and much more fully than Dryden's, beyond any local place. The "events" in his version embody the act of bad writing itself; the actors of them are timeless devices of literature, images, metaphors, genres, gone to Chaos. What makes noise in Pope's picture is not a boy-actor but "nonsense," imagined as a promising infant. Pope's "Cave" is a stage for mental actions, and the action there has bizarre grace, however repellent the results in actual miscellanies from Grub Street. The chaotic action merges into a "mazy dance" of devices, and the loving motion, perversely harmonious and fruitful, makes miracle transformations of the world: "Realms shift their place, and Ocean turns to land." The transformations express foolish fancy, the false sublime, but the sensuous experience is delightful, glamorous:

> Here gay Description AEgypt glads with show'rs,
> Or gives to Zembla fruits, to Barca flow'rs;
> Glitt'ring with ice here hoary hills are seen,
> There painted vallies of eternal green,
> In cold December fragrant chaplets blow,
> And heavy harvests nod beneath the snow.
>
> (I, 73–78)

Enhancing and prolonging the fantasy life of the passage, Pope does not change the sensible evaluation of addled efforts toward sublimity, but does allow for the excitement of wonder in the act of judging. The passage echoes Titania's speech in *A Midsummer Night's Dream* (II.i) not only in chance images but also in the spell-casting effect. For all his Augustan mistrust of fanciful flights, Pope seems closer to Shakespeare than to Dryden in his appreciation for the strange.[8]

Mingling of discriminating "Sense" with genuine enchantment, of urbane wit with excited wonder, distinguishes Pope's early work as well. A reader finishing *The Rape of the Lock* knows very well he is leaving a silly, misguided, sterile world, and he also knows that the world as Pope pictured it was truly charmed, partaking of the airy beauty and motion of the sylphs. Pope's sense for magic in that silly world distinguishes him from its fools and from its limited moralist, Clarissa.[9] The fools in *The Rape of the Lock* worship Belinda's hair as a war-prize or sacred object; the pragmatic Clarissa flattens it to an unreliable piece of equipment: "Curl'd or uncurl'd, since Locks will turn to grey" (canto V, 26). Pope evokes bewitching beauty in it, while making clear that to worship it is silly:

> A sudden Star, it shot thro' liquid Air,
> And drew behind a radiant *Trail of Hair*.
> Not *Berenice's* Locks first rose so bright,
> The Heav'ns bespangling with dishevel'd Light.
>
> (canto V, 127–30)

The distinction between Clarissa's moralizing and Pope's is not a simple one between "grave" sense and "gay" enjoyment of pretty nonsense. Pope's supremacy over a Clarissa consists in ready, acute, and varied response to what he judges. His wondering at folly can include pain, or shock. The futile energy of his mad poet (in the *Epistle to Arbuthnot*) is painful: "Is there, who lock'd from Ink and Paper, scrawls / With desp'rate Charcoal round his darken'd walls?" His rich Pamela (in the "Epistle to Miss Blount, with the Works of Voiture") is another haunting spectacle, so cut off from love, and so allied to finery, that she seems transformed to a jewel herself. "A vain, unquiet, glitt'ring, wretched Thing!" The lines on Pamela occur in one of Pope's earliest epistolary poems, in which he celebrates the virtue of "Good Humour" (synonymous with "Temper"), and shows his early mastery of the Horatian style, the lively and sensible sound of civilized talk.[10] I think this early poem, like the mature epistolary satires, shows how Pope's marvelling can be an important, and healthy, complement to his temperate moralizing.

Notes

1.   *Epistle to Richard Boyle, Earl of Burlington*, line 26. All quotations from Pope are from *The Twickenham Edition of the Poems of Alexander Pope*, gen. ed. John Butt, 11 vols. (New Haven: Yale Univ. Press, 1939–1954), vols. 2–6, line numbers cited in parentheses.

2.   Important works are Reuben Brower, *Alexander Pope: The Poetry of Allusion* (Oxford: The Clarendon Press, 1959), and Maynard Mack, *The Garden and the City: Retirement and Politics in the Later Poetry of Pope, 1731–1743* (Toronto: Toronto Univ. Press, 1968). John Butt also emphasizes Pope's personal identification with a Horatian *persona*: "Pope: The Man and the Poet," in *Of Books and Humankind: Essays and Poems Presented to Bonamy Dobrée*, ed. John Butt (London: Routledge and Kegan Paul, 1964), pp. 69–79. See also Peter Dixon, *The World of Pope's Satires* (London: Methuen, 1968), pp. 38–39; William Bowman Piper, "The Conversational Poetry of Pope," *SEL* 10 (Summer 1970): 505–24; Barbara Lauren, "Pope's *Epistle to Bolingbroke*: Satire from the Vantage of Retirement," *SEL* 15 (Summer 1975): 419–30; Lawrence Lee Davidow, "Pope's Verse Epistles: Friendship and the Private Sphere of Life," *HLQ* 40 (February 1977): 151–70; Thomas Woodman, "Pope and the Polite," *EIC* 28 (January 1978): 19–37.

3.   See Thomas Edwards, *This Dark Estate: A Reading of Pope* (Berkeley: Univ. of California Press, 1963), and Tony Tanner, "Reason and the Grotesque: Pope's *Dunciad*," *Crit Q* 7 (Summer 1965): 1945–60. Also S. L. Goldberg, excerpt from "Alexander Pope," in Judith O'Neal, ed., *Critics on Pope* (Coral Gables, Florida: Univ. of Miami Press, 1968), pp. 37–53; and Piper.

4.   The books by Brower and Edwards, and the articles by Tanner and Piper, point to the darkening tone in later poems. In her study of Pope's imagery, Patricia Spacks associates phantasmagoric passages with a madness that repels Pope and that seems more extensive in *The Dunciad*: see *An Argument of Images: The Poetry of Alexander Pope* (Cambridge, Mass.: Harvard Univ. Press, 1971), especially ch. 7.

It should also be noted that Pope's phantasmagoric imagery has been linked to cool, detached wit and laughter. Two examples are Donald T. Siebert, Jr., "Cibber and Satan: *The Dunciad* and Civilization," *ECS* 10 (1976/1977): 203–21, and W. K. Wimsatt, Jr., "The Augustan Mode in English Poetry," *ELH* 20 (March 1953): 1–14. The laughing view of such imagery ignores or disallows the possibility argued in this essay, of Pope's expressing genuine wonder at the strange.

5.   Pope borrows the first couplet from Thomas Creech's translation.

6.   *The Dunciad*, book I, 83.

7.   In *The Poems and Fables of John Dryden*, ed. James Kinsley (Oxford: The Clarendon Press, 1962).

8.   In his review of the Twickenham edition of *The Dunciad*, reprinted in *The Common Pursuit* (New York: New York Univ. Press, 1952), pp. 88–96, F. R. Leavis suggests that a

sense of wonder is a distinctive characteristic of Pope among Augustan satirists, a characteristic linking him to earlier poets like Donne and Marvell, while harmonizing fully with Augustan values. The pertinence of wonder to Pope's Horatian moralizing seems to me worth further exploration.

9. Many critics of *The Rape of the Lock* have noted the delicate ambiguities that distinguish Pope's narrative stance from what can be expressed in explicit moralizing. Two recent critics who suggest that a prosaic tone limits Clarissa's version of "Sense" are J. S. Cunningham, *Pope: The Rape of the Lock* (Great Neck, NY: Barron's Educational Series, 1961), and G. S. Rousseau, ed., introduction to *Twentieth-Century Interpretations of "The Rape of the Lock"* (Englewood Cliffs, NJ: Prentice-Hall, 1969).

10. John Butt notes this early mastery in "Pope: The Man and the Poet," p. 77.

[from "The Pope Controversy: Romantic Poetics and the English Canon"]

James Chandler

[1]

The point about nature and England is important because although, as I have tried to suggest, it makes some sense to explain the movement to exclude Pope from the canon (or demote him within it) in terms of nationalist interests, the question of Pope's Englishness is almost never raised in the actual controversy over his status. This is the case from the inception of the controversy. The dedication to Warton's *Essay on Pope* does, it is true, announce its concern with locating Pope's rank among "our English poets," but he nowhere directly brings nationalist arguments against Pope's reputation.[1] Warton's method, as readers of the *Essay* will recall, was rather to establish certain major-minor distinctions among the English poets and then to determine "in which of these classes Pope deserves to be placed" (1:viii). Yet the confusions that beset Warton's work are telling, and they survived through much of the subsequent writings about Pope. The ambiguity centers chiefly in the major-minor distinctions. On the one hand, Warton seeks to erect a fourfold hierarchy among English writers, placing Pope in the second group with Dryden, Donne, Denham, Cowley, and Congreve: all writers who "possessed the true poetical genius, in a more moderate degree" than others such as Spenser, Shakespeare, Milton, Otway, and Lee, but who nonetheless "had noble talents for moral, ethical, and panegyrical poetry" (1:vii). On the other hand, Warton wants to make a distinction between the "true poets" and other worthy writers, and to insinuate that Pope was no true poet. After complaining, for example, that his contemporaries do not "sufficiently attend to the difference there is betwixt a MAN OF WIT, a MAN OF SENSE, and a TRUE POET," Warton goes on to ask about Donne (grouped with Pope in the fourfold scheme) and Swift, "undoubted men of wit, and men of sense": "what traces have they left of PURE POETRY?" (1:ii). That Pope is implicated here is clear from a later question, in which Pope is named specifically. After asserting that "the sublime

James Chandler, "The Pope Controversy: Romantic Poetics and the English Canon." Reprinted from *Critical Inquiry* 10 (March 1984) by permission. Published by The University of Chicago.

and the Pathetic are the two chief nerves of all genuine poetry," Warton asks pointedly: "What is there very sublime or very pathetic in Pope?" (1:vi). It was to this latter sort of invidious distinction that Johnson was responding in a celebrated question of his own: "If Pope be not a poet, where is poetry to be found?"[2] This confusion, as I said, lasted for decades; in his 1818 *Lectures on the English Poets*, Hazlitt could still declare that "the question, whether Pope was a poet, has hardly yet been settled."[3]

Whichever way we understand Warton's distinctions to cut, however, it remains clear that they do not specifically introduce Pope's national loyalty into the controversy, directing attention instead to the relative "purity" of his poetry. How strongly Warton was actually influenced by the desire to find the enchanted ground of English poetry on English soil is a difficult matter to decide. But it is fair to say that many readers have suspected that Warton's stated reasons for demoting Pope do not correspond to his actual motives. Lipking captures this suspicion in his suggestion that "the interest of the *Essay* can only depend on the search for principles according to which Pope is to be excluded from the first rank of his art" (p. 365). The desire to unseat Pope is represented here as having preexisted definitions (of "pure poetry" and the like) employed for the purpose.

We have seen how far Bowles, as early as 1791, was willing to identify himself in print with a Burkean English nationalism and a corresponding distrust of French cultural influence. Yet when he steps up to mediate the quarrel between Warton and Johnson, the issue of nationalism never emerges. In Bowles' 1806 edition of Pope, the headnote to the "Concluding Observations on the Poetic Character of Pope" explains that Bowles' aim is to "state the grounds of this difference [between Warton and Johnson] upon principles which . . . will be easily recognised."[4] These two principles are stated outright in the ensuing discussion: first, "that 'all images drawn from what is beautiful or sublime in the works of NATURE, are more beautiful and sublime than any images drawn from ART'; and that they are therefore, *per se*, more poetical"; and second, that "in like manner, those *Passions* of the human heart, which belong to Nature in general, are, *per se*, more adapted to the *higher species* of Poetry, than those which are derived from *incidental* and *transient* MANNERS."[5] In these two notions, specifically articulated for the purpose, Bowles claimed to have found the means of establishing the rule by which we would estimate the "general poetic character of Pope" and thus of determining once and for all his proper rank as an English poet: that is, right at the top of the class of second-rate poets. When Campbell sought to reestablish Pope among the very greatest of English poets in the preface to his 1819 *Specimens*, Bowles responded by restating these same two propositions and by rechristening them with the Coleridgean phrase, "The Invariable Principles of Poetry."[6] Insofar as the ensuing controversy had critical substance, it took these principles, either by themselves or in their relation to the case of Pope, as constituting the main item on its agenda.

Many participants in the debate, on both sides, saw that Bowles' principles resembled those by which poets like Wordsworth and Coleridge defended their own poetry. We think of such principles ourselves, I believe, as central to the poetics of high English Romanticism. It is of course possible to explain the emergence of such principles—as Samuel Monk, Walter Jackson Bate, M. H. Abrams, and many since have done—in terms of critical or aesthetic history.[7] Such an account would show the debt of these principles to Longinus, John Dennis, the Edmund Burke of *A Philosophical Inquiry into . . . the Sublime and the Beautiful*, the theoreticians of the picturesque, and so on. As I suggested earlier, I do not propose to argue the extreme case that the principles of Romantic poetics can be explained solely as an ad hoc contrivance to justify the ouster of Pope. And I would not want to deny that many participants in the Pope controversy of the 1820s accepted Bowles' representation of his commitment to these principles at face value—that is, as categories independent of any prior, or extrapoetic, attitude toward Pope. There were, however, two pamphleteers who argued otherwise: Isaac D'Israeli, man of letters and father of the later prime minister, and Lord Byron. Their positions are the ones that merit particular attention here.

D'Israeli's critique of Bowles, which appeared in the July 1820 issue of the *Quarterly Review*, elaborates a central claim in Johnson's response to Joseph Warton decades earlier. This claim, as quoted by D'Israeli himself, is that "To circumscribe poetry . . . by a definition will only shew the narrowness of the definer."[8] In D'Israeli's hands, however, the Johnsonian apothegm expands into a full-blown assault on those who place their trust in theoretical principles. The question at issue for D'Israeli comes down to a choice between what we have been calling the poetic canon and what he, following others before him, calls "canons of criticism" (p. 410). He suggests that where the critical canon, in the form of "invariable" or universalized principles, comes into conflict with a duly canonized poet such as Pope, the former must give way. Obviously, the notion of whether a poet is indeed duly canonized is a problem for this account, but it is not one about which D'Israeli has much to say.

D'Israeli's early summary statement indicates what concerns him most in Bowles' response to Campbell: "Mr Bowles has adopted a system which terminates in an exclusion of a great poet from the highest order of poets" (p. 408). Whether or not we take D'Israeli to be insinuating that Bowles deliberately developed a theory that would demote Pope, he makes it very clear that he bothers to address Bowles' "Invariable Principles" only insofar as they affect the fate of Pope in the canon. This latter issue is indeed a momentous one in D'Israeli's eyes: "How this wonderful operation [the exclusion of Pope] has been carried on, it is of some importance to state—it is the history of the past, if Mr. Bowles triumphs; or the history of the future, should good sense and good taste return to Pope" (p. 408). In order to save Pope, and guarantee a future for English poetry, D'Israeli undertakes to show where Bowles goes wrong.

Perhaps the clearest expression of D'Israeli's priorities is the assertion that he offers as axiomatic for his discussion: "It is clear to us that a theory, which frequently admitting every thing the votary of Pope could desire to substantiate the high genius of his master, yet terminates in excluding the poet from 'the highest order of poets,' must involve some fallacy" (p. 410). One immediately wants to say to this what Bowles in effect says himself in later pamphlets, that the votaries of Pope may be mistaken in their poetic criteria. They might simply be praising Pope for trivial or mistaken reasons. D'Israeli anticipates this objection with the skeptical argument that we have no reliable means of establishing the kinds of principles by which an erroneous view might be categorically refuted. He is especially skeptical about Bowles' specific strategy of refutation, the appeal to "Nature":

> What are we not told of "Nature"! What chimes and changes has not the delighted critic rung on "Nature," on "General Nature," on "External Nature," and on "Moral Nature"—and so on! "Nature" is a critical term, which the Bowleses have been explaining for more than two thousand years—and they still throw us into that nervous agitation of spirits which always arises when we sit down to our favourite studies of squaring the circle, or beginning the perpetual motion.
>
> (P. 409)

D'Israeli is careful to suggest that the "Bowleses" have increased in both number and influence over recent years and that they included both Wordsworth, "who is often by genius so true a poet" and "by his theory so mistaken a one," and Coleridge, who is implicated in Bowles' reference to Kant's verbal mystification (p. 411).[9] The grounds upon which D'Israeli can call these theories "mistaken" is, again, a question not itself addressed in his discussion.

In his account of the causes or motives that he sees leading to the malignant opinions of Bowles and the Bowleses, D'Israeli nowhere says that their invidious, pseudonatural principles are motivated by nationalism as such, but what he does say is nonetheless quite compatible with such a conclusion. The root of the problem, as he explains it, is a self-blinding self-centeredness: "It has frequently been attempted to raise up such arbitrary standards and such narrowing theories of art; and these 'criterions' and 'invariable principles' have usually been drawn from the habitual practices and individual tastes of the framers; they are a sort of concealed egotism, a strategem of self-love" (p. 410). Burke, in his attack on the allegedly bogus cosmopolitanism of the French, had argued that self-love grows inevitably into the love of nation. But we needn't rely on Burke to make this sort of connection, for it is suggested by the direction in which D'Israeli himself takes the discussion when he goes on to charge Bowles, and by implication the Lake Poets, with intellectual provincialism:

> We have frequently observed that *rural* editors and writers often incur the danger of effecting discoveries which are not novel, and are apt to imagine that

they have completed their journey, when they have only proceeded as far as they were able to go. Plutarch long ago declared that an author should live in a great and populous city, which only could supply him with that abundance of books he requires, and with that traditional knowledge which floats in the memories of men of letters. Matters have by no means altered in this respect, for even at this day, there are some works, particularly an edition of Pope, which cannot properly be prepared in a country town.

(P. 411)

D'Israeli's notion is that provincialism, like egotism, leads to a kind of solipsism in literary judgments—"Provincial authors . . . are liable to a sort of literary hypochondriasm, where they see nothing but the creation of a morbid fancy, a phantom in a dark room" (p. 411). Nationalism, then, would represent just an extension of this same debility with similar consequences.[10] (We note, in this connection, that D'Israeli cites a *classical* author to make his point.)

D'Israeli's discussion of Bowles and the Bowleses probably owes a great deal to Byron's *Don Juan*, a poem whose genesis simply cannot be fully explained without reference to the Pope controversy.[11] In April 1818, Byron wrote to Murray of "the unjustifiable attempts at depreciation begun by Warton—& carried on to & at this day by the new School of Critics & Scribblers who think themselves poets because they do *not* write like Pope."[12] On this occasion Byron's invective seems to trail off in fatigue: "I have no patience with such cursed humbug—& bad taste—your whole generation are not worth a Canto of the Rape of the Lock—or the Essay on Man—or the Dunciad—or 'anything that is his' but it is three in the matin & I must go to bed" (*LJ*, 6:31). It was probably late one night just weeks after this that Byron began his witty polemic against the Lakers in the dedicatory stanzas to *Don Juan*. We cannot take it for granted that D'Israeli read the 1818 letter, though he is in fact praised in it and was a member of the circle at Murray's among whom Byron's letters from Italy were circulated.[13] It is probably not even reasonable to assume that D'Israeli saw the suppressed dedicatory stanzas, though their existence was widely known by 1820 and he seems to echo them in the article in Murray's *Quarterly Review*. But D'Israeli would unquestionably have known canto 1 proper of *Don Juan*, with its satire on Lakist system-building and its famous canonical imperative: "Thou shalt believe in Milton, Dryden, Pope; / Thou shalt not set up Wordsworth, Coleridge, Southey."[14] Indeed, the general drift and tone of D'Israeli's critique of Lakist provincialism and self-absorption are too Byronically mordant to be explained as coincidence.

If D'Israeli's 1820 discussion thus develops points initially articulated by Byron, Byron's *Letter to Murray* pamphlet of 1821 may in turn be read as extending what D'Israeli had printed the year before. Byron not only read D'Israeli's article, he even uses its mention of a dinner exchange between himself and Bowles as his explicit point of departure in the *Letter*. We also have evidence that Byron had already been an admirer of D'Israeli's work and that he knew it well enough to identify D'Israeli—Bowles, to his embarrassment, failed to do so—as the author of the anonymous piece in the *Quarterly*.[15] Here is Byron to his friend Francis Hodgson soon after its appearance:

> The Scoundrels of Scribblers are trying to run down *Pope*, but I hope in vain. It is my intention to take up the Cudgels in that controversy, and to do my best to keep the Swan of Thames in his true place. This comes of Southey and Turdsworth and such renegado rascals with their systems. I hope you will not be silent; it is the common concern of all men of common sense, imagination, and a musical ear. I have already written somewhat thereto and shall do more, and will not strike soft blows in the battle. You will have seen that the "Quarterly" has had the sense and spirit to support Pope in an article upon Bowles; it is a good beginning. I do not know the author of that article, but I suspect *Israeli*, an indefatigable and an able writer.
>
> (*LJ*, 7:253)

A month earlier Byron had written to Murray even more unequivocally: "D'Israeli wrote the article on Spence—I know him by the mark in his mouth—I'm glad that the Quarterly has had so much Classical honesty and honour as to insert it—it is good & mtrue" (*LJ*, 7:223).

One point that Byron seems to have found especially good and true in D'Israeli's remarks is his debunking of universalized "canons of criticism." Characteristically, Byron is both more emphatic and more personal in his enunciation of the position that D'Israeli only partly spelled out:

> I now come to Mr. B's "invariable principles of poetry." . . . I do hate that word *"invariable."* What is there of *human*, be it poetry, philosophy, wit, wisdom, science, power, glory, mind, matter, life, or death, which is *"invariable"*? Of course I put things divine out of the question. Of all arrogant baptisms of a book, this title to a pamphlet appears the most complacently conceited.
>
> (*WB*, 5:543)

Putting D'Israeli's skeptical critique of critical principles so explicitly leaves it even more vulnerable to the sorts of objections we noted in the case of D'Israeli. In his review of Byron's *Letter*, Hazlitt coolly exposed its weaknesses and inconsistencies, especially Byron's attempt, after renouncing invariable principles, to substitute a set of such principles of his own.[16] What is especially germane about the *Letter* here, however, is that Byron also extends D'Israeli's suggestion about the nature of Bowlesian provincialism and about the way a parochial attitude defends itself on universalized principles.

In the concluding paragraph of the *Letter to Murray*, Byron develops a hypothetical case to point up the nationalist motives that underlie the work of the scoundrels who praise system and damn Pope:

If any great national or natural convulsion could or should overwhelm your country in such sort as to sweep Great Britain from the kingdoms of the earth, and leave only that, after all, the most living of human things, a *dead language*, to be studied and read, and imitated by the wise of future and far generations, upon foreign shores; if your literature should become the learning of mankind, divested of party cabals, temporary fashions, and national pride and prejudice;— an Englishman, anxious that the posterity of strangers should know that there had been such a thing as a British Epic and Tragedy, might wish for the preservation of Shakespeare and Milton; but the surviving World would snatch Pope from the wreck, and let the rest sink with the people. He is the moral poet of all civilisation; and as such, let us hope that he will one day be the national poet of mankind.

(*WB*, 5:560)

Like Keats' survey of English literature in "Sleep and Poetry," this passage should probably be read as responding to Wordsworth's remarks in the 1815 *Essay, Supplementary*. Byron's apocalyptic vision of an England in ruin invites us to view the canon of English poetry, much as Wordsworth's Preface does, from the perspective of future generations. But unlike Wordsworth, Byron asks that we become a "posterity of *strangers*" (my emphasis) toward English poetry and that we therefore regard it as part of a canon of international classics. From this perspective, he claims, not only the Bowleses of the world (and of course the Wordsworths, the Keatses, and the Southeys), but even Shakespeare and Milton, will be less highly cherished than Pope.

That this alien or cosmopolitan perspective is to be understood as Byron's own is clear from the pronouns: "*your* country," "*your* literature." Whether or not we accept his implied claim to being above "party cabals, temporary fashions, and national pride and prejudice," we must admit that Byron was perhaps uniquely qualified for the difficult role he tries to play. What other English writer living in 1821 could boast a position sufficiently alienated from contemporary English life to recognize the nationalistic premises of its literary arguments? Who else had so little to lose in exposing them to the world?[17]

[2]

Byron's *Letter to Murray* seems, then, to offer stiff opposition to the movement to establish a specifically native poetic canon; there is certainly no evidence that Byron thought any such canon would argue for the superiority either of England's national character or its poetic genius. What he urges instead looks like a return to Pope's own notion of a classical canon that cuts across national boundaries and rises above national interests. There is an important difference, however, in the way in which Byron's and Pope's respective classics bear on the practice of poetry. Pope and Pulci cannot be for Byron what Homer and

Virgil were for Pope, and the reason lies in the skepticism Byron shared with D'Israeli about "invariable principles."

To see this difference plainly, we need only recall the two celebrated imperatives of Pope's *Essay on Criticism*. This is the first:

> First follow NATURE, and your Judgment frame
> By her just Standard, which is still the same:
> *Unerring Nature*, still divinely bright,
> One *clear*, *unchang'd*, and *Universal* Light,
> Life, Force, and Beauty, must to all impart,
> At once the *Source*, and *End*, and *Test* of *Art*.
>
> (ll. 68–73)

Here is a power that Pope is, in effect, willing to call "invariable." In terming its light "divinely bright," Pope certainly does not mean to suggest that, like Byron's "things divine," it should be "put . . . out of the question." On the contrary, this invariable force is also invariably essential to success in the human work of writing poetry. According to Pope, the great poetic rules that poets ignore only at their aesthetic peril are but nature self-methodized. "*Nature*," as he says, "restrain'd / By the same Laws which first *herself* ordain'd" (ll. 90–91).

Pope argues further, however, that we discover these rules by perusing the great works of the classical tradition. In the most famous formulation of the second imperative, Homer stands as a synecdoche for this canon:

> Be *Homer's* Works your *Study*, and *Delight*,
> Read them by Day, and meditate by Night,
> Thence form your Judgment, thence your Maxims bring,
> And trace the Muses *upward* to their *Spring*
>
> (ll. 124–27)

Anticipating those who would question the consistency of these imperatives, Pope recommends the example of Homer's greatest student, Virgil, who is portrayed as initially falling prey to the same suspicion. Starting out on his great work, Virgil is supposed to have thought himself "*above* the Critick's Law, / And from *Nature's Fountains* scorn'd to draw" (ll. 132–33). Pope then quickly explains that Maro's "boundless Mind" was too keen to remain unbound for long: "But when t'examine ev'ry Part he came, / *Nature* and *Homer* were, he found, the *same*" (ll. 134–35). The moral of this parable would be clear enough even if Pope had not spelled it out: "Learn Hence for Ancient *Rules* a just Esteem; / To copy *Nature* is to copy *Them*" (ll. 139–40). Pope's view, then, is that not just Nature and Homer but also Nature and Homer and Virgil—by implication even Nature and Homer and Virgil and Pope— are the same. They are always "still the same." Together they make up one clear, unchanged, and universal light. The canons of criticism and the canon of classics, in this scheme of things, are one in nature.

In the Romantic period, this doctrine no longer carries weight with either side of the quarrel over Pope. Writers are forced, as it were, to take sides on this matter, too. In elevating the national canon over the classical one, Bowles, Keats, and the Lakers insist on the universality of their critical principles. Seeing in this move a glorification of provincialism in the name of nature, Byron and D'Israeli insist upon a universalized canon of classics but surrender the notion that this canon embodies universally applicable principles.

D'Israeli's version of this argument in the *Quarterly Review* essay is that one must maintain the full range of the canonized classics precisely because they are so various. He holds universalized canons of criticism suspect precisely because he sees the great poets responding *variously* to various historical conditions. This position is sketched out in his account of why an "artificial test" (such as Bowles and the Lakists propose) for poetry must be "repugnant to the man of taste who can take enlarged views":

> In the contrast of human tempers and habits, in the changes of circumstances in society, and the consequent mutations of tastes, the objects of poetry may be different in different periods; preeminent genius obtains its purpose by its adaptation to this eternal variety; and on this principle, if we would justly appreciate the creative faculty, we cannot see why Pope should not class, at least in file, with Dante, or Milton. It is probable that Pope could not have produced an "Inferno," or a "Paradise Lost," for his invention was elsewhere: but it is equally probable that Dante and Milton, with their cast of mind, could not have so exquisitely touched the refined gaiety of "the Rape of the Lock."
>
> (P. 410)

Genius finds its merit not in its fidelity to a changeless Nature but rather in its adaptability to the mutations of society and the concomitant variations of culture. According to this historicist "principle"-against-principles, Pope's own representation of the classical canon is just one of many such possibilities among which we cannot readily discriminate a hierarchy.

In making an argument similar to this one, Byron is, again, both more emphatic and more personal than D'Israeli. The emotional climax of his *Letter to Murray* is a passage occasioned by his charge that the present enemies of Pope "have raised a mosque by the side of a Grecian temple of the purest architecture; and, more barbarous than the barbarians from whose practice I have borrowed the figure, they are not contented with their own grotesque edifice, unless they destroy the prior, and purely beautiful fabric which pre-ceded, and which shames them and theirs for ever and ever" (*WB*, 5:559).[18] The climatic moment assumes the form of a confession and a subsequent qualification:

I shall be told that amongst those I *have* been (or it may be still *am*) conspicu-
ous—true, and I am ashamed of it. I *have* been amongst the builders of this
Babel, attended by a confusion of tongues, but *never* amongst the envious
destroyers of the classic temple of our predecessor. I have loved and honoured
the fame and name of that illustrious and unrivalled man, far more than my
own paltry renown, and the trashy jingle of the crowd of "Schools" and upstarts,
who pretend to rival, or even surpass them.

(*WB*, 5:559)

How is it that Pope's fiercest advocate and most loyal defender can end up
at work on the same poetic enterprise as Pope's detractors? How is it, to be
specific where Byron is not, that the satirist of *English Bards and Scotch Reviewers*
could praise Pope's classicism to the sky in 1809 and then spend the next two
years writing and living the life of Childe Harold, that most Romantic of
Romantics? The reason can only be that Pope's own principles must themselves
somehow cease to apply. Pope's poetic temple should outlast the applicability
of the principles by which it was constructed. It is to be admired but not
imitated. Byron saves Pope not for the history of the future but only for the
history of the past.[19]

We touch here, I believe, on the reason why in *Don Juan* Byron can only
parody the laws by which Pope swears. We can tell by the tone not to take
him seriously when, midway through canto 1, the Byronic narrator comments:
"as I have a high sense / Of Aristotle and the Rules, 'tis fit / To beg his pardon
when I err a bit" (1.120). The joke becomes more obvious toward the end of
the canto when he promises a work in which he will "carry precept to the
highest pitch" (1.204) by setting down his poetical commandments. The title
he proposes for this work makes it out to be the epitome of poetic anarchy:
"Every Poet his own Aristotle" (1.204). The joke is easy to get but hard to
interpret, especially in view of Byron's later comments about how the degrada-
tion of Pope by the leveling "poetical populace of the present day" is tied to
their obsessive jockeying for fame and recognition: Juan has a vision in canto
11 of "the eighty 'greatest living poets,' / As every paltry magazine can show
its" (11.54). Byron cracks off in a letter to Murray in 1820 about "the fifteen
hundred first of living poets" (*LJ*, 7:168). Perhaps it was this suspicion about
an unseemly ambition beneath the surface of their populist rhetoric that led
Byron, the most radical Whig among the Romantics, to denounce Wordsworth
and his colleagues as too democratic in their poetics, as for example in canto
3, where Byron describes the Lakers as "Jack Cades / Of sense and song"
hissing above the graves of the majestic Pope and Dryden (3.100).

Indeed, in a degenerate age such as his own, Byron seems resigned to
seeing a despot emerge from the anarchy, just so long as it is not the hypocrite
Wordsworth. "Did you read [Hunt's] skimble-skamble about [Wordsworth]
being at the head of his *profession* . . . ?" asked Byron of Moore in 1820. "He

is the only one of us (but of us he is not) whose coronation I would oppose. Let them take Scott, Campbell, Crabbe, or you, or me, or any of the living, and throne him;—but not this new Jacob Behmen" (*LJ*, 6:47). Of course, Byron would prefer that the despot be himself. He seems to admit as much when, with a characteristic renunciation of hypocrisy and cant, he sums up the poetical commandments of "Every Poet has his own Aristotle":

> Thou shalt not write, in short, but what I choose:
>   This is true criticism, and you may kiss—
> Exactly as you please, or not, the rod,
> But if you don't, I'll lay it on, by G——d!
>
> (1. 206)

The noble lord was perhaps not altogether uneasy in the role of an enlightened despot thrown up by what he saw as a failed revolution—or as he described himself later in this same poem, "The grand Napoleon of the realms of rhyme" (11.55). But what uneasiness we do discern in Byron's posture—elsewhere in canto 11, for example—sometimes takes the form of a melancholy awareness of the contradictions in his position. And when it does, it can make his high-handed pronouncements seem a kind of twisted elegy for the passing of those fixed laws that guided Pope.

Notes

1. Joseph Warton, *An Essay on the Genius and Writings of Pope*, 2d ed., 2 vols. (London, 1762), 1:vii; all further references to this work, with volume and page numbers, will be included in the text.

2. Samuel Johnson, *Lives of the English Poets*, ed. George Birkbeck Hill, 3 vols. (Oxford, 1905), 3:251.

3. William Hazlitt, *Complete Works*, ed. P. P. Howe, 21 vols. (London, 1930–34), 5:69.

4. Bowles, ed., *Works of Pope*, 10:362.

5. Ibid., p. 363.

6. See Bowles, *The Invariable Principles of Poetry . . . Particularly Relating to the Poetical Character of Pope* (London, 1819). Bowles begins by simply quoting verbatim his statements of 1806 (see p. 6).

7. The classic critical histories of the rise of Romantic poetics are Samuel H. Monk, *The Sublime: A Study of Critical Theories in Eighteenth-Century England* (New York, 1935); Walter Jackson Bate, *From Classic to Romantic: Premises of Taste in Eighteenth-Century England* (Cambridge, Mass., 1946); and M. H. Abrams, *The Mirror and the Lamp: Romantic Theory and the Critical Tradition* (Oxford, 1953). An example of important recent work in the area is Thomas Weiskel, *The Romantic Sublime: Studies in the Structure and Psychology of Transcendence* (Baltimore, 1976).

8. Isaac D'Israeli, review of *Anecdotes of Books and Men* by Joseph Spence, *Quarterly Review* 66 (July 1820): 408; all further references to this work will be included in the text.

9. See also p. 409 for D'Israeli's disparaging remarks about the "Kantian transcendental philosophy."

10. For a suggestive recent discussion of classicist ideas about canon-formation and

provincialism, see Frank Kermode, *The Classic: Literary Images of Permanence and Change* (New York, 1975), pp. 15–45.

11.   See McGann's discussion of the poem as Byron's effort at "Counter-Reformation" in *Don Juan in Context* (Chicago, 1976), pp. 51–67.

12.   Byron, *Letters and Journals*, ed. Leslie A. Marchand, 12 vols. (Cambridge, Mass., 1973–82), 6:31; all further references to this work, abbreviated *LJ* and with volume and page numbers, will be included in the text.

13.   On D'Israeli's friendship with Murray, see Samuel Smiles, *A Publisher and His Friends: Memoir and Correspondence of the Late John Murray*, 2 vols. (London, 1891), 1:41–55. Smiles cites a letter of Washington Irving's which describes a dinner at Murray's, with D'Israeli present, at which one of Byron's letters from Italy was brought out (see 2:127).

14.   Byron, *Don Juan*, cited from the variorum edition, ed. Truman Guy Steffan and Willis W. Pratt, 4 vols. (Austin, Tex., 1957), 2:canto 1, st. 205; all further references to this work will be to canto and stanza from this edition and will be included in the text.

15.   Bowles ascribed the *Quarterly Review* piece to Gilchrist, whom he then attacked in "A Reply to the Charges Brought by the Reviewer of Spence's *Anecdotes*, in the Quarterly Review," *Pamphleteer* 17 (1820): 73–102. This set off a further exchange between the two men, from which I quoted above.

16.   See Hazlitt, *Complete Works*, 19:62–82.

17.   Peter Manning rightly warns me against over-stating the case for Byron's literary expatriotism. "He was a poet," as Manning puts it, "who declared that his hopes of being remembered 'were twined with my land's language.'"

18.   Byron's use of the figure of the second temple is reminiscent of Dryden's conceit, which has been so effectively elaborated by Bate, *The Burden of the Past and the English Poet* (New York, 1970), pp. 3–27. But the Romantic edifice that Byron regards as the second temple is discussed by Bate as the third (see pp. 95–134).

19.   And once we understand the logic of D'Israeli's (Byronic) position, it is not clear how, by saving Pope, he can claim to be saving the poetic history of the future, either.

20.   "Jack Cade," as Pratt's note explains, "led the rebellion of commoners against the misrule of Henry VI and his council in 1450" (*Don Juan*, vol. 4, p. 101).

[from Introduction to *Pope: New Contexts*]

DAVID FAIRER

In the past few years the study of eighteenth-century English literature has become the location for lively methodological debate, exemplified by two impressive collections of essays: the tercentenary of Pope's birth was marked by G. S. Rousseau and Pat Rogers's *An Enduring Legacy*, and the previous year (1987) saw the publication of *The New Eighteenth Century* edited by Felicity Nussbaum and Laura Brown. The contrast between them is a conceptual one. It is clear that the notion of an "enduring legacy" is as polemical as a "new eighteenth century." The first implies the sustaining of a sure line of inheritance just as clearly as the second implies a break with the pre-owned. Where Rousseau and Rogers preface their collection by locating its origins in a sociable walk around the gardens at Stourhead, Nussbaum and Brown argue for a criticism which decentres and destabilises. One volume aspires to permanent value, the second aims to initiate debate. The contrasting discourses of these texts—continuity and revolution, authority and revisionism—are striking and each on its own terms fulfils its aims.

By breaking down barriers between so-called major and peripheral texts, those which express the dominant culture and those which find a voice outside it, *The New Eighteenth Century* offers a challenge to the kind of criticism whose ultimate concern is in the editors' words, "the preservation and elucidation of canonical masterpieces of cultural stability." Inevitably, to present a collection of essays on Alexander Pope seems to declare a resistent "old" eighteenth century with Pope still enshrined at the centre of his age. One of the aims of *Pope: New Contexts*, however, is to challenge both the cultural stability of the eighteenth century and Pope's centrality or representativeness within it, and to do so by locating the power of his work in its resistance to discourses of coherence and stability. The present volume recognises that there is a wide range of methodologies available and that acts of recovery through history need not be embarrassed by engaging with newer critical practices, indeed that they can co-operate in the same enterprise.

In a recent article, "English in crisis?," Ian Small and Josephine Guy

David Fairer, "Introduction" to *Pope: New Contexts*. Reprinted from *Pope: New Contexts*, edited by David Fairer (Hertfordshire, England: Harvester Wheatsheaf, 1990). U.S. rights granted by Barnes & Noble Books. World rights granted by Harvester Wheatsheaf.

argue that the current, well-documented "crisis" in literary studies is one in which irreconcilable epistemologies are struggling for mastery. This present collection obviously contributes to such a crisis, and confidently so. The volume has in Small and Guy's terms no "common epistemology," nor does it attempt some kind of "resolution" in the way they suggest:

> For a theory to rebut or refute contending theories there has to be a common epistemology, or at least the conditions for an agreement about epistemology. . . . / either English as a discipline will exist in a state of continuing crisis, *or* a dominant epistemology and therefore a dominant intellectual authority will begin to re-emerge. But for this to occur, an initial debate about epistemology has to take place: *these* are the grounds for an intellectual debate, and perhaps for its resolution.[1]

The medical connotation implied here (crisis as the condition of a patient on the threshold of what may be either death or recovery) is unfortunate. The patient's condition is not "critical" in quite this sense: indeed, the present debate should indicate a state of health. Perhaps the last thing criticism needs is an authorised epistemology which establishes agreed principles of meaning and truth, allows the emergence of a new consensus to refute aberrant theories, and sends the critical project virtuously on its way. We should recall that both crisis and criticism are rooted in the Greek *krinein*, to distinguish, decide, judge, and the "critical" task has traditionally flourished in such a context of choice and dispute.

An epistemological consensus was certainly not something that the eighteenth century offered Pope. The historical moment in which he wrote was a time of fierce epistemological debate: contending theories of knowledge set idealist and materialist ideologies against each other, Shaftesbury and Hutcheson against Hobbes and Mandeville; in philosophy, Bishop Berkeley was taking issue with Locke's notions of abstraction, matter and human perception; in religion the clash between deism and revelation remained controversial; in literary studies the "affective" criticism of Addison and Dennis challenged the Aristotelian inheritance; aesthetics, sublimity, "sympathy," "enthusiasm," "taste" offered a new terminology and with it new criteria, and the "grounds of criticism" like the grounds of philosophy, religion and social theory, were being urgently fought over. From our present-day perspective it is possible to see these disputes as aspects of a sustained and wide-ranging epistemological debate contending for the location of truth, meaning and value.

After his death, Pope himself became the locus for competing ideologies. But the well-known Byron–Bowles controversy of the early nineteenth century was merely the culmination of decades of argument about the principles not just of literary judgement but of truth, meaning and value. The debate on Pope was inaugurated by the *Essay on the Writings and Genius of Pope* (1756) by Joseph Warton, who grounded his judgement on the central role of imagination and inspiration in poetry, and therefore consigned Pope to the "second rank" of poets (the "moral and ethical"). Dr Johnson's championing of Pope's *Homer* as the peak of poetical achievement was part of his wider project to declare 1660–1744 the great age of English poetry, and this involved the demotion of the work of the early Milton, whose rediscovery had encouraged the shift in poetic taste during the 1740s of which Warton had been a part. In response, Joseph's brother Thomas Warton produced his 1785 edition of Milton's early verse to confront Johnson's "specious" judgement and explicitly elevate the "school of Milton" above the "school of Pope." William Lisle Bowles, a pupil of the Wartons, continued the debate in overtly anti-Popeian terms, questioning whether Pope should be regarded as a poet at all. Byron's championing of Pope, like his aversion to Keats, was correspondingly a function of his distaste for the Warton–Bowles poetry of sensibility which had established itself in the mid-eighteenth century. These are just a few related contributions to what was not merely a debate about Pope, but a prolonged disagreement over standards of literary judgement and their consequences for the canonising and demoting of specific texts. It was fundamentally a clash of epistemologies, of underlying principle regarding the subjective, affective elements of poetic meaning, the status and function of imagination, the issue of art's allegiance to an empirically-perceived "reality," the location of meaning in relation to the interplay between author, text and reader—and it could never be resolved because there was no common ground.

Much of our contemporary critical debate finds itself echoing the canonical and epistemological issues underlying eighteenth-century controversy. To author, text and reader we would now wish to add history and society as constituents of an intricate force-field within which meaning can be located, and although the forces are more complex and the terminology vastly expanded, the critical struggle, the crisis, goes on.

In adding history and society, I am conscious that the relationship between text and context is a lively issue in the current debate, and that the hitherto serene placing of text *within* context is now in question. Which is the text and which the context? Can the text "write" the author, in the sense that the "author" is no longer originary, but contingent? Is the complex freight that words carry (contextualisation via usage, etymology, association, etc.) in any sense under control, and if so by whom or what? Few poets have been so insistently contextualised as Pope, and the relation of his "poetry of allusion" to current debate about text/context is a fascinating one. With its title of "New Contexts" this volume partly draws on the traditional notion by placing Pope's poetry in less familiar settings and regarding it from unexpected angles. But etymology can usefully remind us that *text* as well as *context* is a "weaving," a texture, and that *context*, rather than seen as detachable, was considered to represent the full weaving-together of meaning. When Milton in 1642 speaks of "that book, within whose sacred context all wisdom is infolded,"[2] he is asserting the completion, entirety—even plenitude—of meaning-as-truth within the Bible: the truth is in the seamless weaving-together of each part. In such terms the context could be the whole structure, the connection and coherence of any text: it was not something within which a text resided or was placed, but implied a kind of totalised reading. Criticism can probably never return to its old confidence in an available totality, yet our currently more comprehensive ideas of text allow us to examine discourse as overriding the traditional text/context distinction, expressing meanings which are totalised not in the sense of "universal" but as signifying a complex system of culture, individual and society, and speaking concurrently for, in and through its language.

The traditional notion of Pope's context is, of course, "Augustanism," a category still used to shape university literature courses on both sides of the Atlantic (and often to ensure that the eighteenth century remains persistently unpopular); the term seems to make sense of a contradictory period and can be useful in preparing the way for a glorious romanticism. Like any "movement" romanticism needs a "structure" to overturn, and Augustanism (which has never been graced with the title of "movement") has always offered itself up as structure (Blake found this useful); but the need for the term tells us more about ourselves as readers and critics than about the literature of the eighteenth century.

Concepts of "Augustan satire," an "Augustan reader," or one of the many variants on "Augustan ideology" (a compound of stability, balance, correctness, reason, classicism, sociability, etc.) are endemic and useful fictions. The "attitudes and values of Augustan England" (to quote one recent blurb writer) provide the bulwarks for a set of critical, social and moral values which an "Augustan" Pope can articulate for us. Wallace Jackson is right to note how Pope's admirers during the last forty years have tended "to fortify a diminished position, to build it upon the solid foundation of a poetry of allusion, and to hold strenuously the middle ground of high poetic competence."[3] But an "Augustan" Pope can also be invoked when some revisionary enterprise is under way, and it is less than ironic that these discourses are being given a new lease of life in some literary theory. In prefacing Laura Brown's *Alexander Pope* (1985), for example, Terry Eagleton finds it useful to evoke "the age of Pope, with its good sense and fine taste, its appeal to universal Reason, its passion for symmetry and stability" (p. vi). In a subversive critical project, no less than a rearguard defensive one, Pope is useful as a cultural spokesman for his dominant "Augustan" group; hence Eagleton's need to see Pope "at the very centre" (p. vii) and Brown's declaration that, "Pope has been the centre of the canon in traditional eighteenth-century literary history for good reason, it seems. This study keeps him there" (p. 5).[4]

Brown's critique works powerfully from her epistemological premises, but in splitting off in a paradoxical way Pope's conscious and intentional *text* (as exemplary, symptomatic, documentary of his age) from her own subversive

reading of the poems ("remorselessly questioning" the age's ideological structures) she likewise projects a separable *context* in which ideology resides at the
conscious level of Pope's text yet can be undermined through criticism's
scrutiny of its supposedly "suppressed" elements. Her procedure therefore
makes little play with incompatibilities between the age's competing ideologies
or with the rich complexities of contextualised poetic meaning. The latter is
in danger of separating out into the intentional-official and the suppressed-
subversive, with the result that the poet himself ends up being taken hostage
for one cause against another ("This study keeps him . . . as a lever against
the whole canon of eighteenth-century studies" [p. 5]), yet at the same time
being remade and redeemed by the critic as a subversive voice.

Notes

    1.   Ian Small and Josephine Guy, "English in crisis?," *EC*, 39 (1989), 185–95 (p. 194).
    2.   Preface to *The Reason of Church-Government, Complete Prose Works of John Milton*, 8 vols
(New Haven and London, 1953–82), i, 747.
    3.   Wallace Jackson, "The genius of Pope's genius: criticism and the text(s)," in *The
Enduring Legacy*, pp. 171–84 (p. 171).
    4.   Colin Nicholson, in prefacing one of the tercentenary volumes, speaks of "Pope's
evident centrality during his life of writing. His axial significance in a varied convergence of
discourses—from poetics to politics, from economics to ethics, from form to fashion—makes
him at once characteristic of his age and almost correspondingly alien to our own," (*Alexander
Pope: Essays for the Tercentenary* [Aberdeen, 1988], p. ix).

[from "Perils of Articulation: A Review Essay of Maynard Mack's *Alexander Pope*"]

G. S. ROUSSEAU

By the time this review appears, Professor Mack's book[1] will have begun to earn the high reputation and win the awards it deserves. Written by the scholar-critic who has known more about his chosen poet than anyone in this century (comparing him with other, late, leading Popeans: Sherburn, Butt, Tillotson, Brower, Wimsatt), this "life" has been handsomely produced and packaged by Norton. It sits massively in state: 975 pages long, three and one-half pounds of avoirdupois, containing literally thousands of footnotes in well over one hundred pages of very small print, adorned with ninety-seven illustrations, a very extensive index prepared by professional indexers, and written in the impeccably clear and polished prose style with which we have come to associate Maynard Mack, for four decades now, as the supreme literary critic.

As one reads in it (not reads through it from cover to cover, for that would occupy a very long time and require a tireless reader who found himself in a Tolstoyan mood), one experiences a sense of finality, a threnodic sense that both Pope and his best critic to date have now, at last, been put to rest. One also feels an indescribable apprehension, as well as crystalline awareness, that this book has been in some crucial ways the life's work of its author, while at the same time possessing a finality in that it necessarily performs closure on a whole era of Pope scholarship. It is the book's tone that culture will cease after Mack's last page, just as civilization—the author rhetorically implies—seems to have come to an end with the death of Pope. And along this line, it is the felt sense that ultimately the reader's experience will resemble the perception Samuel Johnson arrived at when he composed the concluding lines of his own life of Pope:

New sentiments and new images others may produce, but to attempt any further improvement of versification will be dangerous. Art and diligence have now done their best, and what shall be added will be the effort of tedious toil and needless curiosity.[2]

This intimation of finality derives as much from the book's moment in literary history as from any intrinsic finality in Mack's retrieval of the life of Pope, or from any prescience that nothing more of an original nature will ever be said about Pope's life. Far from it, for Mack's "life" is a perfect product of the golden age of scholarship attained in the 1960s. I was then a graduate student of English literature at Princeton, reading Pope by day and studying him by night—more drearily writing about his life and works in my qualifying examinations. How well I recollect what such an authoritative and massive study would then have meant for us: young Turks, we were given to lamenting (how times have changed!) that Sherburn had terminated his work in 1728— roughly at the time of publication of the first *Dunciad*—and that virtually nothing of a reliable biographical nature had been written about Pope after his composition of *The Dunciad*. Now, approximately twenty years later, we live in a world in which English majors barely know who Pope was (anyone who doubts the statement should conduct his or her own survey); and even if a few do know, it is inconceivable that they could understand to what degree our sense of the mature Pope was shaped by one man: in such obvious studies of Pope's maturity as *The Garden and the City*[3] and also in less well-known works such as Mack's brilliant and intuitive extended review essay of Sherburn's Oxford edition of Pope's correspondence, which lies buried in an obscure place but remains one of the most expressive statements of Pope's romantic temperament.[4] Our understanding also was shaped in the revelatory footnotes that abound in the Twickenham Edition of *An Essay on Man*, which Mack gathered and presented long before interdisciplinary approaches to scholarship permitted scholars easy access to this type of recondite information. More recently our understanding was formed in such meticulous and painstaking scholarship as that found in his study of Pope's manuscripts.[5] With all this Mackean annotation and exegesis, capped now by this gargantuan "life," an era in critical scholarship comes to an end. The threnodic sense proves true after all. Like Pope's own *Dunciad*, which was a work of literature and something more, as more than one critic has noticed, Mack's biography is both a very large book and something else: an epitome of the pinnacle of the golden age of American literary scholarship, as well as a moment in the final, intellectual development of its author.

Even so, Mack's latter-day book produces anxiety and guilt, at least in this reviewer, as a consequence of loss: the knowledge that its publication marks more clearly than we would have wished to recognize to what extent this type of fluency and civility have passed out of the world. I can think of no higher compliment to pay the book in 1987, and no greater homage to make to its author, than to claim that if we could somehow bring back the dead and gather them together with the living at a conference boasting the cream of *Gallican* minds of our times—Barthes, Foucault, Derrida, Lacan, Levi-Strauss—they would be among the first to acknowledge (to the extent that they had ever read Pope in French) that this is a masterful book.

Yet is it too late? The book appears long after the effective demise of the New Criticism (Pope had been a perfect author for the American New Critics because he could be packaged so well into their philosophical precepts and peddled in classrooms) and long after this variety of meticulous scholarship has been widely enough appreciated for it to make any significant dent on higher education: for example, to restore academic integrity for the genre of biography. The fate of Mack's biography is dubious within the academic community; outside academia it will not be read much, notwithstanding its stylistic fluency, for it remains very much a scholar's biography rather than a popular account written for the educated reader. Despite Mack's virtuous motive of constant allusion to our present time, his book remains very much a chronological life uncluttered by the claims and methods of Freud, Marx, Levi-Strauss, and post-structuralism. Mack's practice is noble (especially when we ponder how the purists have lost our audiences by despising the habit of modern analogy), but in itself probably insufficient to change the collective mind about the broad ways we conceive of Pope the man. Mack's book also demonstrates another Antaean hurdle for the modern critic-scholar, to say nothing of professional Popeans, which is even more elusive to grasp let alone accurately to describe. From the first page to the last, Mack's life remains a critic's, rather than a biographer's, biography. These are matters requiring a gloss.

As everyone knows, and for reasons that are hardly mysterious, ours is an age of theory and criticism. Poetry, as the Horatian Pope himself recognized, follows Nature wherever she may lead. Criticism and theory thrive on systems of thought, especially quasi-philosophical systems, rather than on bare Nature; if anything, criticism and theory abhor Nature and her paradoxically simple-minded lessons. Furthermore, after the Second World War the developing social sciences came into their most imperialistic mood and made immense encroachments on the humanities. From them, for example, the now much-touted New Historicism has taken most of its cues. More recently, pervasive social chaos and a heightened moral fragmentation have caused a new type of mass confusion to reign. Among those who try to understand these complex matters and their interconnections, the onus of explanation has been transferred from the humanists to the social scientists, who are now regularly called upon to account for phenomena as diverse as God, man, the earth, terrorism, nuclear disaster, population, starvation—just about everything pertinent to the survival of the race.

The humanists have thus far been omitted—as if they had been missing in action for a whole generation. The most haunting questions of our time (i.e., the last two or three decades) are such that most distinguished humanist scholars, like Maynard Mack, could have addressed them with as much expertise and profundity as the social scientists but elected not to. As a consequence, the educated public has lost much of its earlier fervor for the humanities, to say nothing of our career-minded youth who barely realize what vital energy and power the humanities possessed only a short time ago. Most direly this public has surrendered its former faith in the verve and fiber of the humanities, and with this loss the formerly high reputation of poets such as Pope has also suffered. The remaining great scholars, the Macks, are like priests who preside over temples depleted of worshippers. The essential matter is not that professional, academic literary critics think any less of Pope's poetry today than they did a few decades ago, but rather that poets like Pope have ceased to speak to the educated public, which has altogether shifted its gear vis-a-vis poetry and its symbolic meaning. In our age of anxiety the public's collective angst is not altogether different from the mature Pope's, disturbed as he was about the dissolution of hierarchies in virtually every realm: religious, political, social, economic, even literary. So no matter whose biography Mack had written—it could have been Milton's or Dryden's as well as Pope's—it would still have been too late if presented and packaged in this particular way. The culprit then—if there is any culprit in an impossible situation—is not Pope or Professor Mack but the temper of our times and the status of scholarly biography. These remain, it seems, but a pastime for emeritus professors in America and, in England, a sport for dilettantes and country vicars. It has not occurred to most readers that good biography is one of the most difficult literary forms in which a writer can excel. For this last reason the young eschew it and the old, who are usually incapable of rising to its olympian demands, dispraise it.

All these accomplishments and caveats, including Mack's threnodic tone, are half truths: one can counter them with an opposite position. But if today we live in an age of theory embedded in an age of anxiety, as I will maintain, accompanied by a precipitous decline in practice; and if the questions that continue to haunt us most remain abstract and methodologically grounded, then we must also recognize—as the nominalistic Professor Mack would be the first to do—that however atomistic biography ultimately is, it alone can answer many of these big questions. For biography exists in a realm of its own; as a type of knowledge it is practically unrivalled. It explains precisely what cultural history cannot: the private motives, drives, and grovelling instincts that lie beneath the actions of those who make the history on which the larger claims of culture are based. Even more crucially, biography is difficult to perform; so difficult, and requiring so much background in placing details into their proper compartments while trying to say something new, that most theorists cannot cope with it, let alone understand how to research, compile, and write it. The French theorists listed above and their American epigoni could never have compiled one (can one imagine what a biography of Pope, or even Voltaire, written by Foucault would be like?). Nor do any of these theorists combine the rare explicative skills and narrative talents of a

Mack: critical ability, superb scholarship, and a lifetime's devotion to the subject.

Yet for all these achievements and in the face of the finished product before me, Mack's biography is ultimately a disappointment and its precise flaw must be articulated if one is to understand what Mack has accomplished. The problem does not lie in his scholarship or style (the former practically impeccable, the latter lucid) but in a realm removed far from these: in thé irrefutable recognition that Mack writes biography as if it were criticism—as if it were but a species of literary explication. I do not mean to suggest that Mack's life is "literary biography" in the sense that Boswell's *Life of Johnson* is: " 'Tis a pretty book," Donald Greene, the distinguished Johnsonian, would continue to remind Boswell of his own big book about Johnson, "but you must not call it biography."[6] I mean instead that Mack's book is biography that explicates through the poet's literary works rather than by providing any lasting, overarching portrait of the writer apart from his works: his deepest psyche, his motives, his drives, independent of their dramatization in his poetry. For all Mack's brilliance in the analysis of individual passages and poems, Pope-the-man eludes us in this book. It is as if Mack cannot distinguish them, and as if he would insist, if Mack were compelled to distinguish them, that Pope had no genuine life independent of his poetry. This issue forces us, of course, to come to the very heart of the matter: Pope's genuine self and the transformations of this self in his writing. But Mack somehow can never capture Pope except within Pope's poetry and cannot understand that there are selves other than the one who dramatizes and represents itself. Mack has no new theory of how the historical Pope proceeded from the one realm to the other, granting that there are only these two essential selves. I have no doubt that the biographical Pope is well-harnessed in Mack's imagination, but that vision is not delineated in the pages of this large book. In brief, then, the disappointment is that though he is a superlative critic, he remains an undistinguished biographer. Over and again the reader is deflected from the man he craves to learn about and brought back to Pope's verse: to an analysis of the subtlety of some word, metaphor, pun; to some rhetorical strategy or to the action of a particular poem, but rarely to the poet apart from his lines. Even in historical matters (for example, Pope's appalling behavior displayed to those to whom he had every reason to be grateful), it is a poetic Pope who is always placed under Mack's fine analytical lens. The result is that we are forced to keep asking whether Pope really existed in no other way than through his couplets. Professor Mack apparently believes not.

A distinguished biographer compels you to feel the essential glow of his subject, forces you to understand why his life evolved as it did. He provides all the facts of the life, of course, but also measures the potential of his protagonist: not merely the palpable, but the potential, reality. He rarely reduces his subject's motives to neat patterns that fit paradigms about the age in which he lived or, alternatively, paradigms about its psychology. Most crucially he does not reduce his subject's complexity of package it for a particular audience; the concept of packaging does not suit Pope but makes the point about Mack's implied audience that I am trying to stress here. Distinguished biographers are never too timid to speculate, even when in the face of dark passions or disgraceful patterns of behavior, about their subject's warts (it may be that despite his disclaimers in the preface about not wanting to conceal Pope's warts, Mack has glossed over them too protectively). Aware that he cannot prove everything he wants to say, the great biographer has enough confidence in his grasp of his subject to encourage conjecture as a major approach. He naturally avoids the language of elision, especially where such omission casts doubt on his subject or thwarts the reader's desire to know about a particular aspect. Neither does he suppress his subject's frailties or recoil from them into a camouflage of flaccid prose. He lives to confront his protagonist head on in his most difficult moments.

The problem with Pope, specifically, is that in our time he has been packaged by two opposing groups: the New Critics who obliterated his life altogether and taught, like primitive proselytizers, that his poems were all that mattered; and a small group of literary historians (Sherburn, Osborn, Tillotson, Butt) who anatomized portions of his life and works but who usually were unable to see him whole or to discover the key to his riddled personality: cripple, bachelor, poet, Catholic, supreme manipulator—all the obliquities lumped into one hulk of deformity. Even now it is almost impossible to breakaway from either of these images. College students (the only tiny segment of youth who reads Pope) continue to follow in the former tradition, engaging in what Donald Greene perceptively calls "Pope-Bashing" (i.e., the not so sublime art of denigrating Pope because he represents something he himself never actually was)[7] while professional Popeans (the few there are) inexorably cultivate the second path. Laura Brown's allegedly new image[8]—that Pope was an antiproletarian oppressor who maliciously advocated radical colonialism and imperialism through repressive mercantilism—is biographically so improbable that its course has run out even before being trounced by the professional Popeans.[9] But Mack himself has been responsible in large part for the formation of both the major views: to him, in part, we owe the enduring stability of this binary conception of Pope. During the last three decades he had been in practically a unique position to modify either one, even to alter either subtly; yet on every occasion he has demonstrated to what extent he wishes them to solidify into the accepted, granitic mold of Pope. He would seem to prefer this form of closure and consolidation to any more amorphous alternative that jeopardizes Pope's character by asking too many questions. There is a sense that those who invent new subjects, like Mack who defined a new Pope in the 1940s altogether different from the one identified by Bloomsbury and Edith Sitwell (to say nothing of the Pope of the Victorians), dwell beyond the confines of the categories into which the subjects themselves fit. Viewed within this context Mack has been a member of neither group, but a staunch defender of the tradition of historical research that seeks to leave no stone unturned, and which operates on the premise that the critic's eye, that microscope of truth, discovers all, permits no secret to remain.

A few examples selected from *The Rape of the Lock*, *Eloisa to Abelard*, and the *Epistle to a Lady* demonstrate the point about biography as criticism in the context of Pope's relation to women. Mack's index lists thirteen topics under which he has discussed *The Rape*, most of them literary categories ranging from the origin of the poem to its reception. Among these is the poem's eroticism. The relevant pages affirm that "the erotic shimmer that hangs over the entire poem [is] like a heat haze over a meadow on an April afternoon" (252), and that "eroticism suffuses the poem like a sea, quite appropriately considering its subject, but the insistent delicacy of its strategy calls for a similar delicacy in the reader" (253). These are splendid critical observations, poised in simplicity and soaked in the analogy of naturalism, but their underlying substratum was iterated long ago, if less lyrically, by Cleanth Brooks in his famous article on sex and *The Rape of the Lock*.[10] The more original and biographically germane observation—that Teresa Blount rather than Arabella Fermor remains the genuine inspiration of the *Rape's* eroticism—is found in the last sentence of Mack's chapter dealing with this youthful poetic masterpiece: "What is equally clear, in my view," Mack maintains, "is that the poem's deep currents of affection and sexual attraction . . . owe as much to its author's personal experience of the sparkling young women at Mapledurham as to his [Pope's] imagination" (257). If this is true, as it may well be, then it would seem insufficient in a modern biography of this immense size to say as little as Mack does about the psychological way Teresa fired up Pope's libidinal drive. The same is true of the biographical dimensions of the other poems where Mack identifies a similar degree of sexual inspiration generated by the Blount girls. Holding that *Eloisa to Abelard* is a personal, autobiographical pouring out, Mack quotes many amatory couplets to substantiate his poet's "objective correlative," stating that:

> To put the affinities of life with poetry in these terms is to put them too baldly,
> I am well aware. Yet the poem does open, I think, at some obscure subterranean
> level, a window on Pope's sense of his situation at this time, and marks, perhaps,
> a personal urge to come to terms, imaginatively, poetically, dramatically, by
> means of an objective correlative, with the austere future that lay ahead. It is
> interesting, at any rate, that he never again undertook a poem so amorous of
> content, or so passionate of style.
>
> (330)

Why never again? What dynamic process in Pope's psyche rose to a pitch at this and no other juncture of his life, subsequently resolving itself in a way that the poet "never again undertook a poem so amorous?" These are not questions Mack apparently asks, though we might expect Pope's most expert biographer to answer them. The glance at "the objective correlative" of the New Critics (after all, there are other ways to explain the relations between literature and life) would not be disappointing in itself if these questions had been put and provisionally answered, but what most disappoints is the abrogation of the biographer's responsibility by the substitution of a note of chronological interest ("It is interesting. . . .") as the surrogate of biographical analysis of the young poet's sex drive.[11] The words trip off Mack's deft pen as we expect them to flow from a supreme critic, but they reveal rather little about the psyche of the creative imagination which is, after all, the subject of this life, and still less about the erotic drive of the young man who articulated the poems. If Mack's treatment of Pope's life in relation to the *Epistle to a Lady* is even less successful than either of these discussions, we can excuse the lapse on the grounds that Mack's intellectual stance was formed before the development of contemporary feminism. We can overlook his endorsement of Pope's treatment of the sex who have "no characters at all" by his substitution (again) of a poised critical voice that shuns all shrill opinions demanding the vocabulary of excoriation (there are readers who find Pope's poem appalling). Mack's discussion, illuminating as it is in its reference to the paintings of women that may have influenced Pope's descriptions in this poem, is adumbrated for ten pages (626–35). It culminates on the anticlimatic note that the poem's ending is not at all about "a woman's character as woman in the poem has been hitherto understood; for she [the woman at his side] is androgyne" (635). Androgynous she may be, in the terms that Pope and his contemporaries could construe sexual androgyny, but Mack seizes no opportunity in this disclosure to explore the implications of androgyny in Pope's own life. A sentence is all we get—apparently enough for the biographer as critic.

In conclusion then, Mack's accomplishment, though weighty, is not free from defect. If his biography is more inclusive and better written than any previous life—more perfect than any life of Pope we are likely to have for a long time—it nevertheless remains a critic's view that has not solved all the enigmas of Pope's complex personality. From my vantage virtually all Mack's research was completed and digested long ago, lending an impression that, except for the material (796–801) about "Amica," who idolized Pope and whose identity remains unknown, no fresh research is to be found here. Nor has Mack sought to change our mind about the late, mature Pope: the Pope who wrote in the chronological years after Sherburn left off. Mack's Pope after 1730 remains virtually consonant with the ethical and urbane poet of *The Garden and the City*. There is no new interpretation of the way Warburton came to replace Bolingbroke in Pope's imagination during 1739–41, years that have been least understood by the Popeans. Finally, Mack has not gone beyond the position he himself staked out, long ago, in relation to Pope's dramatization and recreation of his various selves. The images Pope generated of his persona and the relation of these images to his own, felt, true self must await a Popean whose cast of mind differs fundamentally from Mack's. As I have continued to urge, there is a great deal to admire in this magisterial performance. But these matters remain to be resolved by others, and it may be that another type of book—written in a medium altogether different from this critical analysis—will be required to cope with them.

Notes

1. Maynard Mack, *Alexander Pope: A Life* (New York: Norton, 1985), pp. 975, $22.50.

2. G. B. Hill, ed., *Lives of the English Poets by Samuel Johnson*, 3 vols. (Oxford, 1935), 3:251.

3. M. Mack, *The Garden and the City: Retirement and Politics in the Later Poetry of Pope 1731–1743* (Toronto, 1969).

4. M. Mack, *PQ* 36 (1957): 388–99.

5. M. Mack, *"The Last and Greatest Art": Some Unpublished Poetical Manuscripts of Alexander Pope* (Delaware University Press, 1984).

6. Donald Greene, " 'Tis a Pretty Book, Mr. Boswell, But—," *Georgia Review* 32 (1978): 17–43.

7. Greene, "An Anatomy of Pope Bashing," in Pat Rogers and G. S. Rousseau, eds., *Alexander Pope: The Enduring Legacy* (Cambridge, forthcoming).

8. Laura Brown, *Alexander Pope* (New York, 1985).

9. See, for example, the harsh review by Howard Weinbrot, *SEL* 25 (1985): 692–94.

10. C. Brooks, "The Case of Miss Arabella Fermor," *The Well-Wrought Urn* (New York, 1947), 80–104.

11. For an interpretation of this poem very different from Mack's, see John Trimble, "The Psychological Landscape of Pope's Life and Art," Ph.D. diss., University of California, Berkeley, 1971.

ESSAYS

◆

Beyond Consensus: *The Rape of the Lock* and the Fate of Reading Eighteenth-Century Literature

ROBERT MARKLEY

A student of mine recently remarked that trying to explain the literary "significance" of *The Rape of the Lock* was a bit like trying to explain a dirty joke to a group of divinity students. "You either get it," she said, shaking her head, "or you don't." This is, I have come to think, a more probing assessment than it first seems. Underlying it is a basic premise of much of the traditional criticism of Pope's poem: the assumption that "it"—meaning, significance, or satiric intention—is self-evident; in other words, the poem both describes and enacts the literary and cultural values that we have been instructed to attribute to Pope: balance, irony, the satire of human foibles, and so on. In this sense, "you either get it or you don't" can be read as a laconic twentieth-century version of what is implied by Pope's remark in the *Essay on Criticism* that sound must echo sense—if we take "it" or "sense" to encompass not simply "self-evident" literary platitudes but a set of complex ideological factors that inform both Pope's poetry and the critical values that, over the past fifty years or so, have been both extrapolated from and read into his work.

The history of Pope studies in recent years, and particularly criticism of *The Rape of the Lock*, suggests that a fair number of recent scholars—among them marxists, feminists and deconstructionists—are questioning exactly what the "it" is that we are supposed to "get." In one sense, what is happening to Pope may be no different from what is going on elsewhere in literary studies— the questioning of what makes an author canonical, of the values that allow us to "get" certain authors and to walk away, shaking our heads, from others. But the debates about Pope seem, if anything, more contentious, less given to scholarly mediation than those that swirl around other figures because, I suspect, Pope—as poet, critic, translator of Homer, and editor of Shake-speare—embodies the values we have been taught to associate with the study of literature.[1] For this reason, debates about seemingly trivial things in his verse are ultimately broader and value-laden debates about the great things

Robert Markley, "Beyond Consensus: *The Rape of the Lock* and the Fate of Reading Eighteenth-Century Literature." 1988 by Loyola University, New Orleans. Reprinted by permission of the *New Orleans Review*.

that trouble our profession. My interest in investigating the metacritical debates about *The Rape of the Lock*, in this regard, does not lie in the fruitless task of trying to decide who "gets it" and who doesn't but in examining the significance of these debates for teaching and writing about Pope, for the eighteenth century, and at least by implication for literature itself. More specifically, my purpose in focussing primarily on reviews is intended to demonstrate three points: that the process of reviewing the works of our colleagues (traditionally a suspect, almost sub-critical mini-genre) has in recent years become increasingly fragmented, politicized and chaotic; that the rhetoric of disinterested assessments of others' works masks deep-seated political disagreements about the nature and purpose of literary study; and that our models of what literary criticism should be—reverent, objective and rational—are in need of a serious overhaul.

At the risk of simplifying a complex process, we might say that the purpose of any critical account of Pope's poem—or that of any canonical work—is to demonstrate its "value," its potential to instruct us about something, whether life, manners, human vanity, the nature of women, or the sources of the cosmetics on Belinda's table. In turn, the strategies by which Pope has been rendered "significant"—an object worthy of intense critical speculation—tell us a good deal about the values of the literary culture and the critical profession that value the *Rape*. My assumption is that neither Pope nor his poem has an *intrinsic* literary worth, that is, a value on which theoretically "all" scholars can agree. Rather, as the recent criticism demonstrates, Pope's poems have become the site of dialogical debates about the values he has been traditionally taken to represent. "Dialogical" debates, though, need to be differentiated from the anything-goes pluralism of much contemporary criticism.[2] Obviously critics have always disagreed about specific interpretations of Pope and about specific problems in reading his verse: note, for example, the various responses to Clarissa in *The Rape of the Lock*. But these disagreements have taken place on fairly narrow grounds that, I would argue, ultimately lead to an implicit acceptance by most critics and their readers of liberal-humanist values. What distinguishes contemporary debates about Pope from the controversies of the 1960s and 1970s is precisely the challenge that some marxist and feminist readings pose to the values that underlie traditional readings of individual poems. The dialogical forces at work in contemporary Pope criticism, in this regard, cannot be easily tamed or assimilated into familiar assumptions about literature, criticism and culture. As the books and reviews that I shall discuss below indicate, we seem to have arrived at a point beyond consensus from which there may not be an easy way back to the collegiality of old-fashioned scholarly debate.

In the past few years there have been a number of critical studies of Pope that, in one way or another, seek deliberately to challenge conventional ways of reading his work.[3] Two of the more controversial—and significant—of these rereadings call into question rather than simply reaffirm the nature of the poet's achievement. Rather than contenting themselves with reworking the interpretations of previous studies, they seek to reassess the assumptions and values of the critical culture that celebrates Pope's significance as a canonical poet. Ellen Pollak's *The Poetics of Sexual Myth: Gender and Ideology in the Verse of Swift and Pope* (1985) and Laura Brown's *Alexander Pope* (1985) both offer rereadings of Pope and, in a larger sense, of the problem of assessing literary value. I would strongly recommend both books, and not simply for what I see as their critical virtues. Anyone who neglects to read them and merely skims the reviews of these two studies is likely to come away far more puzzled than enlightened. Particularly in the case of Pollak's study, the reviews offer a troubling variety of contradictory and self-contradictory assessments, vapid generalizations, miscitations, and distortions of the author's arguments that suggest many reviewers cannot be bothered to examine critically either her theoretical framework or her polemical purpose. Both self-confessed and closet conservatives, in reviewing Pollak's and Brown's books, frequently retreat to the battlements to protect Pope as though he were a religious icon to be saved from the post-structuralist hordes. In a recent review essay of full-length studies of Pope, John M. Aden begins by condemning what he calls "a new species of Pope Burnings, in effigies of cause ranging from feminist outrage, Marxist defacement, deconstructionist sabotage to a pedantry of microscopic dismemberment and incrimination."[4] Mixed metaphors aside, this sentence is noteworthy both for the vehemence of its attack and for the certainty with which it links Pope criticism to a nearly apocalyptic vision of humanist literary culture under siege. But the responses to Brown's and Pollak's studies do more than reveal a straightforward "us-versus-them" mentality. Comments like Aden's testify to fundamental ideological divisions within eighteenth-century studies and within academe at large.

Laura Brown's *Alexander Pope* appears in the Blackwell series "Rereading Literature" edited by Terry Eagleton. In his preface to Brown's study Eagleton concisely sums up her argument: Brown produces "a Pope whose poetry is less magically free of social and ideological contradiction than in part consti-tuted by it; a Pope whose writing, in the very act of lending its voice to imperialist power and social oppression, finds itself curiously, unwittingly diverted into affirming something very like the opposite" (vii). As the title of Eagleton's series, "Rereading Literature," implies, Brown is concerned to reassess Pope's poetry from a materialist or marxist perspective. In re-examin-ing the canonical work of a canonical poet, she subjects Pope to a dialectical analysis which demonstrates that the very form of his poetry registers the contradictions within the ideology of eighteenth-century mercantile expan-sionism. To some, like Aden, this attempt at "demystification" can have only one purpose—"the unmasking of the capitalist pig lurking behind all the major poems" (662). Aden's metaphor here is interesting (even if one resists trying to visualize a pig suddenly being unmasked). He presupposes that there is a fundamental distinction between ideology and poetry, that Brown is imposing a historical and irrelevant notions of class antagonism and conflict on a text that should be approached with sympathy and humility, if not reverence. Yet this is precisely what Brown says she is not doing: her "critique is not an attack on Pope from the outside, from the wiser perspective of a later historical moment. It seeks instead to find *in Pope's poems themselves* the signs of their ideology, to define the structures of belief by which their systems of value are sustained" (3; emphasis added). For Brown, as for Eagleton and all other marxists, poetry and ideology cannot be neatly separated or compartmentalized; in fact, as Michael McKeon argues, poetry *is* ideology.[5] Aden's wrath is directed ultimately not merely at Brown's treatment of Pope but at what he perceives is the cause that she represents—a deterministic marxism.

In addition to the fundamental difference in their views of what poetry is, Aden and Brown also differ about what the purpose of her study or of any of the "new species" of Pope criticism is or should be. After indicating that he finds Brown's "whole account . . . a tissue of Marx-speak," Aden concludes that the only purpose of so radical a study must be defilement of the poet and all who appreciate him: "It is not enough to discredit Pope: one must discredit his critical following as well" (662). But if he assumes that Brown's purpose is another public burning, it is surprising that he does not note that the fires she supposedly seeks to kindle never quite get going. Brown states explicitly that

> Pope has been the centre of the canon in traditional eighteenth-century literary history for good reason, it seems. This study keeps him there. But it keeps him as a subversive, as a lever against the whole canon of eighteenth-century studies. In that sense my reading is not a last word or a full or final evaluation, but barely a beginning, an essay towards that subversion.
>
> (5)

This is a suspiciously inadequate way to discredit either Pope or his admirers, unless one backpedals and accuses Brown (as Aden implies) of a covert hatred for the eighteenth-century canon, for poetry, and ultimately for literature itself. But to make this rhetorical move, one would have to close one's edition of Pope before one chances upon *The Dunciad*, which itself displays (among its other attributes) something of an animus for much of the writing that was going on between 1726 and 1744. In fact, Brown's argument hinges on her reading of Pope's poetry as performing a complex double function. *The Rape of the Lock*, for example, satirically "attack[s] commodities [specifically the array on Belinda's dressing table] and their cultural consequences while it extols imperialism. It can praise the battles of imperial expansion while it condemns the consequences of capitalist accumulation" (22). As this passage suggests, far from seeking to discredit Pope, Brown is intent on reassessing the reasons for his central position in the canon of eighteenth-century studies. In this regard, she is more detailed and specific in arguing for Pope's historical and ideological significance than many of his earlier critics—Cleanth Brooks, Aubrey Williams and Earl Wasserman, for example—who assume that Pope's technical skill is evidence enough of his sociohistorical importance as well as his literary merit.[6] Her analysis of the *Rape* is grounded in her belief that Pope develops a sophisticated poetic mode for registering the political as well as social complexities of the early eighteenth century.

The Pope who emerges in Brown's study is not the miniaturist, the technical virtuoso, or the craftsman who refurbishes classical values and poetic modes but instead the self-divided genius who creates an "elegant fantasy" about the culture of his day that paradoxically creates a "classical 'past' out of his own present beliefs" (26). Pope is drawn to the *Aeneid*, for example, not because he is searching for models or seeking to display his learning but because the "very ambiguities" in Virgil's poem offer "a subliminal and subversive [model] . . . for the implicit ambivalence of Pope's imperialist poems" (27). Pope the champion of drawing room civility is replaced by Pope the incisive commentator on the political ambiguities of his day. By inserting *The Rape of the Lock* into the history of mercantile expansion, Brown seeks to demonstrate that the poem becomes an active constituent of the ideological "reality" of the early eighteenth century rather than a passive if witty reflection of the vagaries of upper-class existence. In this respect, her historicizing of Pope's poetry may be seen as a strategy of re-valuing rather than re-evaluating it, of offering a new means by which to account for the significance of the poem and the poet. In fact, if there is an ideological criticism which could be made of Brown's study it would not be that it has burned or discredited Pope but that it has not gone far enough in demystifying him as an exemplar of English culture in the eighteenth century. My guess is that Brown and Aden basically agree about how crucial a poet Pope is for the study of Augustan literature; the basis of his attack on her book is political: same poet, different ideological perspectives.

Pollak's *The Poetics of Sexual Myth* in both its execution and implications seems more radical—at least as concerns the problem of literary value—than Brown's. Its basic premise is that Pope's poetry plays an important role in codifying antifeminist ideology in the eighteenth century, what she terms the "myth of passive womanhood." The question that her study raises—one which has led at least some of the book's reviewers to condemn it in fairly violent terms—focuses on the relationship between canonical poetry and repressive values: can Pope be both a great poet and a misogynist? Where Brown re-evaluates the reasons for Pope's being at the center of the canon of eighteenth-century verse, and implicitly to the canon if we find that ideologically the center cannot hold. In some respects, then, her book seems paradigmatic of the challenges which radical feminist criticism poses for the study of literature: can we value aesthetically what we condemn politically? In general, the responses to this question—and, as significantly, the refusals to confront it—that one could glean from the reviews of Pollak's study suggest that as a discipline we are ill-equipped to deal with fundamental problems of political value and literary evaluation. The reviewers' widely divergent views of what Pollak has or has not accomplished ultimately result less from disagreements about her abilities as a reader of Pope and Swift than from disagreements about the extent to which literary criticism can tolerate challenges to the equation of moral and literary values that underlies our notion of the canon.

Early in her study, Pollak rejects the myth of the "ideological innocence" of literature in order to explore "the question of how the 'personal' is itself shaped by conventional ideological imperatives" (19). Like Brown, she refuses to drive a wedge between art and ideology, arguing that rather than passively reflecting the ways of the world a poem such as *The Rape of the Lock* actively constitutes the ways in which individuals perceive themselves and respond to their socioeconomic environment. Pope's satire in the *Rape*, she argues, does not merely poke fun at the superficial values of eighteenth-century society; it participates in shaping attitudes towards the relationship between men and women within a world of "sterile fetishism." For Pollak, "Pope's satire on a culture that objectifies individuals is itself a pretext for his own objectification of the female" (77). Therefore, the poet's "ironies function monologically" (90) to emphasize the fetishized nature of the female as an object of desire, not to call into question the ideology of masculine prerogatives that symbolically turn Belinda into "a complex manifestation of male prowess itself—its inspiration, its conquered object, its result" (96). Ultimately, Pollak argues that those qualities of balance and good humor that have traditionally been invoked to praise *The Rape of the Lock* are themselves dependent on the poet's metaphorically turning women into an ornament, a trophy, a symbol of male vanity: "although Pope criticizes the sterility of a world in which the signs of things have become substitutes for things themselves, indeed where people live in a materialistic and metonymic void, he never does controvert the premise that female sexuality is a material property over which man has a natural claim" (97). In effect, the "metonymic void" of the material world is, in part, predicated on the ideological make-up of a patrilineal society that reduces women to the determinant existence of sexual objects.

For defenders of the orthodox critical faith, Pollak's reading of the *Rape* poses an enormous difficulty: to attack it, one must defend Pope by arguing that the poem is in fact not basically antifeminist, that the satire of Belinda is not gender-specific, that she does not have to have an "interiority" of character given the generic conventions of the poem, that she is not really the butt of the satire, or some combination of or variation on these themes. Aden tries to finesse the problem by insisting on the separation of art and sexual ideology: Pollak, he asserts, "is interested not in poetry but in sexism",; she "writes abundantly by buzz-word"; she never encourages us "to think of Swift and Pope as poets, but only as exhibits in the history of sexual miscreance" (662). Pope apparently cannot be a sexist because he is, well, Pope, the canonical poet. An equally spirited, even violent, attack on Pollak's feminist critique is launched by Nora Crow Jaffe.[7] Pollak, she claims,

> has only one context in mind: the condition of women. Her narrowness and her ordering of priorities leave room for a dismaying innocence about the rest of history, especially literary history, and for perverse and anachronistic readings that precipitate her own feminist and Marxist program into defeat. Worse yet, her tendentiousness endangers the efforts of those who wish to combine feminist goals with a sympathetic and responsible appreciation for poets like Swift and Pope.
>
> (245)

To attack Pollak's "unsympathetic" and "irresponsible" treatment of Swift and Pope, Jaffe invokes "common sense interpretation[s]" of the two poets that invariably turn on the minutiae of where commas should or should not be, first versus second definitions in the OED, and melodramatic condemnations of Pollak's "relentless driving toward ideological goals" (247) and alleged lack of knowledge about "eighteenth-century ideas about mock-epic, epic, and history" (248). To drive home her point, Jaffe closes by implying that Pollak's reading "plays into the hands of those who deny a woman's autonomy by offering to relieve her of responsibility for the choices she has made" (248). Presumably, *The Poetics of Sexual Myth* represents "irresponsible" feminist inquiry because it fails to demonstrate its "responsible appreciation" for canonical poetry and the values that support it. Pollak, then, is not simply mistaken in her readings of particular poems; her work "endangers" efforts to bring "feminist goals" into the fold of humanist inquiry. These "goals," for Jaffe, however, seem to be restricted to concocting new ways of praising what has already been praised, new ways of shielding Pope and Swift—under the guise of "eighteenth-century ideas"—from ideological critique.

Jaffe's attack is typical of what happens when conservatively oriented critics turn a perjured eye from the implications of radical questions asked by marxist and feminist criticism. Her purpose—in effect to reclaim Swift and Pope *for* one version of feminism and *from* another—represents another version of Aden's attempt to insulate poetry from politics. By condemning Pollak's "irresponsible" brand of feminism, Jaffe must also cast beyond the pale of "responsible" "feminist goals" those critics who praise Pollak's study: Terry Castle ("*The Poetics of Sexual Myth* is intelligently conceived, beautifully written, and approaches its difficult, incendiary subject with a fine balance of scholarly scrupulousness and critical daring"); Catharine Stimpson ("A deft and subtle text, [this study] balances intellectual energy and grace"); Kristina Straub ("[Pollak's] book is pleasurable to read as well as an excellent argument for the importance and credibility of incorporating an awareness of the political problems of gender in our understanding of eighteenth-century texts"); David

Nokes ("Pollak's book . . . is one of the most persuasive and stimulating works of feminist literary criticism that I have encountered"); Anne Himmelfarb ("A lucid, sometimes brilliant application of feminist theory to a group of poems not usually treated by feminists"); Brean Hammond ("a highly intelligent and challenging book, the first to bring to its subject the resources of an adequately theorized feminism"); Janet Todd ("an extremely enlightening and enlivening work which, on the whole, skillfully draws on the insights and language of modern formalist criticisms to illuminate the ultimately historical problem of the representation of women"); and Harold Weber ("Pollak's book is exhilarating . . . not only for its own contribution to eighteenth-century studies, but because it promises a renewed energy in the field as scholars attempt to come to terms with Pollak's method and conclusions").[8] Underlying Jaffe's objections to, say, Pollak's reading of the word "affectation" as an attribute (according to Steele) of both the coquette and prude is a fundamental difference between these two critics about what we mean by feminism, ideology, poetry, and criticism. Although Jaffe accuses Pollak of driving towards ideological goals, her review is not less committed, no less ideological than *The Poetics of Sexual Myth*. But where Pollak combines a re-reading of Pope with a metacritical examination of traditional critical methods and values—of the nature of ideology and masculinist discourse—Jaffe retreats to the bulwarks of common sense and embattled humanist ideals to avoid precisely the issue which Pollak's study confronts: what is the relationship between canonical poetry and repressive ideologies?

The radical nature of this question virtually ensures that it can be answered (or evaded) from other critical perspectives. In marked contrast to Jaffe's insistence that Pollak, laden with her ideological cargo, has sailed off the edge of the earth, Felicity Nussbaum, while praising Pollak's readings as "scholarly, energetic, and engaging in their conviction," argues that she has not gone far enough: her "use of authorial intention," for example, "conventionalizes Pollak's vigorous readings and threatens her compelling thesis."[9] Although Nussbaum acknowledges that Pollak "raises issues which are crucial, even urgent, for eighteenth-century scholars and for the humanities," she nonetheless laments that *The Poetics of Sexual Myth* "steps back from forging a new historicism which would acknowledge the way writing narratives of history is an interpretive act, and the way representations of reality . . . construct as well as reflect a material world" (369). In other words, what for Aden and Jaffe is dangerously radical is for Nussbaum too conventional. And yet Nussbaum's review is not simply a case of one critic trying to outflank another on the fashionable critical left, what we might call the "leftier-than-thou" mode which, over the past few years, has increasingly pitted literary critics against each other to test the limits of political tolerance within academe. Nussbaum's earlier study, *The Brink of All We Hate: English Satires on Women, 1660–1750*, has been castigated by reviewers for its lack of theoretical sophistication and criticized by Pollak (208, n. 9) for its attempt to redeem Pope's

Rape and the "Epistle to a Lady" from charges of misogyny by arguing a Jaffe-like position that "each [poem] is ambiguous and complex in its use of eighteenth-century conventions and commonplaces" about women.[10] The difference in theoretical orientation between Nussbaum's book on satire and her review of Pollak's study involves more than an individual critic's move to a more ideologically self-conscious position. In her review, Nussbaum is, in effect, reformulating the problem of poetic value in ideological rather than (as in her earlier study) formalist terms. The constructivist position that she implicitly maintains in her critique of Pollak does not so much question the relationship between poetic value and ideology as equate them. In effect, Nussbaum, even as she praises Pollak's readings of Pope, invites us to see *The Poetics of Sexual Myth* as a kind of catalyst that, having demystified the workings of gender and ideology in *The Rape of the Lock* and other poems, needs itself to be challenged for its supposed failure to call into question the notion of authorial intention.

As the incompatible responses of Jaffe and Nussbaum suggest, Pollak's feminist critique, perhaps even more than Brown's Marxist study, asks its readers to take sides, to examine their own positions on the problems of misogyny and poetic value. This is not simply a matter of declaring a straight-forward political allegiance, as Aden, Jaffe and Nussbaum, although in very different ways, maintain. It is significant, in this regard, that reviewers' attitudes towards the Pope and Swift chapters in Pollak's work differ de-pending on their critical allegiances to one or the other of the poets. Aden, for example, having lambasted Pollak's reading of Pope, is willing to grant Pollak at least this much. She finds in Swift something that gives her comfort doctrinally, and so—save where he still comes off ever so psychopathic and, what is worse, an admirer of Pope—he fares pretty well at her hands. Her reading of *Cadenus and Vanessa* is a good and useful commentary on that poem and one deserving of commendation (663). Contrast his praise to Nussbaum's terse comment: Pollak's "interpretations of Swift's verse are less convincing" than her readings of Pope (*Southern Humanities Review* 368). Although Nuss-baum is not really explicit about why they are less convincing, the implication is that they rely too heavily on a notion of authorial intention. Jaffe, who published her own book on Swift in 1977, takes time out from her scattershot attack to acknowledge that Pollak's chapter on *The Rape of the Lock* is "vivid and interesting," although not focused enough on the issue of eighteenth-century notions of mock-epic.[11] The pattern that emerges as one reads through the reviews of Pollak's study is that Popeans are uncomfortable with a feminist critique of Pope, Swiftians with a radical rereading of Swift. The most forth-right acknowledgement of this dilemma is John Sitter's in his review of Pollak's book: "For reasons having less to do with differences of methodological commitment than of poetic sympathy (but which I trust are nonetheless arguable), I find the Popean middle of Ms. Pollak's study less persuasive and helpful than the chapters on gender debates or on Swift's poetry."[12] He then accurately sums up Pollak's contrast of Pope the "bourgeois liberal" to Swift the "radical," but goes on to charge her with violating her own theoretical agenda in her readings of Pope's poems when she asks for "an interiority of character generically improbable then and theoretically suspect now" (61). But the "interiority" that Pollak finds lacking does not seem to me to be an assertion on her part that violates eighteenth-century conceptions of genre or twentieth-century conceptions of the de-centered self; it is a relational idea that she refers, quite sensibly, I think, to the explicit distinctions that Pope makes between the characters of men and women in the *Moral Essays*. In short, as Sitter recognizes, his critique of the book's sections on Pope rests on differences in "poetic sympathy." Even as he recognizes the bases and biases of his response, Sitter seeks a means both to praise Pollak's study—"an intelligent and important contribution"—and to recuperate Pope's reputation (60).

At this juncture, having surveyed a variety of reactions to two important critical works, we might find ourselves tempted by scholarly convention to intone solemn platitudes about the pluralistic nature of the profession, the wide variety of responses that "great" poetry can still provoke, and the need for further studies to clarify this unfortunately muddled situation. But the usual pieties cannot paper over the fundamental differences that separate Jaffe from Pollak and Straub or Aden from Brown. In an important essay that introduces a special issue of *The Eighteenth Century: Theory and Interpretation* devoted to Pope, David Morris argues persuasively that no single theory can possibly "sum up" or "capture" Pope, that the poet, like any great writer, is complex enough to resist being co-opted by a single critical or theoretical perspective.[13] The analogy he makes is a fascinating one: the criticism of Pope is likened to the "Bootstrap Theory" of the Berkeley physicist Geoffrey Chew, who argues that our notion of single theories to explain the subatomic structure of matter should give way to a series of interlocking theories—bootstrap theories. Each theory seeks to explain only a portion of the relevant data; at its boundaries of explanation it gives way to other theories which, in turn, explain different sets of data or anomalies in the original theory. Chew's image of bootstrap theory is finally one of a grand mosaic, though constantly redefining the relationships among its constituent elements, and never quite offering a firm teleological hope that the "truth" is just around the corner, over the horizon, or beyond the next experiment.

Morris's view of Pope criticism as a dynamic and incomplete mosaic is, I think, both brilliantly evocative and historically plausible. It provides a valuable means to theorize a mass of otherwise contradictory and self-contradictory commentary that turns Pope into a Rorschach test for various critical "-isms." And yet, as Morris notes, in theoretical physics nowadays bootstrap theory (first advanced by Chew some twenty years ago) is old hat—certainly not disproved, certainly not contradicted by new sets of data, but simply unfashionable.[14] While literary critics ponder the metaphoric richness of bootstrap theory, theoretical physicists are caught up in the quest for a unified field theory—a single formulation to explain *all* the workings of matter, gravity, strong and weak forces on the subatomic level, and electromagnetism. No one has formulated a unified field theory; no one knows what one will look like. But the lure of comprehensiveness, of mystical truth, of a final summation of everything we know hovers over the enterprise of theoretical physics probably to no less of an extent that it haunts the dreams of literary critics. For the latter, the buzzwords that define critical praise are never those of bootstrap theory but of that teleological phantom, the definitive interpretation. Note, for example, Aden's assessment (in my mind, quite accurate) of Morris's *Alexander Pope: The Genius of Sense*: "unquestionably the most original and seminal overview of Pope's poetry as a whole that, Maynard Mack excepted, I can recall" (667–68).[15] Yet another of the ironies of criticism in the eighties: Morris, the critic most fascinated by the issue of Pope's seemingly infinite variety, is the one labelled as the most capable of providing an overarching view of the poet's work as a consistent, humanistically-based "whole."

But any theory of Pope criticism—or of literary criticism, in general— that attempts to hold widely divergent views in some form of dialectical cohesion may be too optimistic. On the level of praxis, of what goes on in the classroom, the differences among Pollak, Jaffe and Nussbaum seem too fundamental to subsume under a convenient rubric such as "feminism" or "eighteenth-century studies." Suppose, for example, that you had an eighteen-year-old daughter, intending to major in English, whose choice of colleges came down to Smith and Syracuse. Suppose further that your daughter, having whizzed through the Advance Placement exam in literature, walks in on her first day of college to a survey of eighteenth-century literature taught either by Jaffe (at Smith) or Nussbaum (at Syracuse). The vocabulary of these two professors might be the same—Pope, eighteenth-century society, role of women, literature, and so on. But if their responses to Pollak's study are any indication, the courses that they teach would be vastly different: Jaffe presumably would seek to confirm Pope's status as a canonical poet, Nussbaum to identify and demystify the patriarchal ideologies which her colleague at Smith would either pass over in silence or indicate were somehow part of what Pope was satirizing rather than promoting. Depending on her choice of colleges, then, your daughter would be getting fundamentally different views of Pope—and of the process of reading literature. My point here is not necessarily to indicate that in some absolute sense one of these critics is "right" and the other "wrong" but to indicate that there may finally be no way to reconcile their views either of Pollak's study or of eighteenth-century literature, no way to subsume their differences within a unifying rhetoric of scholarly consensus.

There may be, however, other metaphors besides Morris's invoking of bootstrap theory to explain what is occurring in Pope criticism and in the criticism of eighteenth-century literature in general. Like other variants of quantum physics, bootstrap theory is now being, in part, supplanted by contemporary chaos theory.[16] Chaos theory cuts across conventional boundaries of physical and mathematical research and redefines a number of scientific disciplines: fractal geometry, meteorology, non-linear dynamics, irreversible thermodynamics, and many others. In effect, chaos theory studies the transformation of systems from order to randomness, the ways in which minute differences in input (in computer-generated sequences of "pseudo-random" numbers, for example) can relatively quickly (within the space of a few hundred iterations) lead to vast differences in output. In effect, then, chaos theory does not simply redefine relationships between order and disorder; it calls into question both philosophically and mathematically the "common sense" definitions of order and disorder themselves. Chaos theory has the attraction for scientists and mathematicians of employing sophisticated theories and complex models to investigate everyday phenomena, of applying computer-generated functions to problems of predicting the weather, of describing the clouds that cigarette smoke makes in the air, of reassessing the information that can be gleaned from the eye movements of schizophrenics.

And, for us, perhaps the seeming unpredictability of literary criticism. The critics of *The Rape of the Lock* whom I have dealt with in this essay presumably begin from the same data, the Twickenham edition of Pope's poem. Yet what appear to be minute, even trivial, differences in reading single words or lines can and do generate profound differences in interpretations. There is, I think, no way to establish a consensus among Brown, Aden, Pollak, Nussbaum, Straub, and Sitter: in the words of Firesign Theater, you can't get there from here. But I should note that chaos theory does *not* presuppose the kind of nihilistic entropy that Aden laments has overtaken Pope criticism. Anyone who has looked at the fractal geometric constructions of Benoit Mandelbrot recognizes that chaos theory presupposes a kind of Blakean generative energy rather than anomie. For chaos theorists, the true sterility is predictability, the refusal to acknowledge the productive function of iteration, the close-minded division of the universe into static concepts of matter, energy and information. Chaos theory—and I choose this term deliberately—deconstructs the boundaries among these entities.

The critical anticipation of chaos theory in literary studies, though, may belong more to Mikhail Bakhtin than to Derrida, who, after all, published *De la Grammatologie* twenty years after Claude Shannon published his groundbreaking articles on information theory.[17] For Bakhtin, there are no denotative meanings, no single-faceted rhetorical constructs. All understanding is dialogical, our utterances always in the process of defining themselves against prior utterances and against the hostile misconstructions of our social environment. Communication, for Bakhtin, is always an unstable, precarious affair; in the metaphor of information theory, noise and information always interpenetrate in historically specific utterances. Unlike those literary theorists who struggle to pin down meaning, to offer definitive interpretations, Bakhtin offers the dialogics of culture as a contest of competing meanings, of increasing amounts of information that lead to more ideologically various and complex attempts to articulate—and legislate—meaning. Where Bakhtin differs from a wishy-washy form of "pluralism," however, is in his insistence on the historical specificity of utterances, on their ideological nature. For Bakhtin, the exchange of information is always interested, always a political struggle.

So, too, is contemporary criticism of *The Rape of the Lock*. The reactions to Brown's and Pollak's revisionist studies of Pope indicate on one level the breakdown of scholarly consensus that, I would argue, is occurring throughout the disciplines of humanistic study. On another level, however, these books and the responses they have generated suggest that if the breakdown of consensus leads to the falling out of fashion of the heretofore "responsible appreciation" of Pope, it will be all to the good. The problem with the old-line humanist criticism represented by Aden and Jaffe is not that in some metaphysical sense it is "wrong" but that it perpetuates static, reified notions of "responsible" and "irresponsible" criticism that fail to consider the ideological interests of "responsibility." It canonizes Pope at the expense of studying him; by trying to "save" him from Marxist, feminist and deconstructive analysis it renders his verse hardly worth reading by conceding, in effect, what is surely Pollak's most penetrating criticism—that the ironies of his verses on women are monological and coercive rather than, in Bakhtin's sense, dialogical. If Pope's *Rape* does not participate in and, in Foucault's sense, help to disseminate eighteenth-century views of sexuality, what ideological claims does it promote? What values does it accept as "natural"? If Pope, Richardson and other eighteenth-century writers are ideologically innocent—if canonical literature itself resists repressive ideologies—where does antifeminism come from? How is it sustained? Perhaps, to paraphrase Falstaff, misogyny lay in Pope's way and he found it. But to explain away Pope's conservatism, to refuse to interrogate the ideological structure of his verse, as Jaffe tries to do by hauling out alleged eighteenth-century "ideas" of mock-epic, is to eviscerate Pope in a way that, I suspect, would delight the targets of his satire in *The Dunciad*.

It should be obvious by now that my critical sympathies lie with Pollak and Brown rather than with their harsher critics. This does not necessarily mean that I "agree" with them in every instance or that I think either of them is somehow "right" in the absolute sense that is bandied about in Aden's and Jaffe's reviews. The great virtue of their works is precisely their willingness to alter the theoretical and ideological bases on which Pope criticism has traditionally depended. Without questioning the underpinnings of "responsible appreciation" of Pope, we are stuck in a parody of a Laplacian universe, maintaining, whatever evidence to the contrary, that chaos, that dialogic struggle, does not exist. Far from imposing simplistic solutions on a complex poet, Brown's and Pollak's studies open up new levels of discourse to explore, new ways of rethinking the significance of Pope in the dissemination of ideologies which continue to shape our attitudes towards literature and the canon. We do not have to judge between, say, Morris's *The Genius of Sense* and Pollak's *The Poetics of Sexual Myth* in some absolute sense as though these studies were two boxers trying to club the other into unconsciousness, the winner to stand as the champion of definitive interpretation until the next challenger comes along. Instead, the dialogic interplay between two books of this stature can serve as a means to reject both monological readings of Pope and the kind of mushy-headed pluralism that Morris's and my appropriations of bootstrap and chaos theories try to get us beyond. Given the kinds of comments that I have surveyed in this essay, I am a bit less optimistic than Morris in assessing the state of Pope studies because, for all the energy represented by the essays in this issue of the *New Orleans Review* and Morris's special issue of *The Eighteenth Century: Theory and Interpretation*, there still seems to be a lot of bad blood and bad faith among people who write on Pope. How productive this state of chaos will be beyond the old critical consensus may very well depend on how seriously the debates provoked by the contributors to these two special issues are taken.[18]

Notes

1. On the ideological assumptions of Pope's formalist critics see Christopher Norris, "Pope among the Formalists," in *Post-Structuralist Readings of English Poetry*, eds. Richard Machin and Christopher Norris (Cambridge: Cambridge Univ. Press, 1987) 134–61.

2. On the dialogical nature of criticism see Don H. Bialostosky, "Dialogics as an Art of Discourse in Literary Criticism," *PMLA* 101 (1986): 788–97.

3. See particularly G. Douglas Atkins, *Quests of Difference: Reading Pope's Poems* (Lexington: Univ. of Kentucky Press, 1986); A. D. Nuttall, *Pope's "Essay on Man"* (London: Allen and Unwin, 1984); Laura Brown, *Alexander Pope* (Oxford: Basil Blackwell, 1985); and Ellen Pollak, *The Poetics of Sexual Myth: Gender and Ideology in the Verse of Swift and Pope* (Chicago: Univ. of Chicago Press, 1985). The fact that I concentrate in this review on Brown's and Pollak's studies should not be taken, in any way, as a slighting of Atkins' or Nuttall's studies.

4. John M. Aden, "Alexander Pope: Ave Atque Vale," *Sewanee Review* 95 (1987): 661.

5. Michael McKeon, "Marxist Criticism and *Marriage a la Mode*," *The Eighteenth Century: Theory and Interpretation* 24 (1983): 141–62.

6. Brooks, *The Well-Wrought Urn* (New York: Harcourt, Brace, and World, 1947) 146–52; Williams, "The 'Fall' of China," rpt. in *"The Rape of the Lock": A Casebook*, ed. John Dixon Hunt (London: Macmillan, 1968) 220–36; Wasserman, "The Limits of Allusion in *The Rape of the Lock*," *JEGP* 65 (1966): 425–44. See also Donna Landry's comments on Brown's study in her review of Brean Hammond's *Pope* (Brighton and Atlantic Highlands, N. J.: Humanities Press International, 1986) and Rebecca Ferguson's *The Unbalanced Mind: Alexander Pope and the Rule of Passion* (Philadelphia: Univ. of Pennsylvania Press, 1986), in *Eighteenth-Century Studies* 21 (1988): 385.

7. Nora Crow Jaffe, rev. of *The Poetics of Sexual Myth*, in *Eighteenth-Century Studies* 20 (1986–87): 244–48.

8. Castle, cited on the dust jacket of *The Poetics of Sexual Myth* (Ellen Pollak confirms that Professor Castle was one of the readers of her manuscript for the Univ. of Chicago Press and that her comment originally appeared in her reader's report); Stimpson, Foreward, *The*

Poetics of Sexual Myth xi; Straub, "Feminism, Formalism, and Historical Consciousness," *The Eighteenth Century: Theory and Interpretation* 28 (1987): 186–92; Nokes, "Wielding the Gendered Shears," *Times Literary Supplement* 20 Feb. 1987: 9; Himmelfarb, rev. in *The Johnsonian Newsletter* 46.1 (Mar. 1986): 12; Hammond, "Poetry of Gender," *Times Higher Education Supplement* 14 Feb. 1986: 12; Todd, rev. in *British Journal for Eighteenth-Century Studies* 10 (1987): 233; Weber, rev. in *South Atlantic Review* 51.3 (1986): 86–87.

    9.   Felicity Nussbaum, rev. of *The Poetics of Sexual Myth*, in *Southern Humanities Review* 21 (1987): 367–69. For arguments similar to those advanced by Nussbaum see the review of Pollak's study by Donna Landry in *Choice* Feb. 1986: 872, and by Melinda Alliker Rabb in *Philological Quarterly* 66 (1987): 544–47

    10.   Felicity Nussbaum, *The Brink of All We Hate: English Satires on Women, 1660–1750* (Lexington: Univ. of Kentucky Press, 1984) 140. For two critiques of this work for its lack of theoretical and historical sophistication, see Ruth Perry, "Patriarchy's Poetry," *Women's Review of Books* 1.9 (June 1984): 16–17, and Laurie A. Finke, "The Ideologies of Feminism," *The Eighteenth Century: Theory and Interpretation* 27 (1986): 287–92.

    11.   Nora Crow Jaffe, *The Poet Swift* (Hanover, N.H.: Univ. Press of New England, 1977).

    12.   John Sitter, rev. of *The Poetics of Sexual Myth*, in *The Scriblerian* 20 (1987): 60–62.

    13.   David Morris, "Bootstrap Theory: Pope, Physics, and Interpretation," *The Eighteenth Century: Theory and Interpretation* 29 (1988): 101–21.

    14.   I am indebted to Evelyn Fox Keller and David Mermin for their helpful explanations of some of the complexities of contemporary bootstrap and quantum theory.

    15.   David Morris, *Alexander Pope: The Genius of Sense* (Cambridge, Mass.: Harvard Univ. Press, 1984).

    16.   For an accessible discussion of chaos theory see James Gleick, *Chaos: Making a New Science* (New York: Viking, 1987). I am indebted to N. Katherine Hayles for allowing me to read parts of her work in progress on chaos theory and contemporary literary theory.

    17.   I have discussed Bakhtin's significance for literary theory in *Two-Edg'd Weapons: Style and Ideology in the Comedies of Etherege, Wycherley, and Congreve* (Oxford: Clarendon Press, 1988) 19–29. See also Laurie A. Finke, "The Rhetoric of Marginality: Why I Do Feminist Theory," *Tulsa Studies in Women's Literature* 5 (1986): 251–72, and Susan Stewart, "Shouts on the Streets: Bakhtin's Anti-Linguistics," *Critical Inquiry* 10 (1983): 265–81.

    18.   I would like to thank David Morris and Ronald Schleifer for their helpful comments on an earlier draft of this paper.

Pope's Moral, Political, and Cultural Combat

CAROLE FABRICANT

My starting point for this essay is the desire to understand more fully and to come to grips with what have always seemed to me two particularly interesting and in various ways interconnected aspects of Pope's verse: its striking degree of self-preoccupation, and its rather high level of aggression and bellicosity, sometimes channelled thematically into representations of epic or mock-epic warfare (as in his translation of *The Iliad* and *The Rape of the Lock*), but increasingly incorporated into Pope's own stance as satirist and censurer of society, notwithstanding his depictions of himself as a man of peace, moderation, even child-like innocence. Because this self-dramatizing mode and this combative zeal are most dramatically fused in his *Epilogue to the Satires*, I will be referring for the most part to the two dialogues which comprise that poem. My concern here is not with a narrowly generic consideration of Pope's movement from Horatian to Juvenalian satire, about which much of value has already been written,[1] nor even with a specifically literary analysis. Rather I want to reflect upon the different kinds of battles Pope seems to be waging, upon the difficulties we are apt to encounter in understanding them, and upon their relationship to what I perceive as a larger battle that Pope fought throughout his career. My discussion is meant to give rise to some sustained reflection on the meaning of political, ideological, and cultural engagement, both for Pope in his time and for us today.

What are we now to make of the fierce denunciation, the moral outrage and the sense of self-righteousness, the assertion of absolute superiority over the rest of society, the self-portrait of a moral hero completely untouched by the supposed corruptions and degeneracy of the age, which mark the *Epilogue to the Satires*? How are we to understand Pope's characterization of the poem as "the testimony of his own conscience" and as "a sort of PROTEST" against the "depravity" of the times? How are we to respond to his depiction of himself as the "Last of *Britons*," the only man capable of drawing "the last Pen for Freedom" (250; 248): an almost god-like being who strikes fear and trembling into even the most brazen of his impious contemporaries ("Yes, I am proud; I must be proud to see / Men not afraid of God, afraid of me" [Dia.

Carole Fabricant, "Pope's Moral, Political, and Cultural Combat," from *The Eighteenth Century* 29, 2 (1988). Reprinted by permission of Texas Tech University Press.

II, 208–09]) and who unrestrainedly wields the "sacred Weapon" of satire in an aggressive and bloody battle against the army of the damned (Dia. II, 212–19)? Do we today find the tone and the role(s) in which he portrays himself palatable, sympathetic, justified? Would we still find it so if we didn't come to these poems specifically as Popeians—i.e., with a predisposition toward accepting Pope at his own word (and on his own self-image), with an inclination to perpetuate the strain of self-apologia and self-exaltation that runs throughout his poetry—or as formalist critics willing to ratify Pope's myths by justifying them in terms of satiric conventions and techniques?

It strikes me, frankly, that there are serious obstacles to endorsing Pope's own self-portraits as satirist. The exaltation and authorizing of self can be a profoundly moral act, but it can also be profoundly arrogant and solipsistic, as regularly charged by contemporary opponents of Pope, and as demonstrated in the many satiric depictions by Dryden, Swift, and Pope himself of the Miltonic Satan's alternately tragic and comic megalomania. Most of us, I think, recognize that occasionally situations arise that demand a special kind of moral heroism (perhaps even martyrdom) in the face of threats to humanity, to civilization, or to a cherished way of life. Such extreme situations would to our minds justify linguistic if not physical violence directed against existing political institutions or policies, as well as call forth a stance of uncompromising dissent from contemporary practices and attitudes, based on individual conscience and personal vision. At the same time, because the elevation of personal vision and judgment over public laws and policies can as readily produce the madman as the saint, the charlatan as the *vir bonus*, we invariably feel that certain conditions have to be met before we are prepared to credit the claims of moral outrage and the actions or verbal attacks growing out of it. One of the most important conditions is that we be able to accept the external provocation, e.g., the extent of political evil or social degeneration, as sufficiently serious and compelling. In our own century the Nuremberg trials, in response to the Nazi holocaust with its "crimes against humanity," have established grounds upon which the individual conscience is not only justified but morally obligated to speak and act in defiance of laws of the state that are deemed criminal when measured by a "higher law."

Dryden, whose position bore certain resemblances to Pope's, particularly during the final years of his life as a Catholic living under King William III, celebrated several examples of a heroic stance of dissent in his late verse, taking pains to justify the acts of civil disobedience via reference to specific historical circumstances. His "Good Parson," modelled on Chaucer's, sacrifices his benefice to wander penniless through the land because he refuses to accept the authority of a king lacking an inherited title; and his portrait of Sir Erasmus Driden presents a model patriot who was ". . . so tenacious of the Common cause, / As not to lead the King against his Laws; / And, in a lothsom Dungeon doom'd to lie, / In Bonds retain'd his Birthright Liberty, / And sham'd Oppression, till it set him free" (*To My Honour'd Kinsman, John Driden,*

190–94).[2] Swift, in his own expressions of moral outrage or political protest, characteristically eschews Dryden's moral exempla in order to present fictive speakers who resort to linguistic violence and verbal excess to register the intensity of their feelings. Even more than Dryden, however, Swift is concerned to convey to us the enormity of the evils confronting him, the sense that there is both specific and overwhelming provocation for his *scaeva indignatio*: clearly identifiable historical circumstances that fuel the satirist's rage. For example, in poems such as the *Verses occasioned by the sudden drying up of St. Patrick's Well* and *A Character, Panegyric, and Description of the Legion Club*, the respective speakers' fierce invective and vehement repudiation of society (as well as, in the case of *The Legion Club*, the speaker's obscenity, which calls to mind Pope's "filthy Simile" and "beastly Line" in the *Epilogue* [171–81]), is ultimately seen to be justified by their specific condemnations of British conquest, the absentee landlords, Wood's project, the loss of Irish liberty, and the Irish Parliament's traitorous role in Anglo-Irish affairs—all adding up to forceful critiques of English colonialist exploitation and oppression.[3]

We might look at a more recent example which can also be profitably compared with Pope's stance in the *Epilogue* as a man delivering "a sort of PROTEST" and offering "the testimony of his conscience." Although this protest concerns actions rather than printed words, the widespread use of satire as a form of political action in Pope's time and the linguistic sub-text of many political actions in recent times justify a comparison. I refer to the case of the Ploughshares 8, in which eight Catholic anti-war protestors hammered on and poured their own blood over the head of a nuclear missile cone in the General Electric nuclear facility in King of Prussia, Pennsylvania. (Eventually they were sentenced to up to ten years in prison for their "criminal" act.[4]) The defendants chose to represent themselves in court, and in his self-apologia to the jury one of the protestors, Father Daniel Berrigan, employed several "satiric" defenses reminiscent of Pope's in the *Epistle to Dr. Arbuthnot*, ranging from his Juvenalian statement that "he couldn't *not* do what he did," compelled as he was to act by the enormity of the external evil—the threat of nuclear annihilation, the ultimate "crime against humanity"—to his presentation of an Horation ethos, the *vir bonus* whose pious, hardworking parents passed on to him a legacy of Christian dedication and selfless service to the community.[5] In his remarks Berrigan dealt with a number of issues which have a direct relevance to issues treated or implied in the *Epilogue to the Satires* and *To Fortescue*: the relationship between man-made and divine law, the role of the individual conscience vis-à-vis society and the human community at large, the choice between submission and resistance to duly constituted authority, and the role of the courts as instruments in promoting the interests of the political and economic establishment, which renders the very idea of a fair trial obsolete.

Some may wish to take exception to Berrigan's position, but certainly the enormity of the provocation and the magnitude of the issue which moved him to speak and to act as he did rescue his political protest from the realm of mere self-indulgence or deluded heroism. In the case of both Swift and the Ploughshares 8, the specific issues that provoked the protest have profound moral implications, and the protestors are anxious to make clear the ethical (and, in Berrigan's case in particular, the religious) grounds of their resistance; but in neither case do the issues depend for their force or validity simply on the moral status of the protestors.

The same cannot be said for Pope's political protest and fierce denunciations of society in the *Epilogue to the Satires*. I suspect one reason why many readers see Pope's late poems as "Juvenalian" or as reflections of his "romanticism"[6] is that (among other things) the poems appear to lack a convincing objective correlative for the moral outrage and invective expressed, an absence which leaves only the image of a dramatic, bloated, all-consuming, sublime Self that takes over center stage while all else becomes primarily a backdrop which highlights, through contrast, the speaker's virtuous self. The focus of the *Epilogue* is, finally, on the poet as satirist in his various fascinating and self-fascinated poses, in his alternating roles of impotent but truthful observer, enraged flailer, Christian warrior, moral hero, and author of "immortal" verse. We look in vain for a clear and concrete issue (or constellation of issues) that would substantiate and justify the extremity of Pope's denunciation, the sweeping extent of his rejection of society. Without the sense of a specific social evil to address, his historical references risk becoming little more than pretexts for a series of poetic texts on and about Pope.

It is not that Pope ignores the general question of motivation and justification, of course:

> Ask you what Provocation I have had?
> The strong Antipathy of Good to Bad.
> When Truth or Virtue an Affront endures,
> Th' Affront is mine, my Friend, and should be yours.
> Mine, as a Foe profess'd to false Pretence,
> Who think a Coxcomb's Honour like his Sense;
> Mine, as a Friend to ev'ry worthy mind;
> And mine as Man, who feel for all mankind.
> (Dia. II, 197–203)

Even here, however, Pope's self-justification does not spotlight matters external to the self but turns into another concentration on (and exaltation of) the self. The echoing of the word "mine" emphasizes both the main subject of these lines and the extent to which all things in the outside world, including all moral values, seem determined by their relationship to the poet. The relation works both ways; ostensibly Pope is defined and measured in the light of virtue and truth, but the reverse seems equally to apply: truth and virtue assume a special meaning and value through their identification with Pope, who "possesses" them and equates their honor with his own.

Whereas the imagery of combat in the above instance suggests chivalrous action, elsewhere this imagery is more closely linked with blatant aggression as Pope, the self-appointed scourge of virtue, uses his satiric "weapon" to prod society's traditional guardians out of their inertia (Dia. II, 216–19), in a continuation of the one-man war declared earlier in *To Fortescue* (69–76). His pen becomes an instrument of battle, of violent intervention and punishment: "What? arm'd for *Virtue* when I point the Pen, / Brand the bold Front of shameless, guilty Men, / Dash the proud Gamester in his gilded Car, / Bare the mean Heart that lurks beneath a Star" (105–08). The sense of force and aggression conveyed in such descriptions is quite striking. It seems to me it requires a very clear identification of the external provocation, of the specific and (presumably) overwhelming threat to which Pope is responding, if the reader's attention is not to be drawn to the ironic, some might say grotesque, disproportion between the vivid extremity of Pope's response and the cloudy, unspecified situation that occasioned it. Instead we are given descriptions that operate on a level of generality (and moral generalization) bordering at times on the symbolic or allegorical (e.g., "To rowze the Watchmen of the Publick Weal, / To virtue's Work provoke the tardy Hall, / And goad the Prelate slumb'ring in his Stall" [Dia. II, 217–19]). There are, of course, the oblique—and increasingly, not-so-oblique—allusions to Walpole during the period when Pope's commitment to the anti-ministerial Opposition becomes more open; but these innuendoes and veiled references are not likely to persuade anyone of overwhelming external threat who is not already in the Opposition's camp and therefore capable of responding to Pope's topical allusions as political slogans employed for emotive effect (e.g., epithets such as "Jonathan Wild," "a kind of Screen," and "the Great Man" to denote Walpole).[7] The problem becomes clearer if we compare the Imitations of Horace with Dryden's political satires or with a good deal of Swift's verse from 1720 onward. Although in these two instances the grounds of the satirist's attack are shown in relation to the melodrama of virtue versus corruption that on some level informs almost all of the satires of this period, Dryden and Swift bring us into the presence of specific and compelling threats that in certain contexts effectively validate the recourse to such melodramatic oppositions, in other contexts spotlight the existence of concrete constitutional, legal, and political issues independent of these reductive oppositions.

With the focus of the *Epilogue to the Satires* so emphatically upon the censurer of society rather than on the precise objects of his censure, certain questions are thrust to the fore in the reader's mind: What is Pope's special warrant for claiming to be truth's representative both in the courtroom and on the battlefield? What is his sanction for donning battle dress and dispensing "justice" according to his own lights? To put the question in a deliberately exaggerated way, what saves the lone warrior Pope from being an eighteenth-century Charles Bronson, moved by various paranoias to take the law into his own hands—which is also to say, to elevate himself above the law—and unilaterally punish all those he deems guilty of assorted (often unspecified) sins and crimes?

A forceful critique of society, particularly of its judicial operations, might have provided a partial answer to these questions, might have served to complement and justify the figure of the railing satirist and vigilante-hero. In Pope's various references to the law (going back as far as *The Rape of the Lock*: "The hungry Judges soon the Sentence sign, / And Wretches hang that Jury-men may Dine" [III, 21–2]) we find the *potential* for just such a critique of the legal institutions and apparatus of state, of their role as instruments for political manipulation and domination, and of their subservience to arbitrary power. As a Catholic and suspected Jacobite, friend of the banished "traitor" Bishop Atterbury (at whose trial he testified), and brother-in-law of a man apprehended for a capital offense under the infamous Black Act, Pope might have been expected to be particularly sensitive (if only because particularly vulnerable) to the abuses and shortcomings of the prevailing legal system. But this critique never develops beyond a series of one-liners—becomes deflected into attacks on individual personalities (*To Fortescue*, 82) or moral diatribe (Dia. II, 147–48)—no doubt in part because of Pope's basically conservative temperament, which naturally shied away from outrightly subversive (as opposed to merely censorious) treatments of society. But an additional explana-tion—and this is my main concern here—is Pope's overriding obsession with self, which transforms the courtroom into a stage for his performance(s), an arena in which he can display his intellectual dexterity and verbal wit. Thus larger and more objective issues are obscured by the various aspects of Popeian self-dramatization, and absorbed into matters of personal predilection and sensibility: "Each Mortal has his Pleasure: None deny / *Scarsdale* his Bottle, *Darty* his Ham-Pye; / . . . I love to pour out all myself, as plain / As downright *Shippen*, or as old *Montagne*" (*To Fortescue*, 45–6; 51–2). Our attention becomes riveted above all on Pope's roles as the avenger, the god-like bully, the warrior tilting in the fields of corruption, the potent, bigger-than-life hero: an ironic and outrageous and touching contrast to the figure Pope actually cut as a physically fragile, deformed, almost dwarfish poet who walked about in frequent fear for his safety.

I am not alone, of course, in drawing attention to the self-centered focus of the Horatian Imitations, though other critics are generally concerned to resolve the problem of excessive subjectivity in Pope's favor (so to speak), and ultimately to deny that it *is* a problem. Wallace Jackson, for example, argues that Pope triumphs over—even as he occasionally shows himself vulnerable to—the "egotistically sublime" or narcissistic threat through his appeals to an authority outside the self, such as to the community of good men commemorated in his verse.[8]

It seems to me, however, that Pope's exalted tributes to his private grotto society, "grace[d]" by "the best Companions" (*To Fortescue*, 125 f.) and his memorials to individual friends in his *Epistles to Several Persons*, as well as the extensive lists of supposedly exemplary individuals he incorporates into his verse, hardly constitute an escape from the self-concern and subjectivity that forms the core of these poems. The poems' definition of virtue, and of those who follow it, is a curiously circular one: Pope allies himself with particular persons or groups because they are virtuous, and they in turn are virtuous because they have chosen to ally themselves with Pope, the zealous defender of goodness in a land of rampant corruption. The *Epistle to Arbuthnot* underscores this "vicious cyclicality" by bestowing glowing approval specifically on those by whom he had himself been "approv'd" (143). The fact that the very terms "corruption" and "virtue" were, within the context of the times, highly charged political labels, appearing regularly in Opposition propaganda to denote the pro- and anti-Walpole camps respectively, highlights the subjective and arbitrary nature of Pope's moral categories.[9] If his appeals to a "virtuous" community represent a tempering of purely egotistical concerns, they nevertheless may be seen to reinforce narrowly partisan and self-interested ones. Pope's arrogation of Horace's *uni aequus virtuti atquae ejus amicis* (originally spoken about Trebatius) to himself in *To Fortescue* (121) crystallizes these several interrelated problems and underscores the extent to which his laudatory references both to "virtue" and to his community of friends are extensions of and variations on, rather than a transcendence of, his self-tributes and self-preoccupation in the Horatian Imitations.

My point, following up earlier remarks about Swift and the Ploughshares 8, is that Pope's concern with self and his habit of encoding ideological issues in moral terms help to shape a body of poems whose polemical stance depends for its force and validity precisely and exclusively on the exalted moral character of the protesting speaker. Larger ideological issues, if they exist for Pope, are subsumed in what seem narrowly partisan causes. In effect, like Dante sorting out the various dwellers in Heaven and Hell, Pope in the *Epilogue* provides us with lists of the saved and the damned. Scarborough, Pelham, Sommers, Halifax, Carleton, Stanhope, Pulteney, Chesterfield, Wyndham: these and others are put forward as members of a saintly band opposed to the rampant evils of the day (see Dia. II, 63–93). The poem "works" only to the extent that its audience, then and now, perceives Pope and his circle as men greatly good, Walpole and his henchmen as greatly bad. Without this distinction, Pope's entire position—unlike Swift's or Berrigan's—collapses. Without it, there is no convincing way to defend him against the charges leveled by his enemies: that the only difference between the "Patriot" and the "Courtier" is that "the former wants to get what the latter has"[10]—a charge raised by Pope himself in Dialogue II through an adversarius (and wittily parried but never satisfactorily answered): "I think your Friends are out, and would be in" (123).

It is not, of course, that there were no concrete issues separating the Whigs in power from the Tories and Opposition Whigs, nor was Pope unaware of their existence (although he did subscribe to the Bolingbrokean thesis that traditional party distinctions had become obsolete). His failure to address these issues clearly and directly even in verse obviously concerned with politics may be attributed to several different factors in addition to his preoccupation with self: his desire to maintain a pose of neutrality despite his partisan involvements, both for self-protection and as a rhetorical tactic; his interest in personalities and in individual character more than in public policy[11] his decision to imitate a Horatian model of satire, which on the whole avoids engagement with single political issues; and not least (something I will return to in my concluding remarks), his sense of himself as a man speaking through his writings to future generations rather than to a more limited audience of his contemporaries. The point of the discussion here is obviously not to criticize Pope for not being Dryden or Swift—i.e., for not writing a particular kind of political, issue-oriented satire—but rather to understand why it is we are apt to encounter difficulties when we read Pope's later poetry for effective and convincing satire. One major problem, I think, is that this poetry demands contradictory things from its readers: it demands a certain level of political engagement and partisan commitment (as a prerequisite for a "proper" response to the satire) and at the same time a stance of withdrawal from and transcendence of all such temporal and partisan involvements. Another way of putting this problem is to say that Pope writes political poetry while denying its political character and while refusing to take responsibility for the political choices it affirms and implicitly recommends to others. Specific issues are fleetingly alluded to and then hastily incorporated into general moral reflection or diatribe, before they can be understood in relation to deeper ideological convictions and ethical imperatives.

Another problem is that many of the specific issues of the day did not lend themselves to the kind of satire Pope was trying to write; they did not provide suitable subject matter for a poet seeking both to translate complex ideological issues into clear-cut moral categories and to address posterity. Taking a stand on the most topical issues—such as the Excise Bill of 1733 and the war with Spain several years later—would hardly provide a stirring testimonial to Pope's transcendent moral vision. Pope was clearly willing to go down in history for celebrating peace and prosperity in *Windsor-Forest*, but he wasn't about to devote a poem to urging war on behalf of England's overseas trade and in order to avenge Captain Jenkins's severed and pickled ear, despite his support for such a war. (Perhaps in recognition of the inevitably farcical overtones of any poetic reference to this matter, Pope puts in the mouth of the "Friend" rather than himself the statement that " . . . the *Spaniard* did a *waggish thing*, / Who cropt our Ears, and sent them to the King" [Dia. I, 17–18].) The Licensing Act of 1737 was an issue of considerable moment (especially for writers), and Pope of course alludes to it at various points in his verse, but he never really explores its weighty implications for questions about freedom of speech and press, never really marshalls his satiric rage against Walpolian censorship—perhaps because of his own ambivalent attitude toward the uncontrolled production and dissemination of the printed word; because of his general anxieties, dramatized so vividly in *The Dunciad*, about the bibliographic deluge that he saw engulfing the land. Typically, Pope's most memorable reference to the Licensing Act transforms the policy into one more pretext, one more backdrop, for heroic self-dramatization: "Yes, the last Pen for Freedom let me draw, / When Truth stands trembling on the edge of Law . . ." (Dia. II, 248–49).

Other broader issues were equally (if differently) problematical for Pope's Horatian–Juvenalian satires. Court patronage was a genuine scandal because carried out to lengths unprecedented in past governments, but the moral force of Pope's attacks on patronage was necessarily diluted by his own at least partial embrace of Horace, the court poet of Augustus Caesar, and by his friendship with writers (such as Gay) who enjoyed many different forms of support, including court patronage. Pope himself had of course benefited from a Treasury grant and from a gift Walpole extended for his translation of *The Odyssey*. Moreover, Pope could *afford* to spurn Walpolian patronage because of his own wealth—and rejecting something one doesn't need isn't exactly the highwater mark of virtuous renunciation or disinterested moral censure. Other issues separating Whig and Tory, or the Court and Country elements, such as the conflict between land and money, were also problematic because not amenable to the kind of black-and-white contrast Pope would have us believe operated on a moral level. His own complicity in the new capitalist system—his status as entrepreneur and member of the nouveaux riches, the "first business man among English poets,"[12] sometime speculator in the stock market (owner of shares in the South Sea Company), the renter of a small suburban villa who owned no land of his own—made Pope's position vis-à-vis Court and Country ideology ambiguous, even paradoxical, and rendered it impossible for him unequivocally to exalt one and reject the other, despite the rural aristocratic myth that underlies much of his verse. As David B. Morris observes, "Pope could not wholeheartedly share the perspective of Bolingbroke and the landed tradition. . . . Despite his affection for the great land owners Lord Burlington and Lord Bathurst, Pope lived in a different world, made his living by his pen, cherished his independence. Only by considerable distortion, therefore, can Pope be transformed into the spokesman for civic humanism."[13]

Moreover, the relationship between Court and Country ideology was itself full of ambiguities that undermined clear-cut antitheses between the virtuous and the corrupt, as embodied in Pope's portrayal of the Twickenham grotto society and the official seat of government respectively. As H. T. Dickinson notes, "Court and Country co-existed in a symbiotic relationship."[14] J.G.A. Pocock delves further into these interconnections in examining the paradoxes and dualities of the Opposition's stance, observing (for example) that the most astute financiers were often landowners, pointing out that Tory language "often was radical and republican Commonwealth as well as country," and suggesting the possibility that Toryism in the first half of the century was "if anything more urban than rural."[15] These contradictions and complexities didn't, of course, overrule the black-and-white contrasts of Opposition rhetoric, but they complicate and undermine our own faith in the rigid moral oppositions that Pope establishes in the *Epilogue to the Satires*.

We may well be inclined to agree with Pope that there was substantial corruption in Walpole's ministry, but even this agreement need not commit us to the moral contrast between good and evil depicted in Pope's satire. It is not clear precisely how widespread the corruption was, how much of it was necessary for the kind of political stability and consolidation Walpole achieved, to what extent (if any) it was overshadowed by positive aspects of Walpole's tenure. Such questions have been the subject of considerable debate in recent times (as, indeed, in the eighteenth century): a debate that by no means divides along clear ideological lines.[16] I have no intention of adding to the debate here except to observe in passing that, for all of Walpole's numerous documented sins, to my mind he comes out rather well in his lengthy holdout against the growing popular clamor (fanned in no small part by Opposition propaganda, and often supported by patriotic cant and shibboleths of the worst kind) to embark on yet another war for the greater glory and trade of England. Moreover, his proud assertion in 1734 that thanks to his peace policy 50,000 men were "slain this year in Europe, and not one Englishman" strikes me as a more palatable boast than most for a politician.[17] But regardless of how we choose to view Walpole's political performance and its ethical dimensions, the striking diversity of opinion about him that we see today might well tell us something about the difficulties Pope faced in his attempts to paint a convincing black-and-white picture of the time—to define and categorize a situation which for a variety of reasons did not truly lend itself to clear-cut moral labels.

Pope's eventual decision to stop writing Horatian Imitations is most obviously attributable to very pragmatic considerations of personal safety. But I think it is also in the context of the problems described above that we have to understand this decision, along with Pope's accompanying resolve to express his vision of contemporary society in a different genre and format. It is in this context as well that we need to consider the poem *One Thousand Seven Hundred and Forty*, a work almost wholly neglected by Pope critics, presumably because it is deemed a "fragment." But as John Butt rightly notes, "it seems probable that the poem was intended to end where it ends in the printed version. It is 'ruined' rather than incomplete, for the blanks indicate that Pope feared for what he had written, rather than that he was undecided what to write" (*TE*, 4:331). Obviously the fear Butt refers to is the danger of government reprisal: more specifically, Pope's assessment, as expressed in the final note to the *Epilogue*, that writing satire had "become as unsafe as it was ineffectual." But there may be a different sense in which it is appropriate to discuss Pope's fear for "what he had written." I refer to the poem's subversive implications for his own earlier writings. *One Thousand Seven Hundred and Forty*, while still retaining the clear-cut distinction between virtue and corruption—if anything, *intensifying* the distinction—lashes out indiscriminately at both followers of Walpole and members of the Opposition, whose ranks are now seen to be filled with timeservers and hypocrites, to the extent that "the Patriot Race" not only rhymes with but mirrors the "wicked men in place" (3–4). Pope casts pointed barbs at Opposition politicians such as Pulteney, Carteret, Chesterfield, and Sandys, at Jacobite leaders such as Shippen, who in *To Fortescue* was placed alongside "old Montagne" as a model of honesty and simplicity, and at friends such as Bathurst and Cobham commemorated in his Moral Essays.[18]

Perhaps most damning of all, Pope represents the country gentlemen of the Tory Opposition—the grid not only of his political allegiance but also of the rural aristocratic ideal informing so much of his verse—as spineless, self-involved, ineffectual politicians incapable of an independent thought or act. They are little more than puppets whose strings are being pulled by Pulteney and Carteret—much like the placemen and pro-government scribblers who continually bow to Walpole's power: "So geese to gander prone obedience keep, / Hiss if he hiss, and if he slumber, sleep" (35–36). Pope, of course, had already hinted of doubts about certain Opposition figures two years earlier, in the *Epilogue to the Satires*.[19] But in that poem such reservations are carefully contained and marginalized so that the idea and the embodiment of virtue can be preserved intact. In *One Thousand Seven Hundred and Forty* the margins become the body of the text, and the whole Opposition enterprise is called into question. It might be said that the implied message of the poem is that "the only good Patriot is a dead one": Pope basically reserves his praise for the recently deceased Earls of Marchmont and Scarborough and for Sir William Wyndham, whose death in June of that year particularly affected Pope. Hence his outcry, "The plague is on thee, Britain, and who tries / To save thee in th' infectious office *dies*" (75–76).

The poem in a sense has two endings: the first, concluding at line 84, presents an apocalyptic vision of irreversible decay and destruction, an Uncreation that is the political counterpart of the cultural Uncreation in Book IV of *The Dunciad*; and the second, concluding with the final fourteen lines, heralds the coming of a messiah-king as the sole hope for England's salvation: "Whatever his religion or his blood, / His public virtue makes his title good. / Europe's just balance and our own may stand, / And one man's honesty redeem the land" (95–98). These lines seem almost to belong to another poem, so abrupt is the shifting of gears, the change of tone and focus. Inspired by Bolingbroke's *The Idea of a Patriot King*, which Pope had read in manuscript shortly before composing the poem, they presumably refer to Frederick, Prince of Wales, although some might argue that Pope had the Pretender in mind.[20] Either way, the actual historical figure falls hopelessly short of the role and mission ascribed to him in the poem, wholly incapable of sustaining a messianic symbolism. The verse seems to be indirectly acknowledging this absence, for its conclusion lacks conviction, sounding peculiarly listless and formulaic. Dustin H. Griffin makes the rather intriguing suggestion that these final lines might refer to Pope himself.[21] Certainly the suggestion is consonant with the self-referential focus of the Horatian Imitations, with Pope's characteristic method of transforming historical events and situations into occasions for spotlighting and dramatizing the poet. If so, the ending is nonetheless a highly diluted variant of the conclusion to the *Epilogue to the Satires*, where Pope clearly affirms heroic stature for the poet and immortality for his verse. *One Thousand Seven Hundred and Forty* is a poem in search of a hero, and the fact that there are several different candidates for the job—several possible residents for the "one alone" on whom "our all relies" (85)—only serves to underscore the inability of any one figure to rise to the occasion and occupy center stage as the nation's (and, implicitly, humankind's) redeemer.

However painful it may have been for Pope to compose, *One Thousand Seven Hundred and Forty* is a poem he had to write—in order to safeguard his ethical credentials for posterity, to leave as a record of his impartiality as moral critic. The self-proclaimed defender of virtue had to show himself as willing to expose his errant political allies as to attack the Whigs in power. At the same time, it was a poem he couldn't have published in his own lifetime (it did not appear in print until 1797), for even if government censorship had suddenly disappeared, publication would in effect have undermined the grounds of his earlier satires, called into question their entire moral topography and grounds for being.

What was at stake in *One Thousand Seven Hundred and Forty* was more than simple disillusionment with particular individuals. It is possible, after all, to express such disillusionment while at the same time reaffirming the cause with which the specific persons are (or were) associated. But because in Pope's verse the virtue of individuals *is* the cause, once this virtue is impugned little if anything remains; there are no larger causes or issues clearly independent of moral character left to sustain the vision. The only option is desperately to seek yet another "man of virtue" to replace those exposed as no longer worthy. Once God is dead, however, there cannot be another God to take his place, only a potentially endless substitution, a continual recycling of gods whose divine credentials are equally questionable. Hence the weak and shadowy figure of the patriot king, with the faintest glimmer of the no longer abashedly heroic patriot poet flickering behind him, that we see at the end of *One Thousand Seven Hundred and Forty*.

In actual life Pope did of course continue to support the Opposition, turning to such men as Lyttelton and (the younger) Marchmont as replacements of sorts for Pulteney and Company. My preceding comments refer specifically to the internal rhetorical and thematic logic of his poetry, which (I am arguing) made it impossible for him to continue writing the kind of verse he had been throughout the 1730s. With *One Thousand Seven Hundred and Forty*, Pope had come to the end of the line; he couldn't have gone any further in using the varied and mingled cadences of Horace and Juvenal to commemorate and elaborate the myths of the virtuous community and of the lone heroic poet battling vice upon the stage of history.

My essay up to this point has been exploring the problematical nature of Pope's characterizations of himself as a heroic figure "arm'd for *Virtue*," whether we choose to interpret them in moral or in political terms, or in some combination of the two. I would now like to suggest a perspective that might help explain why, in spite of these problems, the Horatian Imitations have nevertheless achieved something like the "immortality" anticipated in the *Epilogue*, and why the myths propagated by these poems have gained such wide acceptance and validation in literary criticism to this day.

Specifically, I want to suggest that we think of Pope, in the context of his heroic self-projections, less as a man armed for moral and/or narrowly partisan warfare and more as a writer armed for *cultural* combat, an arena in which he achieved stunning success, which is why it seems only right that he should have ended his career with *The Dunciad*, one of the greatest cultural documents in history. The melodramatic oppositions governing the *Epilogue to the Satires* are not absent from this work but rather, transformed and subsumed by an encompassing cultural critique which provides a far more effective vehicle for Pope's satire. Maynard Mack, referring to Pope's self-appointed task "to write in a public idiom, and always within a program of reference calculated to draw poet and reader into a community of experience," talks explicitly of Pope's carrying the culture with him,[22] but in certain ways Pope went well beyond this, actually *creating* and *defining* the culture as we still think and talk (and disagree) about it today, establishing the categories that have been so influential in shaping our cultural perceptions. As Brean Hammond has argued, in an age that still regarded all types of printed matter as literature "Pope was determined to make a significant ideological rupture. It was Pope as much as anyone else who established the distinction between 'classic' and 'popular' writers and writings. . . ."[23]

This is not the only distinction Pope was concerned to establish, although it perhaps underlies many (if not most) of the others. As G. Douglas Atkins notes, "Pope insists that distinction is the key to social and cultural survival. . . . As he lambastes Augustan society throughout the [Horatian] satires and epistles for its increasing failure to distinguish, Pope tries, in and through his writing, to make a difference."[24] I would add that one of Pope's primary ways of making a difference was to literally *make differences*—to affirm or create distinctions (different but related sets of distinctions in the Horatian Imitations and *The Dunciad*) to separate the (moral/social/cultural/aesthetic) wheat from the chaff: the true from the false, the enduring from the transitory, the virtuous from the corrupt, the moderate from the extreme, the independent poet from the professional hack, polite society from the "mob," creators from mere laborers, "high" from "low." Most if not all of these distinctions are on some level subjective and self-serving, "necessary" not in any ontological sense but for Pope's own ambitious cultural project; yet all have become incorporated into the ways in which many critics regularly assess his age and the place he occupied in it. Pope's arts of discrimination, held up as the noble alternative to the gross and grotesque levelling process comically depicted in *The Dunciad*, while "discriminatory" in every sense of the word, have more often than not been used as the "objective" grounds for determining what is refinement and what is its opposite, what is civilization and who are its discontents, its would-be destroyers and subverters.

We need to understand these distinctions in a much more critical way than they have traditionally been accepted. For example, Pope was a man very much at home in, and profoundly dependent upon, the same world of print that he is now best known for satirizing. In *The Dunciad* he masterfully exploits the very medium that he damns and produces a popular bestseller that attacks the very conditions that make such a phenomenon possible. The poem's form and format give Pope the opportunity to emerge as the (ostensibly unwilling) prophet of the new technological age while remaining the heroic upholder of the old one; they allow him to embrace and embody the very energies and literary democratization that he is repudiating. In this way Pope made himself a writer who could not easily be dismissed or ignored by future exponents either of high *or* popular culture. He achieved this feat "armed" with a printing press as well as with a pen—as befit a poet who, as Mack points out, succeeded in "becoming to all intents and purposes his own publisher"[25] a writer who exploited the technology of the "new order" in order to disseminate the myth of himself as a man of the "old order," a myth whose power and effectiveness is readily apparent in the extent to which professional Popeians and other traditional eighteenth-century literary scholars perpetuate it in the present day.[26] Pope's determination to "Publish the present Age" (*To Fortescue*, 59) and his expansion of Horace's *scribam* to affirm its modern, plural sense, "I will Rhyme and Print" (100), are consistent with someone as acutely aware as Pope was of the extent to which those who owned and managed the technology of print possessed the power to define reality—to put forth a private version of persons and events that would subsequently be taken as a public statement of fact (as, indeed, the fictions of his Horatian Imitations still often are).

It is customary to see Pope and Walpole as figures "representative of divided and distinguished world":[27] the disinterested artist, man of polite letters and classical refinement, versus the king of the philistines, head of a vast propaganda machine. But I would argue that Pope, himself a propagandist *par excellence*, in fact beat Walpole at his own game because he understood propaganda in a much broader, more sophisticated way: he understood that it was not limited to the activity of party hacks trying to put an attractive gloss on a particular policy of the moment but was, rather, a striving to shape the perceptions and judgments of generations to come—to put forth an interpretation of current affairs and of the contemporary social and political situation, but one of many such interpretations, after all, that would prove compelling and persuasive enough to be accepted as the truth by posterity, while all other interpretations would come to be rejected or suppressed. Pope ultimately "defeated" Walpole (though the latter, as an eminently practical politician, would have viewed the matter differently, of course) because he realized that local, purely political victories and the immediate exercise of power through the manipulation of state machinery were not enough—that the actual battlefield, the real arena where victors and losers would finally be determined, is the cultural and ideological battlefield, where words and ideas necessarily have an edge (literally and figuratively) over political bribes or the winning of a particular election: the arena where state and military domination must give way to the more deeply rooted and lasting forms of cultural, technological, and intellectual hegemony.[28]

Seen from the perspective of Pope's cultural–hegemonic battle, the personal and historical myths in the Horatian Imitations acquire a new level of meaning. Armed with pen (and printing press), Pope is determined to re-create both history and himself—straighten and touch up the image of both, in the same way he kept revising his own writings and having successive portraits of himself painted—in order to minimize Walpole's own historical testimony, to wrest the judgment of posterity away from those (unlike Pope) who were closest to the center of power but who were not necessarily prescient or skilled enough to parlay their immediate political power into a more lasting influence. The self-reference so pervasive in Pope's verse is in fact closely allied with this sense of hegemonic struggle; as Pope remarked in a letter to Ralph Allen, "I have two great Tasks on my hands; I am trying to benefit myself, and to benefit Posterity."[29] It is characteristic that Pope should make so easy an equation between himself and the future of mankind, should imply the two are so closely identified that what is good for one will necessarily be good for the other. Despite the disingenuous disclaimer that follows ("not by Works of my own God knows"), it is clear that the "two great Tasks" Pope posits are (for him) really one, both to be achieved through the production of works of Literature that would endure through successive ages and continue to "profit" him—if no longer financially, as they did so spectacularly during his lifetime, then by vindicating his own way of seeing and interpreting the world, by enabling his own words to prevail while silencing (or ridiculing, or distorting) the words of his opponents, "uncreating" them as he attempts to do so memorably in The Dunciad.[30]

"We who are Writers ought to love Posterity, that Posterity may love us," Pope declared in a letter to Gay,[31] and if that statement sounds calculating and self-serving, if it smacks of the same self-centered circularity we have seen in his treatment of virtue in the Horatian Imitations, it nevertheless points to a pact with himself that has indeed "benefited" both, creating for him an at times small but always faithful band of followers eager to continue his own defense of himself before successive "juries" through the ages, in an ongoing "tribunal" growing out of and expanding upon the mock-trial in *To Fortescue*. The most recent example of this is the fervent advocacy of his latest biographer, who explains (because Pope "has suffered long enough" from the criticisms of his detractors) that he intends to discuss Pope's life and work in a manner that could lend itself to being viewed as "special pleading."[32] If Pope's self-dramatizations may be said to have an objective correlative, it is precisely this concern for hegemonic control in the future—the desire to continue waging his war, and defending his case, in the battlefields and courtrooms of the future. This more than anything else constitutes his "political program" and "commitment" (which is undoubtedly one reason why we encounter a vacuum when we try to identify specific topical events and issues to explain his satiric agenda). to be sure, this concern for hegemonic control does not rescue Pope's obsessive focus on self from the solipsistic cycle I've discussed earlier; nevertheless, it raises his self-interest to a higher level, broadening its historical scope and significance beyond solely a desire for personal justification and aggrandizement, elevating it above the desire for immediate gratification of ego.

Pope's success as a cultural warrior, then, grows out of a prophetic sense that was at the same time eminently shrewd and practical, dependent upon his masterly deployment of ideological weapons to counter the more narrowly political weapons of his opponents. But, finally, his success cannot be explained simply as the result of combative skills, for it also grows out of the fact that we are hardly likely to confuse a poem by Pope with the works of Concanen or Smedley or Oldmixon, even if we don't necessarily accept Pope's own grounds for distancing himself from such writers. Some readers may disagree (as I do) with Pat Rogers's disdainful rejection of "the dirty goings-on down Smithfield alleys" and his unqualified ratification of Pope's own view of Grub Street;[33] they may prefer (as I do) Raymond Williams's critique of the mass-culture/decline-in-standards thesis (which he traces back at least to 1730) and his argument for a broader conception of culture that encompasses a wide diversity of skilled and creative activities.[34] But talent, wit, even genius: these things come back to haunt (and delight) even the most unreconstructed egalitarians and democrats and Marxists among us, demanding to be acknowledged even if we don't quite know how to explain them, even if we haven't entirely figured out how to fit them into our theoretical arguments on behalf of diverse equivalencies rather than hierarchical differences in aesthetic standards and taste.

I remain unconvinced that Pope was any more virtuous or patriotic or "humanistic" (as that term is too often sloppily or sloganishly, not to mention quasi-religiously, invoked) than the rest of his society, but I *am* persuaded that he was far shrewder, more prescient, and more poetically and rhetorically gifted than the vast majority of his contemporaries, and that the concrete manifestations of this gift—*The Rape of the Lock, The Dunciad*, and many other works—would deserve to occupy a prominent place in our literary heritage even if Pope hadn't been so skillful a propagandist for his own cause, so successful a salesman of his literary wares on the marketplace of posterity. All of which means that this essay can conclude with either of two seemingly opposite but in fact closely interconnected statements: Pope was really in (the Devil's, Grub Street's, the capitalist and commercial age's) camp without knowing it, or at least without acknowledging it and while proclaiming himself to be on the side of the angels, allied with True Art and with a world of traditional noblesse; *Or*: many of us are really in Pope's camp without realizing it, even as we feel impelled to demystify the autobiographical and historical myths promoted in his verse, and even as we continue to challenge the validity of the battle lines Pope himself did so much to inscribe into our cultural consciousness and history.

Notes

1. See, e.g., Howard D. Weinbrot, *Augustus Caesar in "Augustan" England: The Decline of a Classical Norm* (Princeton, 1978), esp. 182–217; and his companion volume, *Alexander Pope and the Traditions of Formal Verse Satire* (Princeton, 1982). Weinbrot argues for Juvenal rather than Horace as the political and rhetorical model for Pope's later satires. Of course, these satires' Juvenalian qualities were first noted long before such recent works of criticism. See, for example, William Warburton's comments about Pope's "strik[ing] with the caustic lightening of Juvenal" rather than applying the tamer ridicule of Horace, in *Pope: The Critical Heritage*, ed. John Barnard (London and Boston, 1973), 365.

2. *The Poems of John Dryden*, ed. James Kinsley, 4 vols. (Oxford, 1958), 4:1534. *The Character of a Good Parson, Imitated from Chaucer* also appears in this volume, 1736–40.

3. The poems referred to here may be consulted in *The Poems of Jonathan Swift*, ed. Harold Williams, 3 vols., 2nd ed. (Oxford, 1958). Irvin Ehrenpreis explicitly compares *A Character, Panegyric, and Description of the Legion Club* to Pope's last satires in the vehemence of its outrage against a society's overwhelming corruption, in *Swift: The Man, His Works, and the Age*, 3 vols. (Cambridge, Mass., 1962–1983), 3:831.

4. Mainstream media coverage of both the protest action itself and the subsequent trial was virtually nonexistent. For brief accounts of both see Ann Morrissett Davidon, "Warheads into Ploughshares: When is a 'crime' a prophetic act?," in *The Progressive* (May 1981): 49–51; and Mary Meehan, "Order in the Court," in *Commonweal* (Aug. 28, 1981): 468–69.

5. My comments are based on a 1982 film dramatization of the trial entitled "In the King of Prussia," which was directed by Emile D. Antonio and starred Martin Sheen as Judge Samuel W. Salus, with the defendants playing themselves.

6. Aside from Weinbrot see G. K. Hunter, "The 'Romanticism' of Pope's Horace," rptd. in *Essential Articles for the Study of Alexander Pope*, ed. Maynard Mack (Hamden, Conn., 1964), 553–68; and Thomas R. Edwards, Jr., *This Dark Estate: A Reading of Pope* (Berkeley, 1963), which locates in Pope's later verse a shift away from "Augustan" modes of expression and experience to modes that Edwards terms "grotesque."

7. For Pope's involvement with Opposition propaganda and his use of politically charged epithets for Walpole in his satires, see Bertrand A. Goldgar, *Walpole and the Wits: The Relation of Politics to Literature, 1722–1742* (Lincoln, Neb., and London, 1976), esp. 69–74; 106–09; 166–69; and Maynard Mack, *The Garden and the City: Retirement and Politics in the Later Poetry of Pope 1731–1743* (Toronto, 1969), 129–36.

8. Wallace Jackson, *Vision and Re-Vision in Alexander Pope* (Detroit, 1983), 119–47 *passim*. For an extended discussion of Pope's preoccupation with self see also Dustin H. Griffin, *Alexander Pope: The Poet in the Poems* (Princeton, 1978). Griffin justifies this preoccupation on generic grounds, arguing that "Pope's late satires set forth what might be called a self-centered or egocentric theory of satire, which perhaps constitutes his distinctive contribution to the form" (215).

9. See Paul Gabriner, "Pope's 'Virtue' and the Events of 1738," in *Pope: Recent Essays*, ed. Maynard Mack and James A. Winn (Hamden, Conn., 1980), 585–611; and H. T. Dickinson, *Liberty and Property: Political Ideology in Eighteenth-Century Britain* (1977; rpt. London, 1979), 169–75.

10. See Goldgar, *Walpole and the Wits*, 26.

11. For an extended discussion of Pope's concern for character see David B. Morris, *Alexander Pope: The Genius of Sense* (Cambridge, Mass. and London, 1984), 179–213. According to Morris, "Pope's most innovative contribution to English theories of character is his effort . . . to shift the locus of character from external actions or social roles or physiological humors to the mind" (199).

12. See Hugo M. Reichard, "Pope's Social Satire: Belles-Lettres and Business," in *Essential Articles on Pope*, 694.

13. Morris, *Alexander Pope: The Genius of Sense*, 193, 194. For a more sustained ideological analysis of Pope's equivocal class outlook, see Laura Brown, *Alexander Pope*, Rereading Literature (Oxford, 1985).

14. H.T. Dickinson, *Liberty and Property*, 169.

15. J.G.A. Pocock, *Virtue, Commerce, and History: Essays on Political Thought and History, Chiefly in the Eighteenth Century* (Cambridge, Eng., 1985), 245.

16. Compare, e.g., the respective assessments of Walpole in J.H. Plumb, *The Origins of Political Stability: England 1675–1725* (Boston, 1967), and E.P. Thompson, *Whigs and Hunters: The Origin of the Black Act* (London, 1975). Stressing Walpole's positive influence in securing a stable parliamentary system of government, Plumb concludes that he was "a man of uncommon judgement, political insight, and capacity for decision" (189). Thompson, on the other hand, contending that "political life in England in the 1720s had something of the sick quality of a 'banana republic' " (197), cites approvingly Bishop Atterbury's scathing judgment that " '[Walpole's] whole administration is built on corruption and bribery, which he has carried to a greater height than any of his worst predecessors ever did . . . ' " (215). In this regard see also P.G.M. Dickson, *The Financial Revolution in England* (London and New York, 1967), esp. 174–76, 199–215; and Isaac Kramnick, *Bolingbroke and His Circle: The Politics of Nostalgia in the Age of Walpole* (Cambridge, Mass., 1968), esp. 48–55; 111–36. The degree to which evaluations of Walpole's rule elude division into clearly defined ideological "camps" becomes evident if we compare Thompson's highly negative view with Perry Anderson's insistence on England's good fortune in having been governed by Walpole in the spirit of the Whigs rather than by Bolingbroke in the spirit of the Tories. See Anderson, *Arguments within English Marxism* (London, 1980), 97.

17. See W.A. Speck, *Stability and Strife: England 1714–1760*, The New History of England, 6 (1977; rpt. London, 1984), 233.

18. Names in this poem are indicated by first initial only, and several of the attributions (Shippen's in particular) are somewhat conjectural, although most can be identified with reasonable certainty from the context.

19. See the Friend's comment in Dialogue I, "*Patriots* there are, who wish you'd jest no more—" (24) and Pope's note to this line glossing the word "*Patriots*": "This appellation was generally given to those in opposition to the Court. Though some of them (which our author hints at) had views too mean and interested to deserve that name."

20. For Pope's possible links to Jacobitism, see Howard Erskine-Hill, "Alexander Pope:

The Political Poet in His Time," *Eighteenth-Century Studies* 15 (Winter 1981–82): 123–48; and Brean S. Hammond, *Pope and Bolingbroke: A Study of Friendship and Influence* (Columbia, Mo., 1984), 92–95. Neither Erskine-Hill nor Hammond mentions *One Thousand Seven Hundred and Forty* in this context, however.

21. Griffin, *Alexander Pope: The Poet in the Poems*, 210n.

22. Maynard Mack, *Alexander Pope: A Life* (New Haven and London, 1985), 87.

23. Brean Hammond, *Pope*, Harvester New Readings (Brighton, 1986), 129.

24. G. Douglas Atkins, *Quests of Difference: Reading Pope's Poems* (Lexington, Ky., 1986), 100–01.

25. Mack, *Alexander Pope: A Life*, 124.

26. See, e.g., Alvin B. Kernan's characterization of Pope as a man "somewhat stained perhaps by print but still the last great writer of the old order," in *Printing, Technology, Letters and Samuel Johnson* (Princeton, 1987), 16. One is tempted to counter that Pope was likelier to have been "stained" by the ink he was purportedly dipped into as a baby (*Epistle to Dr. Arbuthnot*, 125–26) than by print, a medium by which he was *enriched* and *empowered* rather than soiled.

27. See Mack, *The Garden and the City*, 201.

28. I am using the term "hegemony" in its broadest sense, to denote a form of influence or authority exercised through intellectual, ideological, and sociocultural dominance rather than through state or military power. It might be interesting, however, to consider the more specific applicability of Antonio Gramsci's notion of hegemony, in particular his conception of the hegemonic role played by intellectuals, whom he divides into "traditional" and "organic" types. Pope's relationship to each of these, and his seeming ability to combine the functions of both, deserve further study. See *Selections from "The Prison Notebooks" of Antonio Gramsci*, ed. and trans. Quintin Hoare and Geoffrey Howell Smith (London, 1971), 5–23. It could be argued, of course, that this whole idea of cultural hegemony, with its implication of Pope's ultimate "triumph," is itself an ideological myth and form of mystification.

29. *The Correspondence of Alexander Pope*, ed. George Sherburn, 5 vols. (Oxford, 1956), 4:108.

30. In this connection see Aubrey L. Williams's discussion of the extra-textual paraphernalia of the *Variorum Dunciad* as "a deliberate displacing of history, 'notes toward a supreme fiction', . . . a distortion of history so magnificent and well-conceived that it has imposed upon the dunces a character Pope knew they never actually possessed (though many readers have accepted it as 'truth'). . . ." *Pope's "Dunciad": A Study of Its Meaning* (London, 1955), 60–1 and ff.

31. *The Correspondence of Pope*, 3:135.

32. Mack, *Alexander Pope: A Life*, viii.

33. See Pat Rogers, *Hacks and Dunces: Pope, Swift and Grub Street* (1972; rpt. London, 1980), 15.

34. Raymond Williams, *Culture and Society 1780–1950* (1958; rpt. Harmondsworth, Eng., 1985), 285–300.

Pope Surveys His Kingdom:
An Essay on Criticism

RIPLEY HOTCH

Pope's object in the *Essay on Criticism* is not to say something original about criticism, but to announce himself as a poet. The poem compares the state of poetry to a kingdom, and describes the history of its establishment, overthrow, and restoration. Pope's metaphors are drawn from the language of law and conquest, organized by variations on the supreme symbol of kingship, the sun. By breaking the bounds of the law, false poets have destroyed the kingdom, and it falls to Pope to reestablish the laws without falling into a sterile worship of antiquity. The conclusion of the poem argues that the poetic empire has been restored in England by Pope's mentors Roscommon and Walsh. Since they are now dead, Pope is the logical heir to the throne of poetry. Throughout the poem, however, Pope insists on his humility in order to avoid seeming pretentious, while in fact his practice demonstrates that he is a supremely accomplished poet, worthy of the position he claims.

Pope's two references to himself in *An Essay on Criticism* emphasize his inadequacies: he is "the last, the meanest" of the sons of the immortal poets, and he tells us in his conclusion that his muse is content with "low numbers" and "short excursions."[1] As a complement to this humility, Pope asserts that the poem has nothing original to say on the theory of criticism. Why, then, write such a poem? Most readers are unhappy that so many fine quotations are wasted on a generally inferior and unoriginal thesis. They are also irritated by the poem's generally Olympian tone, which does not seem to sit well with Pope's assertions of inadequacy and unoriginality. But that tone is a clue to the real purpose of the poem. Pope is always present in his works, and we usually find him as the standard against which the faults he attacks are measured, something particularly obvious in the *Epistle to Arbuthnot*, for example. The same is true of the *Essay on Criticism*, which is not about criticism, but about the young poet writing the poem, his situation, and his claim to merit. For the poem is, if anything, not a disquisition on criticism, but a proof of the qualifications of the author to assume his place as head of the kingdom

Ripley Hotch, "Pope Surveys His Kingdom: *An Essay on Criticism*." Reprinted by permission of *SEL: Studies in English Literature, 1500–1900, 13*, 3 (Summer 1973): 474–87.

of wit he describes. Treating criticism as the interpreter of the law which governs the well-ordered kingdom of poetry, Pope vindicates his own qualities as law-giver and ruler, and therefore justifies his own role as heir-apparent to the crown of poetry. The role of standard merges with that of scourger of poetic villainy on one side, just as on the other, the role of heir merges with that of the humble student repeating his lessons. But these ought not to be seen as separate roles, rather as a continuum of expression of a single complex figure.

If Pope had been interested exclusively in laying out a critical theory, those personal references would have been out of place, as they in fact seem to be. But each calls attention to one of the major positions of the poem: that the kingdom of wit has a true succession, in which Pope has a place, and that the kingdom survives only when each individual knows his proper role (the principle of subordination). When the subjects disregard its laws, forget their proper places, the kingdom is destroyed, and must be reestablished. The movement of the poem is one of revolution and restoration in the kingdom. The tone follows this movement by varying from the diffident and respectful explication of "Wit's *Fundamental Laws*" (722) to an Olympian moral scorn proper for the judge who condemns malicious revolutionaries.

The three parts of the poem form a triptych on the general theme of establishment, revolution, and restoration in the realm of poetry. The first part treats the foundation of the kingdom, and the establishment of wit's fundamental laws. The second shows the cause of corruption (which is the cause of political, religious, and moral corruption as well) in the observance of these laws: pride leading to factionalism or to sterile and obdurate orthodoxy. This discussion sets up the third part, in which Pope shows the proper attitude of critics, finally recounting the history of the realm, its fall, and its restoration by Erasmus, concluding with its establishment in England through a *translatio imperii* effected by Roscommon, Walsh, and of course Pope.

In the first part, references to nature deal with its creating and ordering role; it takes the pattern of a kingdom, a pattern reflected in earthly orders. As an earthly order, poetry and criticism form a kingdom of poetry deriving from the order of nature:

> In *Poets* as true *Genius* is but rare,
> True *Taste* as seldom is the *Critick*'s Share;
> Both must alike from Heav'n derive their Light,
> These *born* to Judge, as well as those to Write.
>
> (11–14)

That is, true poets and critics receive their talents almost as a commission, a hereditary title, as "a Critick's noble Name" (47). The province of poets and critics is limited by laws from nature; as inferior monarchs they hold their positions by gift, and are allowed to extend their kingdom only to certain limits:

> Like Kings we lose the Conquests gain'd before,
> By vain Ambition still to make them more:
> Each might his *sev'ral Province* well command,
> Would all but *stoop* to what they *understand.*
>
> (64–67)

Pope here does not make much distinction between the poet and critic, especially since he himself is being a poetic critic. Obviously, too, a poet-critic's power consists in his understanding, or knowledge. He conquers by knowing, which means ordering, the province in his command. The rules of judgment are thus the laws of the poetic kingdom, and their relation to nature is on the same footing with the poet's talent: "Those RULES of old *discover'd,* not *devis'd*" (88) are like nature's own laws, through which she establishes restraints even for herself. The equivalence of poetic talent and rules and nature's laws is shown in the way a poet's inspiration can go beyond its own laws to create new laws which are after all only extensions of the old ones:

> If, where the *Rules* not far enough extend,
> (Since Rules were made but to promote their End)
> Some Lucky LICENCE answers to the full
> Th' Intent propos'd, *that Licence* is a *Rule.*
>
> (146–149)

In constantly using the language of provinces, laws, and conquests, Pope brings us to regard the kingdom of poetry as a kingdom in the fullest terms. Furthermore, it is a hereditary kingdom, reaching back to the ancient and hallowed past. Its laws are not only directly available to the true poet through his talent and learning, but through the classical tradition that learning represents. There is a direct (and priestly) succession from Greece:

> Hear how learn'd *Greece* her useful Rules indites,
> When to repress, and when indulge our Flights:
> High on *Parnassus'* Top her Sons she show'd,
> And pointed out those arduous Paths they trod,
> Held from afar, aloft, th' Immortal Prize,
> And urg'd the rest by equal Steps to rise;
> Just *Precepts* thus from great *Examples* giv'n,
> She drew from *them* what they deriv'd from
> Heav'n.
>
> (92–99)

This is the great original of the way all poets receive their inspiration, and that original has a religious force: "Still green with Bays each *ancient* Altar stands, Above the reach of *Sacrilegious* Hands" (181–182). Pope connects himself with these traditions in his appeal for "some Spark of *your* Cœlestial Fire" (195), which is obviously the same as the "Poet's Fire" (100) that the critic fanned in ancient Greece. Pope thus claims a heavenly sanction for his talent at the same time he demonstrates his learning, a sort of reconquering of the province on his own.

The traditional symbol of kingship was for Pope, as it had been for Renaissance poets before, the sun. Nature as the monarch is, like the sun, the giver of warmth, light, life, the source of creativity and of the ordering light of understanding. Everyone's judgment is "at least a *glimm'ring Light*" (21) from nature, and nature herself stands as permanent and unchanging as the sun:

> *Unerring Nature*, still divinely bright,
> One *clear, unchang'd* and *Universal* Light,
> Life, Force, and Beauty, must to all impart,
> At once the *Source*, and *End*, and *Test* of *Art*.
> (70–73)

The derivation of the poetic talent from nature makes the "Poet's Fire" a reflection of that sun, or a recreation of the sun in the poet, a role which is also passed on as indicated in Pope's appeal for a spark of the ancients' "Cœlestial Fire." Thus the ancients, founders of the kingdom, give light like the sun, and their laws like sun kings. They were conquerors in the sense that they extended their understanding over the poetic realm, and left laws for the rest to follow, a role Virgil plays in the third part (645–652). The conqueror image is a part of the political metaphor that Pope uses often—the true poet observes proportion like the "prudent Chief" who

> not always must display
> His Pow'rs in *equal Ranks*, and *fair Array*,
> But with th' *Occasion* and the *Place* comply,
> *Conceal* his Force, nay seem sometimes to *Fly*.
> (175–178)

The main metaphor of the poem is, then, this political one, the parallel of poetic and political kingdoms. Each is a reflection of the other and each affects the other. Each provides a reflection (distorted or true) of the universal order.[2] There are, in this first part, two notions about the establishment of the kingdom of poetry: the creative emanation of divine light that gives one control of a certain province, and the regulative function of natural law codified in poetic rules or laws. The tension between these two aspects is established at the outset of the poem in the watch image: each subject wants to carve out a solipsistic realm for himself—that is, to develop the "glimm'ring Light" of judgment without regulation. Such development in critics causes over-regulation, "*good Sense* defac'd" by "*false Learning*" (25), and in wits (as we find out later) "One *glaring Chaos* and *wild Heap* of *Wit*" (292).

The poem is based on the notions that creation must be limited or it becomes cancerous, and that law must be tempered or it is sterile. Thus creation can have a good aspect or a bad one, depending on a proper observation of limits, while that limiting knowledge must not be permitted to kill through too much restriction. These four possibilities exist at any point in the poem, and only one combination will be proper: true criticism aiding true poetry. The poet who can feel his way among these tensions is alone qualified to assume the role of king, as both the law-maker and the judge, poet and critic. In doing so, Pope shows the distinction to be a false one, and our inability to unite them to be a measure of our insufficiency as compared to him. Pope as poet is "the one who knows," whose knowledge and skill show his worth and his right to talk to others as a superior. In order to prove this he must impress two qualities of himself on the reader: his humility (his knowledge of his limits) and his creative ability (his knowledge of his worth). Thus the tension the poet must manage in himself parallels the tension of creativity and limitation in poetry and in the political realm. Pope can talk about order in large only if he can demonstrate that he himself is, and can create, order in small.

The first part of the poem, concerned as it is with the foundation of the kingdom of poetry and with wit's fundamental laws, therefore stresses the necessity of limiting oneself through self-knowledge as well as knowledge of the rules, so that the creative impulse will not undertake more than it can control or accomplish. That attempt makes one a monster of sorts; the "Poet's Fire" becomes a fruitless lust: "Each burns alike, who can, or cannot write, / Or with a *Rival's* or an *Eunuch's* spite" (30–31). Without knowledge or limitation, the false poet and false critic decline to a position below animal nature because they are distortions of nature. Their origins are mysterious, perverted, probably dirty:

> Those half-learn'd Witlings, num'rous in our Isle,
> As half-form'd Insects on the Banks of *Nile*;
> Unfinish'd Things, one knows not what to call,
> Their Generation's so *equivocal*.
>
> (40–43)

The first part of the *Essay on Criticism* pits itself against this notion of formless invention, by being able to encompass and describe it, and then giving the true foundation of the poetic realm, of which the nation of witlings is a perversion.

The true poet knows the laws of his kingdom, their originals and traditional written sources, and knows that these laws parallel the divine order. He understands the light itself, and has demonstrated his poetic skill in writing. But lest the reader forget that someone is standing behind the poem, Pope puts himself into it, and proves that he knows his limitations and his place, but that his place is important: "Oh may some Spark of *your* Cœlestial Fire / The last, the meanest of your Sons inspire" (195–196). From this assertion of humility and membership in the priesthood of wit, he turns to attack pride, the refusal to see one's proper place, breaking order, resulting in being misled by the wrong light into a false or parody creation:

> Pride, where Wit fails, steps in to our Defence,
> And fills up all the *mighty Void* of *Sense*!
> If once right Reason drives *that Cloud* away,
> *Truth* breaks upon us with *resistless Day*.
> (209–212)

The presence of the sun cannot be doubted, though it may lie behind temporarily obscuring clouds of dulness.

The second part, as the section most indulging in satire, recalls at times *Mac Flecknoe*, which depends on a kingly succession, with a mock-religious sanction and the inverted sun-as-king image. The "lambent dullness"[3] that plays about Flecknoe's face perverts the idea of the halo that surrounds the true priest-king. Pope only just recalls this aspect of Dryden's treatment of Shadwell as the anti-Christ of wit in the recurring metaphor of clouds of dulness covering the face of the sun of truth, and in such lines as these: "As things seem *large* which we thro' *Mists* descry, / *Dulness* is ever apt to *Magnify*" (392–393). We find an equation between pride and dulness, an overstepping of natural bonds that are established by knowledge and self-knowledge. Dryden's linking of pride, dulness, and irreligion in *Mac Flecknoe* is an indication of the kind of connections Pope is making. he does not want to make them too strongly at the beginning of the second part—he builds through the section so that he can create pressures that will call for the critic's moral role in the third part. But the mere use of the term *pride* recalls the greatest Christian sin, and delicately establishes a connection between political rebellion, Adam's rebellion, and poetic rebellion that finally issues in the assault on heaven of "Witt's *Titans*" (552). In the realm of poetry, the refusal to keep to one's natural limits represents a perversion of divine gifts, therefore an oversetting of the natural order of one's own bodily microcosm that must spill over into a larger revolt. Thus the second part begins:

> Of all the Causes which conspire to blind
> Man's erring Judgment, and misguide the Mind,

> What the weak Head with strongest Byass rules,
> Is *Pride*, the *never-failing Vice of Fools.*
>
> (201–204)

In this part, a revolt in the state of poetry causes a decline and fall equal to and parallel to the fall of Rome, and echoing the fall of Lucifer and the fall of man from grace. But the setting of the fall is given fully in the various sins committed by false wits, who mistake nature and erect a part for the whole; they "offend in Arts / (As most in *Manners*) by a *Love* to *Parts*" (287–288). Pope's elegant reference to the affected manners of a fop saves his statement from pomposity and at the same time reminds one of the courtly background of the poem. The critic as the true courtier must be graceful in giving his precepts, and not offend by his enthusiasm.

As the problem is insubordination, setting one's unworthy self above one's proper place, the courtly setting is best served by the metaphor of fashion. Fashion, properly seen, is the current appearance that as a whole seems most natural. The distortion of a part of this whole shows the pride of the individual, his absurd attempts at originality, his lack of judgment, and his consequent foolish and unfashionable appearance. The proper attitude in wit is the same as in proper courtly behavior; small faults mean nothing if the whole is proportioned (243–252). On the other hand, excessive ornament only calls attention to its own absurdity: "One *glaring Chaos* and *wild Heap* of *Wit*" (292). False fashion is equivalent to false creation in this case, or to uncreation, a witty reminder of the sacrilege of the presuming false critic.

Allowing a part to govern the whole, and thus creating a foolish appearance, is the prime characteristic of a foolish sectarianism: "*Wit*, like *Faith*, by each Man is apply'd / To *one small Sect*, and All are *damn'd beside*" (396–397). The religious metaphor asserts the psychological unity of parallel kingdoms: bad taste comes from the same impulses that create fanaticism. The same is true of politics, where men with too fastidious taste are offended by the distasteful parts of a general order, and by separating themselves become what they most dislike, a foolish-appearing sect:

> The *Vulgar* thus through *Imitation* err;
> As oft the *Learn'd* by being *Singular*;
> So much they scorn the Crowd, that if the Throng
> By *Chance* go right, they *purposely* go wrong:
> So *Schismatics* the *plain Believers* quit,
> And are but damn'd for having *too much Wit.*
>
> (424–429)

These errors derive from a foolish concern for appearance alone, a modishness that overlooks the true purpose of religion and of social order, as well as of the proper function of dress. Thus Pope joins the images of fashion and of religion: "If *Faith* it self has *diff'rent Dresses* worn, / What wonder *Modes* in *Wit* shou'd take their Turn?" (446–447). The result is to discredit modishness in both, as a matter of distinctions without differences, just as "Parties in *Wit* attend on those of *State*" (456).

These factional results of pride are to be expected, but Pope in his serene confidence regards them as only temporary distortions of the proper order of nature's court, which in the end is only made more glorious by these temporary aberrations:

> *Envy* will *Merit* as its *Shade* Pursue,
> But like a Shadow, proves the *Substance* true;
> For envy'd Wit, like Sol Eclips'd, makes known
> Th' *opposing Body's* Grossness, not its *own*.
> When first that Sun too powerful Beams displays,
> It draws up Vapours which obscure its Rays;
> But ev'n those Clouds at last adorn its Way,
> Reflect new Glories and augment the Day.
>
> (466–473)

Here is the true function of dress: not merely fashion, but that decking out of any personage which augments his glories. No perversion is successful in Pope's scheme here; it can only be temporary. It becomes, in fact, one of those small faults that set off the glory of something much greater.

But the temporary, or temporal, is very much Pope's concern, since modern poetry seems particularly time-bound: "Short is the Date, alas, of *Modern Rhymes*" (476). Pope answers this problem as he answers that of the critic's judgment, which, like a watch, may not tell the same time as others': these are temporary faults, a result of not knowing the universal scheme, which none can know perfectly, anyhow. The clear light is always there, and small differences are of no ultimate importance. Art, however, must take a role in curing the ills it finds in its time. Against the background of this calm assurance, Pope presents the supreme crime that poetry must take a hand in reforming: the revolt against divine order, a futile revolt in ultimate terms, though it might be temporarily successful in one or another earthly realm. The first crime is insubordination, permitted by an "easie Monarch," Charles II, "Seldom at *Council*, never in a *War*" (537). Under such a monarch all degrees of political and moral laxness appear: "*Jilts* rul'd the State, and Statesmen *Farces* writ" (538). This revolt permitted by an easy monarch sets the stage for an even larger revolt under William III:

> Then unbelieving Priests reform'd the Nation,
> And taught more *Pleasant* Methods of Salvation;
> Where Heav'ns Free Subjects might their *Rights* dispute,
> Lest God himself shou'd seem too *Absolute*.
> *Pulpits* their *Sacred Satire* learn'd to spare,

And Vice *admir'd* to find a *Flatt'rer there*!
Encourag'd thus, Witt's *Titans* brav'd the Skies,
And the Press groan'd with Licenc'd *Blasphemies*.

(546–553)

Distortion of order is expressed in linguistic distortion in such juxtapositions as "unbelieving priests" or "licenced blasphemies." The fashionable profligacy is expressed in, and intensified by, a fashionable profligacy in language: the revolt of pride in one kingdom must invariably affect others. But so, Pope contends, does the proper reordering of one kingdom, and he issues a call to arms of his own: "These Monsters, Cricks! with your Darts engage, / Here point your Thunder, and exhaust your Rage!" (554–555).

This supreme revolt, in which British liberty becomes British license, ends the nightmare world of the second part, and provides the pressure for the moral third part. The present times demand a restoration of poetry in the true manner: witty, ordered, and reflective of the universal monarchy of nature, and therefore moral. Such a reformed poetry will contribute to the political and moral stability of a kingdom once again in harmony with nature. The third part completes the triptych in a restoration of this ideal as the sun reappears from behind the obscuring fogs of dulness, and the enormities of the preceeding part only emphasize the beauty of this restoration. The movement is exactly opposite to that of *The Dunciad*.[4]

The satire on various evils creates, as it always does, a pressure for some kind of ideal or standard of proper behavior, and Pope outlines the requirements for the model critic (631–643). He can then move into a grand view of the history of the realm of criticism, and the great line of critics who founded and ruled the kingdom: Aristotle the conqueror and establisher of the laws, the rest graceful rulers and judges. This kingdom falls with Rome, in a way that emphasizes the connections in the various realms:

From the same Foes, at last, both felt their Doom,
And the same Age saw *Learning* fall, and *Rome*.
With *Tyranny*, then *Superstition* join'd,
As that the *Body*, this enslav'd the *Mind*.

(685–688)

It is as though the arrangement of the verses enforced the notion that Rome would never have fallen had not learning fallen first. Erasmus unites in himself both a religious sanction and a scholarly one to reestablish the kingdom and begin a new golden age. This pattern is then repeated, as learning again reconquers the world, with the exception of England, which remained "*unconquer'd*, and *unciviliz'd*" (716). Finally certain critics appear who combine in themselves the requisite qualities of learning and humility, and consequently effect the translation of the kingdom to England:

> Yet *some* there were, among the *sounder Few*
> Of those who *less presum'd*, and *better knew*,
> Who durst assert the *juster Ancient Cause*,
> And here *restor'd* Wit's *Fundamental Laws*.
>
> (719–722)

Foremost among these new rulers are Roscommon and Walsh—now both dead—and their young protegé, Pope, who is left as the only possible heir of the whole line.

The whole poem is designed to show Pope's qualifications for his position, by an exercise of taste, learning, judgment, truth, candor, and tact. The pressure of all of these is felt throughout. The elegant imperative indicates command of his subject—and of his subjects: "Men must be *taught* as if you taught them *not*; And Things *unknown* propos'd as Things *forgot*" (574–575). This is the practice Pope sets himself to follow: he is not really proposing anything new, only reviewing the history of criticism to clarify its fundamental laws, a position he takes at the end: "hence th' Unlearn'd their Wants may view, The Learn'd reflect on what before they knew" (739–740). The form of the poem must also be casual, an offhand way of proposing things as though they had been forgotten. Pope wants to dissimulate his own pretension by emphasizing his adherence to what has gone before.

Modern readers have taken him rather too much at his word, leaving out of account Pope's disingenuousness. Pope was not concerned, or at least concerned only partly, with critical theory, but about the attitude proper to the critic, while he demonstrates that attitude in himself. Taking the humble expressions of unoriginality at face value, most readers regard the poem as a collection of brilliant fragments.[5] On the other hand, Arthur Fenner, Jr., has asserted a formal rhetorical organization for the *Essay*.[6] Such an organization may be there, with all the connections involved, but this too can mislead us from the kind of tone Pope is using. The important thing is not so much what is expressed as a theory, or how it is organized rhetorically, but the attitude of Pope and the underlying metaphor of a divine kingdom paralleled, as in any other earthly kingdom, in the kingdom of wit. Pope knows where the inconsistencies in his position are, but it is his role, as king, to carry out the laws; he must show how he would interpret them, not how he would create a whole new set. A monarch who is succeeding to a throne does not, and cannot, lead a revolution, even if he wants to. He can, perhaps, ameliorate the laws, as Pope does in the *Essay*.

But this larger purpose is pretentious, even if true (we still find it a little disturbing that a poet can so accurately predict the place he was to hold). The overt movement of the poem is therefore opposite to its covert movement, just as the two tones he adopts are complementary, if apparently at odds. Through the elegant imperative he shows his learning, separates true from false wit to show his judgment, attacks immorality to show his candor. Yet when he comes to the translation of empire to England through the laying on of hands by Roscommon and Walsh, the tone shifts to the personal and humble, though he retains the authority of all the previous discussion. Walsh's blessing falls on a poet who well knows the weight of the task:

> The Muse, whose early Voice you taught to Sing,
> Prescrib'd her Heights, and prun'd the tender Wing,
> (Her Guide now lost) no more attempts to *rise*,
> But in low Numbers short Excursions tries.
>
> (735–738)

The last lines reflect the virtues the poem says belong to the proper poet-critic, connecting them particularly to this poet: truth and candor ("Content, if hence th' Unlearn'd their Wants may view"), learning ("The Learn'd reflect on what before they knew"), judgment ("Still pleas'd to *praise*, yet not afraid to *blame*"), and the whole of the last lines emphasizing that here is a poet who will not be carried away by pride, "Still *pleas'd* to *teach*, and yet not *proud* to *know*" (632): "Averse alike to *Flatter*, or *Offend*, / Not *free* from Faults, nor yet too vain to *mend*" (743–744). No one should be fooled by the "low Numbers" of Pope's well-behaved Muse. The question of where to find the next monarch of wit is answered by Pope's character of himself.

It is, I think, only by using himself as an example that Pope is ever able to state what he means. The praise he gives to others he can only give from a throne, even though he claims the throne as modestly as is (for him) humanly possible. The parallels emphasize the fact that Pope always sees the world as a reflection of himself, which, when he can no longer impose on the world, remains as the standard from which all else falls away. Pope is never absent from the *Essay on Criticism*. The progression of the tone carries an implicit argument by which Pope's way of viewing experience can be seen. By referring to himself humbly, Pope can claim to know his limits, a Socratic knowing himself. From there he concludes that he can know nature, that it is then his duty to make others know nature by knowing themselves, all of which comes back to knowing Pope. Anyone who rejects what he says is automatically unqualified to judge. The *Essay* must avoid the charge of arrogance by showing that his skill is in fact commensurate with his claim, so that in the end he can say with modesty that he has done less than he in fact has. That puts him at a rhetorical advantage; he gives more than anyone can take. The apparent modesty of the conclusion points back to the whole poem as a palpable description of his own qualifications for his role, and yet prevents anyone from directly accusing him of pride.

Notes

1. *An Essay on Criticism* in *The Twickenham Edition of the Poems of Alexander Pope*, Vol. I, ed. E. Audra and Aubrey Williams (1961), II. 196, 738. All further references are included in the text.

2. Maynard Mack has called this the "ideal of corporateness": Introduction to *The Augustans* (Englewood Cliffs, N. J., 1950), p. 22.

3. *Mac Flecknoe*, 1. 111.

4. It is interesting that, in spite of his professed respect for Dryden, Pope does not make greater use of *Mac Flecknoe* in the *Essay*, even though Dryden is clearly using the metaphor of a poetic kingdom. But the movement of Dryden's poem is not acceptable to Pope, because it is opposite to his own. Pope turns to *Mac Flecknoe* as a model only when he creates his own perverted kingdom in *The Dunciad*. Pope is not to be swayed from his confidence in the *Essay* that he is refounding poetry; his satiric thrusts in the second part are there for the pressure they exert towards that refounding. *The Dunciad* becomes the natural fulfillment of the movement of Pope's career, when, seeing the world in his own image, he dissolves the kingdom along with himself.

5. William Empson's "Wit in the *Essay on Criticism*," *Hudson Review*, II (1950), 559–577, although it concentrates on the meanings of the word *wit*, eventually asserts through that the importance of the social tone of the *Essay*, but is not concerned with whether that attitude has some larger point.

6. "The Unity of Pope's *Essay on Criticism*," *PO*, XXXIX (1960), 435–446.

[from "The Aesthetics of Georgic Renewal: Pope"]

RONALD PAULSON

Pope . . . chose rather, with his namesake of *Greece*, to triumph in the old world, than to look out for a new. His taste partook the error of his Religion; it denied not worship to Saints and Angels; that is, to writers, who, canonized for ages, have received their apotheosis from established and universal fame. True Poesy, like true Religion, abhors idolatry . . .
—Edward Young, *Conjectures on Original Composition*, 1759.

GEORGIC FARMING AND OVIDIAN METAMORPHOSIS

This chapter approaches Pope the Roman Catholic who had to write within the gap—literally the "yawn"—left by iconoclasm, the iconoclasm of "others," and claimed to do so by way of the georgic cultivation of broken, fallen, season-governed acreage. As far as Pope was concerned, what the Civil War and the Glorious Revolution (and above all, William III, and then George I and II) stood for was iconoclasm. But writing from the position of the iconoclasted, Pope at the same time required an idol of his own in the form of an "Other" against which to react in his own iconoclastic fashion. Perhaps it was impossible to write in England without in one way or another partaking of the iconoclastic tradition.

The central question of *The Dunciad* (1728) is how does a poet make use of iconoclasted materials, by which we mean both the ancient gods iconoclasted by the moderns and the new gods set up by the iconoclasts which are being broken and dispersed by the poet Pope. The answer comes on many levels: as georgic farmer he grows food and flowers from the compost, as Ovidian poet he transforms these intransigent materials (metamorphoses them) into art, and as the Miltonic poet of *Paradise Lost* (conflating the poet and the Son of God) he redeems the fallen world. We would be misunderstanding Pope's

Ronald Paulson, "The Aesthetics of Georgic Renewal: Pope," from *BREAKING AND REMAKING: Aesthetic Practice in England, 1700–1820*. Copyright © 1989 by Rutgers, The State University. Reprinted by permission of Rutgers University Press.

sense of his own poetry if we overemphasized one of these models at the expense of the others. Satire, the fourth term, the one most frequently applied to Pope, is simply the fallen, rather secondary genre (Pope like Horace apologizes for using it) that is at hand for practical use by the georgic farmer who must fill, sow, and reap in the fallen world. The fallen world, we must emphasize, includes both the consequences of modern iconoclasm and of the poet's need to wreak his own havoc.

The poor hacks and their shabby poetry Pope loathes and wishes to obliterate. But he also knows that these dregs are, in one of its aspects, nature—though he would say unredeemed nature, a perversion of nature, or fallen nature plastered over by false art, made into an idol. And for various reasons he is drawn to this subject, perhaps as more interesting, certainly as more viable, more probable, more threatening in the 1700s than, say, the poet's conventional, classical canonical subjects of Hercules, Achilles, and Hector—or (the chief immediate subject of most seventeenth-century poets) the monarch. In the same way, but at a higher level, the world of Belinda, Clarissa, and the Baron in *The Rape of the Lock* is more local and national, as well as trivial, than that of Sarpedon and Glaucos in the *Iliad*. In both *The Rape of the Lock* and *The Dunciad* Pope demonstrates his duty but also his prowess as a poet by absorbing these local, particular, ephemeral, and often ugly materials into the beautiful world of classical learning and art.

The principle of accommodation most clearly enunciated in Pope's poetry is Virgilian georgic, supported of course by its Christian analogues in *Paradise Lost* (and in the Church Fathers' interpretations of Virgil's "Pollio" eclogue). The georgic statements are scattered throughout Pope's poetry. In the *Epistle to Burlington* (1731) he bases the process of landscape gardening on the need to "consult the Genius of the Place in all."[1] This involves first a knowledge of the capabilities of the terrain, that is, its climate as well as soil, from which its beauty and utility can be drawn out by the skillful gardener. It is, in this sense, the genius of the place "That tells the Waters or to rise, or fall, / Or helps th' ambitious Hill the heav'n to scale": It "tells" and "helps," and as the passage continues, it "scoops" the vale and "calls in the Country, catches opening glades, / Joins willing woods, and varies shades from shades." But its relationship with the patron-architect Burlington, to whom the poem is addressed, is reciprocal: "Now [it] *breaks* and now *directs*, th' intending lines; / Paints as *you* plant, and as *you* work, designs" (ll. 57–64, emphasis added). In the course of the poem Pope sets up the addressee and the poet, Burlington and himself, as parallel figures, and the making of a garden and a poem (*this* poem) as analogous acts. Both involve the human inability to create out of whole cloth, by means of either mathematical ratios or the unaided imagination. This collaboration of the gardener with his land and the poet with his indigenous subject matter is couched in the discourse of the georgic farmer.

The analogy was implicit in Virgil's *Georgics* (especially the fourth, between Aristaeus and Orpheus) and emphasized in Addison's essay on georgic and Dryden's authoritative English translation (both, 1697), where Dryden renders Virgil's line, "ignarosque viae mecum miseratus agrestis," literally "pitying *with me* the rustics who know not their way," as "Pity the poet's and the ploughman's cares."

Of course, Pope and Burlington can expect to learn that their "Just," their "Noble Rules" for drawing art out of nature, for fixing the transient in nature by art, will "fill half the land with Imitating Fools" (l. 26). Both poet and Man of Magnificence (or true patron) therefore "make falling Arts [their] care, / Erect new wonders, and the old repair" (ll. 191–92), with the same ironic glance at the duncical distortions and recreations of Timon and the monarch, whose failure of patronage makes necessary the work of the restorers Burlington and Pope.

As the *Epistle to Burlington* suggests, although "farming" carries the bluntness of the georgic intention, "gardening" is the more precise term for Pope. Gardening was more aristocratic by association and implied the remaking of the Garden of Eden with another garden, not some corn or wheat field. Pope's examples are lordly estates and landscape gardens, and they carry a nostalgia for both the Christian and classical pastoral garden. However "natural" an English landscape garden was to become, at least as late as the work of Capability Brown, its "art" in fact predominated.

In the complementary epistle, *To Bathurst* (1733), the Virgilian view of man in *Burlington* is qualified by the Christian, Bathurst's classical ethos with the Man of Ross's *Imitatio Christi*.[2] Bathurst is not a creative restorer like Burlington but a great man who understands the classical virtue of the middle way: "That secret rare, between th' extremes to move / Of mad Good-nature, and of mean Self-love" (ll. 227–28). The Man of Ross, like Burlington but with only limited means, "*hung* with woods yon mountain's sultry brow," "*bade* the waters flow" from dry rocks, not for purposes of grandeur but for "health to the sick, and solace to the swain." He put up seats for the weary traveler, and "taught" a church spire to rise.[3] The language parallels the description in *Burlington* of how the architect-gardener brings out the genius of the place, but added now are Christ echoes that become more insistent as the Man of Ross "divides the weekly bread," feeds the poor, "relieves, / Prescribes, attends, the med'cine makes, and gives" to the sick, and moreover drives out "Despairing Quacks" and "vile Attornies" from the temple (ll. 253–71).

The ideal of the poem emerges in the obscure, hitherto unsung Man of Ross, a private man whose fame the poet (as part of *his* function) draws out, as Burlington drew out the potentialities of a landscape. At the same time Pope the poet is consulting the genius of this obscure man (who died in 1724, "his name almost unknown"), drawing attention to his Christian life, and giving him the "monument, inscription, stone" he lacks: producing in effect a prospective epitaph. He does the same for the antithetical figures of the poem, the Blunts and Sir Balaams, whom he polarizes in his satiric mode as pseudo-Noahs and pseudo-Jobs (and, on the classical side, pseudo-Danaës). But the point to notice is that Pope has associated himself with the Man of Ross, in a subtle way capping the patron of the poem, Bathurst. Three figures play in Pope's georgic drama—the same three as in Virgil's: the poet, the farmer, and the patron. The presentation of this uneasy trio always turns the patron into something of the Other (as we shall see, Pope even turns Horace into a slightly alien Other).

The Christian-classical parallel/antithesis appears at its most striking in the description of Belinda's toilette in Canto I of *The Rape of the Lock* (1712–14). Belinda, carrying (ll. 35 ff.) overtones of Eve before the Fall, is shown looking at herself in the mirror, regarding her own image as Eve lost herself in her reflection in the pool. Pope combines by way of the mirror Belinda's functions as both idol and chief priestess, worshiped and worshiper. In this context, the donning of makeup assumes an Eve already fallen.

First, "awful Beauty *puts on* all its Arms," as Achilles "puts on" his suit of armor. Second, "The Fair each moment *rises* in her Charms"—Beauty "*repairs* her Smiles, *awakens* ev'ry Grace, / And *calls forth* all the Wonders of her Face." The carpenterlike word "repairs" is qualified by the more positively georgic (and organic) "awakens" and "calls forth": that is, from what is already present in the genius of Belinda's face. But the last couplet is the most precisely Christian. Beauty, Pope concludes,

> Sees by Degrees a *purer* Blush *arise*,
> And *keener* Lightnings *quicken* in her Eyes.
> (ll. 139–44, emphasis added)

The "purer" blush is, of course, the "blush" made by cosmetics, which replace, augment, and fix the color at a point where an impure thought could produce a *natural* blush that is in fact less pure than one created by art: but art requires the basis of fact, Belinda's natural beauty, though fallen and so in need of "correcting" by art.[4] (In Belinda's case a blush would only give her away, revealing the crucial fact that she is in love and with whom. Love, we shall see, is in this case the crux.)

Pope wrote his georgic *Windsor Forest* (1713) in the context of his quarrel with Addison, Ambrose Philips, and Thomas Tickell over the way pastorals should be written. The Addison-Philips-Tickell theory of the pastoral recommended a program based not on the international, classical tradition of Virgil but instead on native English poetry and life; not on "heathen" "Fauns, Nymphs and Satyrs," but local superstitions, the "tales of Goblins and Fairies," and proverbial sayings[5] not on the habits of the court and city but the customs of the specifically English countryside. (This is the same contrast outlined by Addison and Steele in the *Spectator* essays on history painting, which they argue should avoid the continental, classical, and antique stories of gods and heroes, replacing these with stories from the Bible and contemporary life.[6])

The Pope-Philips alternative versions of pastoral present essentially different aesthetic modes: Pope's emphasizes art, offering in his "Spring" pastoral both lamb and engraved bowl but clearly seeing his poem as analogous to the bowl that imitates nature in its own decoration, moreover with sky framed by the zodiac and the seasons by emblematic human figures called Seasons. The Addisonian tradition (in this particular respect) wants to emphasize the discontinuities with the past, with the classics, and give us a local, indigenous "art" for the 1700s.

The basic assumption, already established in Addison's essay on georgic, is that the pastoral voices are those of shepherds, whereas in the georgic not the farmer but the poet gives his voice to the homely formulations. The innocence and simplicity of pastoral, according to Tickell, should derive from the "Character of Shepherds":

> Their Minds must be supposed so rude and uncultivated, that nothing but what is plain and unaffected can come from them. . . . Those who have little Experience, or cannot abstract, deliver their Sentiments in plain descriptions, by Circumstances, and those Observations, which either strike upon the Senses, or are the first Motions of the Mind.
>
> —*Guardian* No. 23, pp. 107–08

Tickell's examples juxtapose the poetic diction of a "courtly lover" with the simple proto-Wordsworthian of Philips's shepherd, to the advantage of the latter:

> Come Rosalind, Oh! come, for without thee
> What Pleasure can the Country have for me?

Whereas it is precisely the elevated diction that Addison-Tickell find appropriate for the georgic mode.

Pope'e *Pastorals* (pub. 1709) might at first appear to be Addisonian georgic poems. But neither georgic nor the Virgilian imitation Tickell felt he wrote defines the *Pastorals*. Though Pope employs the strain of dispossession and postpastoral malaise he found in some of Virgil's *Eclogues*, the mode is satiric, the first genre one associates with Pope, inherited from Dryden and sanctioned by parts of Milton's *Paradise Lost*.[7]

The young Pope followed Spenser in making his *Pastorals* seasonal, indeed simplifying twelve months into four seasons. But when he divides his pastorals into four seasons, and begins with spring, he is limiting the unfallen world (the pastoral world) to spring; each of the succeeding eclogues portrays a stage of decline. *Spring*, therefore, with its harmonious conjunction of art and nature, of contesting poets, their loves, alternating songs, and shared prizes, is the only true pastoral of Pope's *Pastorals.*[8] The other three offer indications of representative satiric modes, or at least of elegiac modes on the way to the fallen world of georgic in *Windsor Forest.*[9]

Summer, though a conventional pastoral complaint, already approaches, with its oppressive heat and paranoia. Pope's more characteristic mode. The speaker Alexis, associated by name with Alexander Pope, is the young poet trying to write poetry to his beloved in a world from which the muses have fled (to the fashionable poets of Oxford and Cambridge). The beloved is not to be found, and the only harmony that remains is between the poet and his own rural setting. The dedication is to Sir Samuel Garth, the satiric poet and translator of Ovid, but Garth is invoked as a physician, a body-doctor (as Dr. Arbuthnot will be in Pope's mature *Epistle* to him), yet one who cannot cure the "disease" of love. And mingled with the address to him are the references to the "You" of the ideal that is unattainable in this Miltonic garden in which love is now a "Serpent." Only in the poet's love complaint itself is there an art, already prefigured in the bowl inscribed with the Four Seasons in *Spring*, which cures in a way that Garth's medicine cannot. The present but inefficacious Garth, the absent but longed-for ideal, and the busy poets of the universities will reappear in modified form in the satires of the 1730s.

The most obviously satiric is the third pastoral, *Autumn*, dedicated to William Wycherley, the satirist of *The Country Wife* and *The Plain Dealer*. Here Pope simply sets up a dramatic situation in which Hylas and Aegon, two foolish shepherds, whose loves are absent and unfaithful respectively, maunder on about themselves and project equally delusive visions of happiness and suicide. The poet returns only at the end to note that they sang this way "till th' Approach of Night" and then went to bed without having recovered the mistress or accomplished the suicide. This is a rehearsal for a satiric mode, but not, as it happens, for Pope's. It acknowledges Wycherley's satiric drama and may recall Swift's straight-faced reporting of incriminating documents or voices. Pope, however, except in some of his (unsigned) prose satires, never allows the reader to believe he is merely overhearing the words of a Hylas or Aegon. In his poetic satires we are always aware of the voice and presence of a, or rather *the*, poet. The poet may have many and shifting tones, or be accompanied by other voices or felt presences, but the voice remains normative, encompassing the dramatic scene. Indeed, even the "delusive vision of happiness and suicide" that is projected in Pope's mature poems is made in his own voice.[10]

Winter, Pope's pastoral elegy, is a lament for what was; the "You" of *Summer* is no longer missing but declared dead, with a possible apotheosis in the afterlife but no hope of restitution in this world. *Winter* ends evoking a world in which not Love but "Time conquers All, and We must Time obey," and Thyrsis bids the shepherds "arise" and withdraw. The combination of complaint—or the sense of loss—with the lone counterefficacy of the poem itself will also inform Pope's satiric writings, where the lost loved one has become Astraea.

The crucial eclogue, however, is the *Messiah* (1712), based on Virgil's fourth, "Pollio" eclogue, which furnishes the answer not vouchsafed by the *Pastorals*. The presence of the Messiah projects the pastoral Golden Age into the future—but in the Christian terms of redemption and rebirth. There the disjunctions of the fallen world will be banished and the contraries, including lions and lambs as well as separated lovers, will be reunited.

Pope had a genius for such visionary passages, where the action is a slow unfolding of apotheosis or apocalypse, and the real action takes place in the smallest units of meaning—the words, half-lines, lines, couplets, and their interactions. The Messiah's miraculous act of correction seems to have intrigued Pope almost above all else in the poetic range. It permits the figure *adynaton* ("impossibility") in its commonest "world turned upside down" form of mountains sinking and valleys rising and lions lying down with lambs (summed up in *"Hear him ye Deaf, and all ye Blind behold"*). But a similar use of *adynaton* will herald the approach of Dulness:

> How Time himself stands still at her command,
> Realms shift their place, and Ocean turns to land. . . .
> In cold December fragrant chaplets blow,
> And heavy harvests nod beneath the snow.
> —*Dunciad*, 1.69–76

> The forests dance, the rivers upward rise,
> Whales sport in woods, and dolphins in the skies . . .
> (3.244–45)

This sort of poetry, whose fancy is at the expense of judgment, began for Pope with Ambrose Philips's "natural English" pastorals in which (as he acerbically noted in *Guardian* No. 40) "Roses, Lillies and Daffodils blow in the same Season."

This poetic solecism takes many forms, going back to the hyperbole of Tityrus's claim in Virgil's first *Eclogue* that before he can forget the generous acts of his patron, "stags must take wing and feed in the upper air; the sea roll back and leave her fishes high and dry," and so on.[11] But as Swift's poems repeat the Modern process of breaking and remaking, Pope's repeat the dunces' own fantasticating process—the evil of which Pope is careful to stigmatize— as one of creating graven images out of rubble. And yet Pope seems to acknowledge, in *Windsor Forest*, that poetry inherently depends upon some such trope when he describes the transformation of Lodona, the warlike nymph, into a still mirror of nature consisting of

> The headlong Mountains and the downward Skies,
> The watery Landskip of the pendant Woods;

And absent Trees that tremble in the Floods;
In the clear azure Gleam the Flocks are seen,
And floating Forests paint the Waves with Green.
(ll. 212–16)

An inverted or pseudo Pollio vision is the chief, the best-known mode of his satire from *The Dunciad* to Vice's triumphal procession at the end of the first dialogue of *One Thousand Seven Hundred and Thirty-Eight* (the *Epilogue to the Satires*). There is always the temptation in Pope's grander moments to slip into a messianic pose, but this (we shall see) is accomplished by way of Milton's melding of Son and Poet. In general the Pollio's Messiah becomes an inversion at the hands of dunces, and it is the georgic to which Pope turns for his authority, with the georgic farmer serving as the model for the poet. The poet does not create afresh, like the Messiah; he lets his art draw out the inherent potential, whether in a landscape, in the subject matter of the satirist, or in the texts of his great predecessors Homer and Horace.

Two relevant quotations are, first, Pope's statement in the *Epistle to Burlington* about the "imitating Fools"

Who random drawings from your sheets shall take,
And of one beauty many blunders make. . . .
(ll. 27–28)

and second, Swift's remark to Pope in a letter: "You turn a blunder into a beauty."[12]

For Pope the poetic project was to make a garden out of his tiny estate in Twickenham which was divided by a highway, or to make poetry out of dullness—or even out of his own physical deformity. Only the second is a satiric transformation, and I suggest that Ovidian metamorphosis may be a term that subsumes satire as one of many forms of transformation. All have in common the transformation of a "blunder" into something that is specifically "art." This is an ordering that transcends farming, though it remains closely related to gardening with its vocabulary of sculptures, temples, and poetic allusions and inscriptions.

There was a satiric dimension in Ovidian metamorphosis, which originated as a reaction to the official Virgilian image of Rome and Augustus in the *Aeneid* as well as to the earlier, less imperialist, more pragmatic response to the Civil War in the *Georgics*. It indicated (as Augustus saw) a refusal to serve the state or honor the Augustan principle of utility.[13] Ovid was, compared to Virgil and Homer, even Horace, slightly subversive, and remained (however popular) slightly off the map for Pope's contemporaries. Virgil wrote the official epic of Rome, in which duty wins out over Dido's love. Ovid wrote the *other* epic, the *Metamorphoses*, in which Rome originates in sexual dalliance.

Only partly assimilated (necessarily allegorized) by the Christian commentators, Ovid retained the sense of being amusing, aesthetic, and amoral. He was known for the "truth" of his imitation of nature, especially his depiction of the passions, and in this regard he was a Latin poet to be imitated. But he was also known for his wit, cleverness, and (often) sensuality, and for these qualities he was to be avoided. The Christian allegorization of the stories of Syrinx (bk. 1) and Alpheus-Arethusa (bk. 5) amounted to little more than "virtue pursued by the soul." But when Pope imitates Ovid, it should be emphasized, he always retains the subject of sexuality as at least a blunder out of which beauty can be made.

The georgic fiction is, of course, related to a kind of metamorphosis, but one brought about by hard work in the fallen world, by a realistic appraisal of possibilities and a conscious awareness that without care we can slip back into the bloody civil war and the ploughshare can be replaced by the sword. Where the georgic speaks of truth, nature, earth, and vegetation, Ovid's *Metamorphoses* speaks of love, magic, fiction, and art. In his early poems at least, Pope endows his restorations and re-creations (and/or others' perversions) with the fiction of metamorphosis.[14]

Pope's gardener is always slipping into the Ovidian artist, the Pan who makes a flute of Daphne. It is safe to say that, while Pope may preach georgic, in practice he metamorphoses a blunder—or, in fact more often we shall see, a love/hate object (whether Colley Cibber and Lady Mary Wortley Montagu, or Teresa Blount and Arabella Fermor)—into an instrument specifically of beauty. The Ovidian metamorphoses that Pope evokes are the fables of the artist (or of art): the initial transformation is at the wish of the pursued (Lodona, Arabella Fermor, or Lord Petre), the second by the pursuer himself, who turns Daphne or Syrinx or Arabella into an instrument or product of his art.

Pope's earliest translations and imitations were of Ovid's *Metamorphoses*, and in *Windsor Forest* the georgic readjustments are posed in Ovidian terms. The central metamorphosis is of Lodona, fleeing from Pan, transformed into a river, her flight into a smooth-flowing, contemplative "mirror of nature," in other words poetry, as war is transformed into peace. As Lodona invokes Diana, her patroness, the poet invokes Queen Anne, his Diana-equivalent, to change war (with France, but with memories of the English Civil War, as the Roman Civil War was recalled by both Virgil and Ovid) into peace.[15] And, as author of this poem, the poet invokes his muse to change nature (politics, chaos, and contingency) into art.

The Lodona episode, which compacts the three levels of politics, art, and nature,[16] starts as georgic and ends as Ovidian metamorphosis. The climax of the passage is the upside-down poetic world that results from the metamorphosis of Lodona. Although the poem goes on to represent the political metamorphosis of war into commerce in the speech of Father Thames, it nevertheless returns at the end to the poet: to "my humble Muse," who "paints the green

Forests and the flow'ry Plains," and the poet himself, who with the Peace of Utrecht can "more sweetly pass my careless Days," as both beneficiary, the subject of "empty Praise," and—manifest in the text before us—author of the transformation that has subsumed all of these elements. (He asks his dedicatee Granville to write the heroic; he will write the humble version.)

Metamorphosis involves the substitution, or the dissolution (as with *adynaton*), of categories or essences. Boundaries and limits are broken and reformed—not only of territories but those between hunter and hunted, art and nature, and victor and vanquished—in the ultimate breakdown of rational boundaries in death: "The grave unites; where ev'n the great find Rest, / And blended lie th' Oppressor and th' Opprest" (ll. 317–18).

The sequence leading up to the Lodona episode makes it clear that the hunt that is the sublimation of Williamite chaos nevertheless evokes the pursuit of innocent creatures, the cannibalism of fish, and ("if small Things we may with great compare") military conquest. The hunt is seen through the eyes of the hunted prey, but they are not finally permitted to be innocent. The pheasant "mounts *exulting* on *triumphant* Wings"; his "glossie, varying dyes, / His Purple Crest" and "shining Plumes" make him a symbol of pride and its consequent fall, of vanitas and pathetic loss—in short, an anticipation of the nymph Lodona.

The first two-canto version of *The Rape of the Lock* (1712), written at about the same time as *Windsor Forest*, repeats the form of metamorphosis with Belinda, another Lodona who goes too far, also pursued, her flight merely exciting her pursuer the more. When she loses her symbolic lock it is transformed by the poetic muse into a star. The Baron replaces Pan in the story and, by implication, Belinda's "honor" replaces Lodona's vow to Diana. When she defeats her suitor at cards her "exulting fills with shouts the Sky"; and, as with the "exulting" pheasant, the poet admonishes her pride ("Oh thoughtless Mortals"), followed shortly by Clarissa's shears and the Baron's rude act. The whole poem, it is clear from his Preface, Pope regarded as his own poetic metamorphosis of the Petre – Fermor squabble into peace, of anger into comedy and good feeling, of chaotic reality into art.

The source of Lodona's disaster recalls the love-lust described in Virgil's third *Georgic*, but primarily the love-lust that distinguishes the flawed past of *Georgic 4* (Aristaeus's sin and the similar sin that led to the fall of Antony, to the Trojan War, and so on), which is redeemed in the butchery and maggoty rebirth of the hive.

The similarity between georgic and metamorphosis should now be obvious. If the *Metamorphoses* is filled with surrogate poets, the *Georgics*, as Addison emphasized, are spoken by a poet, not a farmer.[17] Both forms share the subject of the relationship between a rustic and the poet, summed up by Ovid in his combining in the person of Pan both nature and art, attacker and artist. It is a natural urge (often embodied in a natural creature, a satyr, though sometimes a slumming deity) which precipitates the metamorphosis. This metamorphosis is carried out by a supernatural force (a god, muse, monarch, or patron) as a transformation of living flesh into organic nature, and this transformation is recouped—in an almost georgic fashion—by the original perpetrator, who fashions and symbolizes the now inhuman substance into something no longer living but, by art's craft, immortal. The poet-satyr is the important and ambiguous figure at the center of Pope's fiction of poetic making.

In the fourth *Georgic* the farmer and the poet are divided, drawn apart in the would-be rapist Aristaeus and the bereaved Orpheus. Aristaeus has learned why he is being punished—how his satyrish pursuit of Eurydice caused her death and Orpheus's curse, which killed his bees. But the story continues with Orpheus's pursuit of Eurydice to Hades and his loss of her on their return, and then after his murder by the Bacchantes his severed head continues, even now, to lament his loss, calling Eurydice's name. In this ultimate georgic, farming and poetry have been divorced; or at any rate the poet has been shown to be the lamenter of loss, as distinct from the beekeeper who has learned how to recover his hive.

Pope echoes Orpheus's lament directly in his "Ode to St. Cecilia," but ultimately in *The Dunciad* he carries the story one step further than Virgil by picking up Ovid's account of Orpheus's yet-declaiming head which, floating down the stream, comes to rest on a shore where it is threatened by a serpent with widespread jaws—until Orpheus's patron Apollo freezes the jaws in their open, yawning, devouring gesture into immortal sculpture. This is the epigraph Pope attaches to the final version of *The Dunciad* (1743), thereby turning himself into Orpheus, murdered but, even in the act of devourment by the yawning jaws of Dulness, surviving as a poetic voice—while his muse has frozen into the immortality of literature the dunces, hacks, and politicians who have overwhelmed him with personal abuse. This final overview does not cancel the more general sense of *The Dunciad* as a georgic ritual by which life is engendered by the farmer from the maggoty corpse of the bullock or heifer, while the desolate poet (with a dead love in his past) laments his own personal loss.

The large action of Pope's satires takes two general forms. One is the emblematic, allegorical, allusive anti-Pollio vision of chaos and disorder, or of delusion and abject fantasy. The second action concludes with the Horatian *sermo* in which "Pope" converses with somebody. But it begins with the love lament of an Alexis or Orpheus, whose tone is never quite lost, supporting the strong tendency toward apologia, in which the satirist defends himself and at the same time produces satire on his maligners. One action is visionary, the other a dialogic interaction between two or more people. And yet they usually join; the latter is often a frame action for the vision, an "occasion" created for projecting visions of false creation. Pope's career as a satirist begins and ends with fictions of a lone poet complaining of the discontinuities of the world, the victory of Time over love, and projecting a vision of decline—his own and his society's—expressed, however, in the form of something beautiful and lasting which contradicts the pessimistic conclusion of the vision itself. The poetic act, following both georgic and Ovidian modes, is concerned with loss and the healing of that loss through art.

It is necessary now to say something more about the types of transgressive materials transformed by this poet. One is the literary and moral dreck that is farmed or metamorphosed into the beautiful garden of classical art. But another is the satirist's rage itself, an excess not allowed to the "correct" poet (which Caryll advised Pope to become). The rage is directed against those who malign him and, equally, against what they malign in him. As the contemporary attacks (which he collected, listed, and in part quoted in *The Dunciad Variorum*) show, there was obviously a place in the English demonology of that unstable time for his Roman Catholicism (and so the suspicion of Jacobitism), his shortness and bent back, and his too-great brilliance ("wit to madness near allied"). From the first onslaught of John Dennis through the attacks of Lord Hervey and Lady Mary Wortley Montagu, and almost to our own day, these stigmas were represented by images of toad, spider, wasp, and monkey, easily grafted onto the emblem of malicious deformity—a Thersites of Richard III. Even his name allowed him to be called Pope for his religion and Ape (A.P——e) for his poetry. These names must have caused Pope to reconsider seriously the aesthetic that equated beauty and goodness, ugliness and evil. How does a grotesque hunchbacked body—as well as the rage it utters, the satiric venom it produces (one had almost said, adopting the satiric metaphor, excretes)—relate to the classical ideal of order and harmony? Marjorie Nicolson remarks on the growing admiration in these years for mountainous prospects including craggy mountains previously condemned as "hook-shoulder'd" deformities: Pope's shape also called for a new aesthetics or at least an aesthetic accommodation.[18]

Pope's earliest attempt at translation is of Ovid's *Acis and Galatea*, in which the theme of unrequited love in the "Summer" pastoral has been slightly complicated by the addition of a third party. Acis and Galatea love each other, and are not (like pastoral lovers) separated; but the story Pope translates is about Polyphemus the monstrous cyclops, who also loves Galatea, and, seeing the lovers embrace, "Frantick with his pain, / Roar'd out for Rage" and crushed Galatea's Acis, who is then metamorphosed into a fountain.[19]

If *Acis and Galatea* introduces a metamorphosis that is separate from the protagonist, it also introduces rage and the disproportionate body, which are other major elements of *The Rape of the Lock*. The rage of course came as part of Pope's donnée, but both Belinda and the Baron are invested with Polyphemus's fury—Belinda with his "Rage, Resentment, and Despair" and the Baron with his violent action. Belinda's beauty and aloofness, and her "exultant" victory cry, plus a drink of coffee which stimulates "New Strategems, the radiant Lock to gain," lead the Baron to commit the Polyphemus-like act of cutting the lock. If his response is excessive, however, Belinda's too is closer to Polyphemus's than to Galatea's. At first she does not know what to do. Thalestris's speech of poor advice is necessary to get her started, and this is supplemented by Sir Plume's expostulation, most unheroic by comparison, which serves to provoke the Baron to a further refusal to return the lock. And with this chain of provocation Belinda initiates the battle of the sexes, and "all the Prize is lost."

Pope's epic invocation asks the questions of how "dire Offense" can follow from "amorous Causes," "mighty Contests" from "trivial Things," great "Praise" from a "slight . . . subject," "Tasks so bold" from "Little Men," and finally, but above all, "such mighty Rage" from "soft Bosoms." The last two oxymorons closely relate to the Polyphemus story, but that was only one of a series of significant translations, including Chaucer's January and May and Ovid's Sappho and Phaon, which dramatize various kinds of disproportion between a lover and the object of his/her love, and in which the human relationship, ending in failure, nevertheless engenders poetry. In the cases of Polyphemus and Sappho, Pope is working with a story of the way in which poetry gets written, that is, out of loss, frustration and absence of the loved one—plus an act of uncontrolled violence. Polyphemus sings out of longing, but when he sees Acis with Galatea he can only respond with physical violence. And Sappho's story ends with her leap—and Orpheus's, of course, with his violent death at the hands of the Bacchantes (and Achilles' wrath).

Let us begin with "little men," not great heroes but tiny and diminutive, even feminine creatures. *Sappho to Phaon* is Ovid's only heroic epistle from a poet, and in particular a poetess (obsessed with a lover whose young body contains an aged heart), who writes in Pope's version, "Tho' short my Stature, yet my Name extends / To Heav'n it self, and Earth's remotest ends." The Baron is a "little man"; but Pope was also a little man, and the emphasis on the words in the *Rape* should be compared with Pope's papers on the "Club of Little Men" in the *Guardian* of June 1713 (Nos. 91, 92).[20] No. 91 announces:

> I question not but it will be pleasing to you to hear, that a Sett of us have formed a Society, who are sworn to *Dare to be Short*, and boldly bear out the Dignity of Littleness under the Noses of those Enormous Engrossers of Manhood, those Hyperbolical Monsters of Manhood, Monsters of the Species, the tall Fellows that overlook us.
>
> (p. 325).

The "most eminent" members are a little poet, lover, politician, and hero. The poet, Dick Distick, has

> been elected President, not only as he is the shortest of us all, but because he has entertain'd so just a Sense of the Stature, as to go generally in Black that he may appear yet Less. Nay, to that Perfection is he arrived, that he *stoops* as he walks. The Figure of the Man is odd enough; he is a lively little Creature,

with long Arms and Legs; a Spider is no ill Emblem of him. He has been taken at a Distance for a *small Windmill* . . . He hath promised to undertake a long Work in *short Verse* to celebrate the Heroes of our Size

(p. 328).

And this, of course, was called *The Rape of the Lock*.

Interestingly, the poet is linked contiguously with the lover Tom Tiptoe, who goes to bed with a woman who, however, keeps the affair platonic by tying his toe to hers. Maynard Mack has documented the "gay-doggishness" of Pope's early London years, which took the form of the gallantry that defended Arabella Fermor by writing *The Rape of the Lock*—as later Lady Mary Wortley Montagu against Edmund Curll by administering an emetic to the bookseller and writing a pamphlet about it.[21] Even his initial attack on John Dennis in *An Essay on Criticism*, which elicited the first of the horrific personal attacks, must be attributed less to malice than to a sort of self-assertion parallel to his jokes about taking on London "women," which derived from the need to prove himself courageous and "manly" beyond his size and physical capabilities.

Pope also refers to the Little Poet as spiderlike and "stooping" and his translation of Homer's description of Thersites is another case of his dwelling on a figure, here combining deformity and satire, which must—to himself and to his readers—recall his own. Back in the "Summer" pastoral he named the poet Alexis, a conventional name but close to Pope's own. He gave Alexis a hopeless love, and one reason for its hopelessness was said to be his lack of university education (the muses wander beside the Isis and Cam). The reason that Pope could not attend Oxbridge was not financial but political: his Roman Catholicism. Just as the reason that, like the fictional Alexis, he was remote from a love object, was not his lack of university education but of a strong body.

In his reply to Tickell's *Guardian* essays on "English Pastoral," in which he polarizes and exaggerates his own Virgilianism against Philips's Spenserian pastoral, Pope makes two remarkable statements that introduce the personal. The first is when he characterizes himself as one who "takes the greatest Care of his Works before they are published, and has the least Concern for them afterwards." Everything we observe about his career gives the lie to the second clause; in fact, Pope devoted at least as much attention to his works "afterwards" as before publication. The second is when he writes that he "has imitated some single Thoughts of the Ancients well enough, if we consider he had not the happiness of an University Education."[22]

Returning to *The Rape of the Lock*, the "mighty Rage" also calls for some discussion. Although Pope does not always seek out causes, the situation and, more, the effect of the "mighty Rage" are subjects of concern for him: what are the causes of passion and indignant outburst? In this instance they are satirized as excessive all around. But a basic pattern of Pope's satire is established, a pattern not so much of cause and effect as of action and response, provocation and overresponse. Somewhere within the Baron and Belinda and their overreactions is the later obsessive question: what could make an innocent well-brought up poet, indeed one who has his own soul to think about, attack such powerful men as Hervey, Walpole, and even the king? This question is sometimes posed by enemies, sometimes by friends, and sometimes by the poet himself. However different in evaluation, the outbursts of Belinda and the Baron share with the poetic indignation of Pope's satires the apparently spontaneous emotion that has no place in the world of Augustan society and art. While Pope's preparations for his satiric outbursts are always carefully constructed, the construction is based on that of *The Rape of the Lock* and is both a way of getting himself into the position of uttering a Pollio vision and perhaps the only way of creating a poetic effect of an intensity that recalls the great poetry of preceding centuries.

The pattern is considerably clarified in the five-canto version of the *Rape* published in 1714, which adds explanations or motives for the "mighty rages." This version also attempts to distinguish Belinda's rage from the Baron's, making it plain that her rage reflects fear for reputation and appearances ("Hairs less in sight, or any Hairs but these!", while his can be taken to represent a touch of the real world which Belinda the coquette needs—but which she rejects by simply going over from the sylphs to the gnomes.

The addition of Ariel and the sylphs sets up a third agency which explains the way "a gentle Belle" could "reject a Lord," and "dire offenses" can be related to "amorous causes," "mighty contests" to "trivial things." Within this contrast of opposing worlds an action of a different sort takes place, beginning with the vision vouchsafed Belinda in which her guardian sylph Ariel persuades her of (or supports her belief in) her personal sanctity and ideality above "dire" reality. *The Rape of the Lock* begins with these contrasting worlds, or at least ways of interpreting the real world, and a student and her mentor who urges upon her the false interpretation. The sylphs, whether we take them as a level of Belinda's consciousness or a social paradigm of honor, make the essential mediating link between Belinda and her imagined inviolability. Ariel's speeches project a lovely, artificial play world which is meant to replace the real world of marriage and deflowering—a world with its own laws and games that Belinda must obey or be abandoned. They also carry overtones of the temptation of a deluded Eve into seeing herself as godlike when she is a human in a humanly limited situation of courtship, and this temptation is followed by a parody Mass with Belinda officiating before a mirror altar at the "sacred Rites of Pride."[23]

A result of making Belinda a tempted and fallen human being—fallen through pride—is to elicit the exulting hubris of her victory speech, which is the direct stimulus to the Baron's overresponse (prompted only by coffee dreams in the earlier version) of breaking the rules of the game and cutting the lock. The response of Belinda then is hysteria, followed by the Baron's own exulting speech, which in the new context, though excessive, serves a corrective function. Because he has cut the lock, his "Honour, Name, and Praise shall live." Echoing Catullus's "Berenice" and its context of married love, he apostrophizes his sword—his "steel"—which "strike[s] to Dust th' Imperial Tow'rs of Troy," confounds "the works of mortal Pride," and hews "Triumphal Arches to the Ground." In the first version this was empty mock-heroic exulting; now in 1714 with the provocation of Belinda's pride and her own exultant speech, it sounds more like a forerunner of Pope's own vaunt, twenty years later in the *Epilogue to the Satires*: "O sacred Weapon! left for Truth's defence, / Sole Dread of Folly, Vice, and Insolence!" But even in the first version Pope has indicated the odds that are against the Baron, distinguishing between "soon to obtain" and "long possess the Prize"—words that recall the presence of the conqueror Time, with *his* "steel," as well as the power of reputation.[24]

A final addition, made in the 1717 revision of the *Rape*, is the speech of Clarissa, which balances Thalestris's angry outburst with counsels of common-sense and moderation. She is the unheroic and commonsense antithesis of Sarpedon, the hero who goes off to his death. Given the same assumptions about a world dominated by Time in which "frail Beauty must decay," he responds with "great Acts" and "Valour," she with "good Sense" and "Virtue." Clarissa speaks for the acceptance of truth, nature, and reality. Her handing the scissors to the Baron, already present in the first version, represented the same values, though with a militance that is lacking in her 1717 speech. As Pope observed, the latter was introduced to materialize the moral of the poem, but in her realism there is also the germ of a plea for the status quo. If only, the echoes of the *Iliad* seem to say, there were room for a Sarpedon in our world. Even poor Belinda and the Baron are at least fighting for their beliefs, however mistaken, in a losing battle with Time.

At any rate, Clarissa's counsel of moderation, even more than Thalestris's of rage, only serves to provoke Belinda to attack, and the battle of the sexes ensues. She rounds off a fiction of a passionate person who brings down the paragon of pride and affectation, even if it means disrupting the structure around her, violating the laws of politeness, and precipitating a battle. In time, in the age of Walpole, it will become necessary to rethink the alternatives of Thalestris and Clarissa, Clarissa and Sarpedon. The fiction develops through two phases for Pope, first the justification for that "mighty rage," and second the questioning of it as a way of life.

The most obvious, most public transgression of all has not been mentioned: Pope's Roman Catholicism. The anti-Williamite content of *Windsor Forest* is well known. Howard Erskine-Hill has convincingly drawn attention to the Jacobite content of *The Rape of the Lock*, beginning with the game of ombre as itself a metaphor in the 1700s for political affairs. There was a sense (emphasized in *The Key to the Lock*) in which the whole poem was a political allegory: the "rape" also applies to the "rape of a kingdom" by "Foreign Tyrants" that (in Erskine-Hill's words) "yield to what the Jacobites alleged James II's England had yielded to," that is, "The conqu'ring Force of unresisted Steel" (3.179). In this context, Clarissa's speech is added in the aftermath of the Jacobite failure and Hanoverian triumph of 1714 to advocate "the heroism of submission."[25] The Jacobite cause was only more overtly unspeakable material than the personal issues of Pope's body and voice, for which perhaps his Roman Catholicism stood as emblem. . . .

THE POPEAN OTHER

The enveloping fiction of provocation and response informs many of the satires that intervene between the 1729 and 1743 *Dunciads*. The "advertisement" to the *Epistle to Dr. Arbuthnot* (1734/5) explains that Pope had written some observations on the times in a poem but "had no thoughts of publishing it," until he was attacked "in a very extraordinary manner"—"not only my Writings (of which, being publick, the Publick is judge) but my Person, Morals, and Family"—by Lady Mary and Lord Hervey. Within the poem itself it is the slanders ("lies") of Sporus (Hervey) which elicit the climactic utterance of the satire.

But a new Horatian figure, the adversarius, begins to emerge. As he needs an anti-Pope gesture before he can respond, Pope also needs the indifference of those who would let vice alone or come to terms with it before he can give vent to the indignation that adequately captures the false world. Faced with vice itself he can often remain silent. In fact, he never shows himself simply responding to vice—though in conversation with a "friend" he recalls doing so. It is only when a Sporus slanders with his lies, or when a "friend" urges moderation, silence, or flattery of the evil—thus showing the consequences of accepting vice—that he must speak out.

In the Horatian imitations the provocation of the slanderer is moved into the background and its place of prominence taken by the flatterer. The first imitation, of Horace's *Satire* II.i (1732), is presented once again as a response, in this case to the attacks on his *Epistle to Burlington* of the year before. But having been grossly maligned because of imagined satire (supposedly aimed at the Duke of Chandos), the poet is now being advised by his friend Fortescue ("F." = either Friend or Fortescue), a lawyer, against writing anything else that smacks of satire; write praise instead, he is told. This advice allows Pope incidentally to summon up grotesque images of Hanoverian eulogy. But the caution urged by Fortescue has the larger effect of drawing him further out, until the warning for his personal safety—" Alas, young man, your days can ne'er be long, /In flower of age you perish for a song!"—prods Pope into the powerful climactic declaration, beginning "What? armed for Virtue when I point the pen, /Brand the bold front of shameless guilty men . . . ," for which in effect the poem was written.[26]

William Fortescue is symptomatic of the "friend" who now begins to appear in Pope's satires because he was a friend of Walpole as well as of Pope. In the late 1720s he had exerted efforts to keep the two men on polite terms and was in fact, to use Mack's words, "his own and Walpole's long-time intermediary—who would speak with the grave accents of Horace's Trebatius but at the same time with the arguments of the government gazetteers."[27] Dr. Arbuthnot is a more normative "friend" than Fortescue, closer in function to Clarissa in *The Rape of the Lock*, but he advances the pattern established with Fortescue by advising Pope to avoid naming or using living examples and warning him of the personal dangers involved in writing satire. But Pope must name. He is condemned, in this instance like Midas's wife, to act naturally: "Who can't be silent, and who will not lie."

In the *Epilogue to the Satires* the "friend" comes close to being the subject. In all these climactic satires evil emerges as the state of mind of acceptance, the unwillingness to question the idol or the idolatry: the peaceful prosperity of Walpole's long reign, where money and prosperity are sufficient, and art and literature are either forgotten or turned to praise of the regime. This is the same bland acceptance of a new ruler and universal sleep and darkness at the end of *The Dunciad*, together with the same lone cry of the poet who sees the truth.

The effect in the *Epilogue* involves the interaction of P., F., *and* Walpolian vice. The end toward which each dialogue moves is the grand outburst Pope utters, but the subject is this interaction, with the crucial voice now that of the "friend." The voice of commonsense and reason has become utterly despicable, the voice of prudence, of shiftiness, those who join the forces of evil without admitting it, in short, the Other. He is asking for a quiet, peaceful world of flatterers in which satirists do not cause trouble or threaten the status quo by attacking men in place: wait until they are out. The figure of Vice is defined in terms of her acceptance or rejection by others—by the great, by the "friends," by "Fame," or by Pope. For Vice is dangerous only if "Greatness own her," and she is defined only in terms of the great; their flatterers, and the nonsatirists whose acceptance is a necessary condition of her being. Pope represents (and, judging by the last lines of the first dialogue, he is nearly alone) another world of truth, passion, and satire.

He is ironically accepting the role urged upon him by the "friend" when, in Dialogue 1, he describes a world in which satire has a bad name, flattery a good, and the low is taken to be the high, vice to be virtue, and to rise is to fall and vice versa. Here is the pseudo-Pollio at its most powerful, with the removal of distinctions and oppositions, mountains sinking and valleys rising, lambs and lions lying down together. At the end of the first dialogue Pope abandons the ironic impersonation, and in the second dialogue resumes his role of true poet, intensifying the distinctions and making oppositions clear, establishing high as high and low as low, and good *versus* evil. Turning to the whole system of fabrications that is the court, he says:

> The Muse's wing shall brush you all away:
> All his Grace preaches, all his Lordship sings,
> All that makes saints of Queens, and Gods of Kings,
> All, all but Truth, drops dead-born from the Press,
> Like the last Gazette, or the last Address.
>
> (ll. 223–27)

Though an adversarius appears physically in a few of the Horatian satires, such a figure is present explicitly or implicitly in almost every one of Pope's imitations. Even where there is no overt intermediary to elicit his response, Pope suggests the same effect by printing the lines of "delicate" Horace he is imitating on the other side of the page—materializing them over there as a stimulus to a stronger moral vein as well as a source of historic and literary authority. Where Horace's text still applies, we find opposite a literal translation. Where it does not apply, Pope forces the reader to compare his own modernized line.[28] Where in *Satire* II.i Pope speaks out for himself— utters his "mighty rage"—there is simply blank space on the opposite page where Horace's text is printed.

In the opening of Dialogue 1 of the *Epilogue to the Satires*, with its subtitle "A Dialogue Something like Horace," the "friend" begins by accusing Pope of having stolen all his good lines from Horace, but he himself (as Pope points out in a footnote) is the one who steals the only two lines from Horace in the poem: *he* is the Horatian, advocating a Horatian prudence to Pope in the next verse paragraph:

> But *Horace*, Sir, was delicate, was nice;
> *Bubo* observes, he lash'd no sort of *Vice*.
> *Horace* would say . . . [etc.]

It is, of course, also a comment on Pope's satiric object to write a Horatian satire that turns out Juvenalian (or Persian). To evoke the Horatian mask and then prove too large for it, too Juvenalian, is one way of producing passionate response as well as of characterizing the intermediary who provokes it.

The Other who appears in Pope's satires is always external and concrete.[29] The "dialogue" between poet and Other cannot be confused with a Socratic dialogue which involves a certain equality of speech, with the ironist asking questions of his opponent that eventually elicit a response expressing the ironist's own view. Pope's procedure is almost the reverse of Socratic; the opponent elicits the response from the poet himself. The form is far less dialogue than a speech of his own, and the adversarius's function is to provoke the poet, by his words or his mere presence, to the intensity of response which raises the poem above mere exposition. The method is, in fact, parallel to that of Pope's Pollio-visions. The values of the adversarius (whether foe or friend) are questioned and shown to break down under their own load of internal contradictions. But the process is one of creation as well as destruction, and the poet's act of response includes an act of redefinition, which takes the form of a remetamorphosis of folly into truth and poetry.

The adversarius ultimately tends to become conflated with the "You" of the addresses to Cobham, Bathurst, and Bolingbroke. These patrons descend in one sense from the unattainable "You" of the "Summer" pastoral, but in another they are separated off (as Bathurst is from the Man of Ross = Pope) into an Other. Even Milton serves this purpose: Pope needs *Paradise Lost*, now an unattainable ideal and/or a museum piece, in order to write his contemporary version, *The Dunciad*. The relationship between Pope and either his "friends," his Bolingbrokes and Burlingtons, or his poetic models is not a matter of analogy approaching unity; resemblance is less important than the relationship of stimulus and response. The Other is rather something that is already understood or apprehensible, something that is already *there*, by which something new, less readily apprehensible, can be posited which supersedes or corrects the other.

There is always an Other in Pope's world whether he be Homer, Virgil, or Horace; but (even in his translations) this is always a slightly, or markedly, different presence—a too-heroic world or perhaps a too modestly satiric one, but always one that by its difference defines, prompts, and justifies his own in both its similarities and divergences. Take the letters he planted on Curll to make him bring out his piratical edition, the sine qua non for the "correct" edition Pope then published. The latter could only come into existence once a false simulacrum was in existence, as the true image of a weeping Cleopatra could only follow a correction of Augustus's statue of her. One other example among many is *The Key to the Lock* (1715), a work that, while not at all changing the true meaning of *The Rape of the Lock*, produced a counter or additional satiric meaning about contemporary politics, while at the same time satirizing the sort of pedantry or converting imagination (i.e., the attacks on the *Rape*) which could find such preposterously inflated meanings in an innocent poem. The *Key* is only meaningful in relation to the *Rape*, and yet it is a totally independent work because now the stimulus it presupposes is "*The Rape of the Lock*"—in quotation marks, reconceived. In the same way, at each stage of *The Dunciad*'s development something is taken as the real, and this provokes, causes, defines, brings about something else—a sequel, a correction, an explanation—which exists only in relation to it, but once in existence—published and read—becomes a thing itself in terms of which something else is then elicited and defined. The immediate stimulus for *The Dunciad* is presumably Dryden's *Mac Flecknoe*, not because it is a literary source but because Pope corrects and completes it. Every poem exists as a response to another poem in one way or another—whether it is by a friend (Homer, Horace, or Virgil) or by an enemy (Dennis, Hervey, or Theobald). Every poem uses in the georgic sense, or metamorphoses in the Ovidian sense, the matter of these other poems.

It is as if Pope has at every stage to prove his own position to himself by provoking it from something extant, as if without the actual presence of another person or object the sense of his own identity lacks firmness. This is related to the neoclassical stance of seeing reality as a relationship to something already understood, something ontologically and epistemologically secure, however unsatisfactory in itself. The Augustan mode of poetry involves a drawing out or discovery of meaning in an existent rather than the creation of a new object or identity. Pope's identity, and that of his poetry, is seen only as an inference from real, known figures or poems—alike and different in various degrees—or as an extension or realization of them.

Beginning with the paradigm of the *Messiah*, Pope's particular strategy is to take something known and metamorphose or restore it, draw out the true but hitherto unrecognized meaning. Following from the lesson of *The Temple of Fame*, he puts his own Horatian verses on the page opposite Horace's to show that he is again consulting the Genius of the Place, continuing the Horatian entelechy into the 1730s, and establishing for his time the true fame of the Horatian text. He builds on, or brings out the potentialities *as he sees them*, thus producing not exactly a translation or a poem by Pope but rather (if we refer to the Other as X) an X prime or X + P or X − P; but never merely P. Paraphrased, these symbols become the Homer of the eighteenth century; or Horace rendered appropriate for the Age of Walpole; or Boling-broke (in *An Essay on Man*) but less "great" as well as less fallen, less in need of consolation; or Bathurst but a Christ figure, or the Man of Ross but a poet. His own poems may be understood in the same way: once written, *The Dunciad* is regarded as an object that must itself be properly given an "honest fame."

But even this explanation does not cover the friction we feel between Pope and the Other that always reduces it ultimately to an opponent. He has *exceeded* both Virgilian and Horatian models (both of them patronized by the Emperor Augustus), and in a characteristic mock epitaph, to one who was *not* to be buried in Westminster Abbey (as he knew he would not, being a Roman Catholic), he writes:

> Heroes, and Kings! your distance keep:
> In peace let one poor Poete sleep,
> Who never flatter'd Folks like you:
> Let Horace blush, and Virgil too.[30]

In most cases, at least as we approach the satiric end of his poetic spectrum, the Popean meaning is not so much a drawing out of the other's capabilities as a reaction against the Other. It takes a Horatian stance at least partly wrong (or outdated), or a *Dunciad* attacked and misunderstood, to produce Pope's own work, as it takes a property split down the middle by a highway to produce Pope's grotto with its particular symbolic perspective on his peaceful garden on one side and the busy Thames traffic moving toward London on the other. Or perhaps, within the context of iconoclastic discourse, we should conclude that his own inbred Catholic "idolatry" was displaced onto the classical texts, but this was qualified by such factors as his sense of the orthodoxy of iconoclasm, his own quite unclassical body, and (to judge by *The Dunciad*) his deep-seated gothic predilections. As his treatment of Horace shows, the classical text allowed him to keep the idol but distance and correct it.

Notes

1. My text is the *Twickenham Edition of the Poems of Alexander Pope*, 11 vols. (New Haven, 1940–69).

2. I am, of course, indebted to Earl Wasserman's "Critical Reading," in *Pope's Epistle to Bathurst* (Baltimore, 1960), pp. 11–55, with which in general I agree.

3. Howard Erskine-Hill fills in the historical and biographical context of this passage in *The Social Milieu of Alexander Pope* (New Haven, 1975), pp. 27–33.

4. The line is clarified by Swift's lines (164–71) in *Cadenus and Vanessa* (1713):

> From whence that Decency of Mind,
> So lovely in the Female Kind,
> Where not one careless Thought intrudes,
> Less modest than the Speech of Prudes;
> Where never Blush was call'd in Aid,
> That spurious Virtue in a Maid,
> A Virtue but at second-hand;
> They blush because they understand.

5. *Guardian*, ed. J. C. Stephens (Lexington, 1982), No. 23, p. 109.

6. *Spectator* Nos. 29, 83, 249, 555, etc. (ed. Donald F. Bond [Oxford, 1965]).

7. See, e.g., Peter V. Marinelli, *Pastoral* (London, 1971), p. 12. The remainder of this chapter takes off from my article, "Satire, and Poetry, and Pope," in Ronald Paulson and Leland H. Carlson, *English Satire* (Los Angeles, 1972), pp. 55–106.

8. I am indebted in my discussion of Pope's pastorals to Martin C. Battestin, "The Transforming Power of Nature and Art in Pope's Pastorals," *ECS*, 2 (1969), 183–204; rpt. in his book, *The Providence of Wit* (Oxford, 1974), pp. 58–78.

9. We could compare Pope's transformation of pastoral with Virgil's in his *Eclogues:* Virgil appears (in 1 and 9, and also 10) to be writing both pastoral and critique of pastoral, already moving into the more historically determined and characteristic mode of georgic.

10. I am quoting Battestin, *Providence of Wit*, p. 70.

11. *Eclogues*, 1, ll. 59–62; trans. E. V. Rieu (Penguin, Harmondsworth, 1954), p. 25.

12. Swift to Pope, 29 Sept. 1725, in *The Correspondence of Jonathan Swift*, 3 (Oxford, 1963), 103.

13. See, e.g., Ronald Syme, *The Roman Revolution* (Oxford, 1939; ed. 1971), pp. 467–68; Richard Lanham, *Motives of Eloquence* (New Haven, 1976), pp. 48–64.

14. For a somewhat different view of metamorphosis in Pope, see Ralph Cohen, "Transformation in *The Rape of the Lock*," *ECS*, 2 (1969), 205–24.

15. The text says that she calls Father Thames and Diana for help; they cannot help her (she has strayed beyond Diana's precincts). But, it is implied, Diana *can* save her by this transformation.

16. For this conventional analogy, embodied most pertinently by Dryden in poems running from *To Dr. Charlton* to *Mac Flecknoe* and *Absalom and Achitophel*, see Wasserman, *The Subtler Language* (Baltimore, 1959).

17. See Addison's "Essay on the Georgics."

18. Nicolson, *Mountain Gloom and Mountain Glory* (New York, 1959), p. 30.

19. Pope draws upon Polyphemus's lament in Theocritus's eleventh idyll, upon which he also drew for the "Summer" pastoral (both of which were also dedicated to physicians).

20. In one of his *Spectator* papers, Steele had introduced the subject of an Ugly Club, the group that meets to celebrate its members' deformities, including a prominent "Pair of Shoulders." The point, Steele advises, is to be like Paul Scarron, "as merry upon himself, as others are apt to be." Steele also introduces a Merry Club for large mouths, celebrating his own "deformity." (See *Spectator* No. 17 [20 Mar. 1711] and others following, especially No. 32, which mentions Alexander the Great, as Pope does in *Arbuthnot*; Pope also refers to Scarron.)

21. See Maynard Mack, *Alexander Pope: A Life* (New Haven, 1985).

22. *Guardian* No. 40, pp. 160–65.

23. See Wasserman, "The Limits of Allusion in *The Rape of the Lock*," *Journal of English and Germanic Philology*, 65 (1966), 415–44.

24. The Baron's speech about his conquering steel is a less direct version of Clarissa's passage about time: it is after all Time that will "strike to Dust th' Imperial Tow'rs of Troy," and his scissors evokes the Three Sisters as his term "steel" covers a scythe as well as a scissors or sword.

25. Erskine-Hill, "Alexander Pope: The Political Poet in His Time," *ECS*, 15 (1981–82), 130–31. For the prominence of Jacobitism, see, e.g., J.C.D. Clark, *Revolution and Rebellion: State and Society in England in the Seventeenth and Eighteenth Centuries* (Cambridge, 1986), passim., and bibliography, pp. 174–77.

26. This sequence may be thought to correspond in a general way to Mack's scenario for the Popean persona: the ingenu is transformed by contact with the world first into a *vir bonus* who can see and ironically comment and finally, when the stimulus is too outrageous, into a heroic chastiser of evil. (See "The Muse of Satire," *Yale Review*, 41 [1951], 80–92.)

27. Maynard Mack, *The Garden and the City* (Toronto, 1969), p. 177.

28. See G. K. Hunter, "The 'Romanticism' of Pope's Horace," *Essays in Criticism*, 10 (1960), 390–414.

29. For a very interesting essay on Pope's *Bathurst* in terms of an intertwining of different "discourses," see John Barrell and Harriet Guest, "On the Use of Contraction: Economics and Morality in the Eighteenth-Century Long Poem," in *The New 18th Century: Theory, Politics, English Literature*, ed. Felicity Nussbaum and Laura Brown (New York, 1987), pp. 121–43.

30. *Twickenham Pope*, 6.376.

[from "Pope and the Hidden God"]

In Alexander Pope, the young man of twenty-four, we can see immortalizing longings of the same kerygmatic type that gripped Dryden. The "Advertisement" to Pope's *Messiah* (1712) clearly describes his desire to invoke the heraldic powers of both Augustan Rome and biblical Jerusalem. His inspiration came, he tells us, from "reading several passages of the Prophet *Isaiah*, which foretell the coming of Christ and the felicities attending it," and then observing "a remarkable parity between many of the thoughts, and those in the *Pollio* of *Virgil*."[1] The poem, which is indeed a blend of Isaiah and Virgil, constitutes a fleshless but spirited exercise in the reconstructive paradigm of proclamatory verse:

> The Seas shall waste; the Skies in Smoke decay;
> Rocks fall to Dust, and Mountains melt away;
> But fix'd *His* Word, *His* saving Pow'r remains:
> Thy *Realm* for ever lasts! thy own *Messiah* reigns!
> (ll. 105–08)

WINDSOR-FOREST

But Pope's access to a mandate for public proclamation was severely limited.[2] In the opening of *Windsor-Forest* (1713) we observe a poet embarked on a graceful but somewhat desperate circumnavigation toward the harbor of regal authority:

> Thy forests, *Windsor!* and thy green Retreats,
> At once the Monarch's and the Muse's Seats,
> Invite my Lays. Be present, Sylvan Maids!
> Unlock your Springs, and open all your Shades.
> *Granville* commands: Your Aid O Muses bring!

Sanford Budick, "Pope and the Hidden God." Reprinted from *Poetry of Civilization: Mythopoeic Displacement in the verse of Milton, Dryden, Pope, and Johnson.* Published by Yale University Press. Copyright © 1974 by Yale University.

> What Muse for *Granville* can refuse to sing?

The forest represents a point of incorporation where poet and monarch have traditionally been located together. But Pope's muse cannot possibly pretend to any proximate affiliation with the queen. Instead he finds his access to Anne's investitive commands through Granville, who is quickly named twice and whom the queen had just created one of twelve new peers who made possible the Peace of Utrecht, itself the occasion of the poem's publication. Granville thus becomes more than a metaphor for the monarch. In the poem, he is her surrogate.

When the poet speaks "for" Granville, he not only grants a request; he also speaks through the peer's own mind and voice and, by suggestion, through the mind and voice of the monarch (in somewhat the same way Dryden did for Charles II near the close of *Absalom and Achitophel*). It is this system of subrogation that gives Pope's poem authority. The same procedure, in reverse, is used at the end, to depart the poem and to seal its public integrity—in effect, to dislocate it from any mere private authorship. The poet draws in the reins of his inspired muse:

> Here cease thy Flight, nor with unhallow'd Lays
> Touch the fair Fame of *Albion*'s Golden Days.
> The Thoughts of Gods let *Granville*'s Verse recite,
> And bring the Scenes of opening Fate to Light.
> My humble Muse, in unambitious Strains,
> Paints the green Forests and the flow'ry Plains.
> (ll. 423–28)

The distinction between hallow'd flight and unambitious strains is not - flattering fiction. It points to the magic circle of public poetry in which poet and monarch can only conjure jointly. In important ways the poem itself has been Granville's verse; and Granville, in turn, recites the thoughts of gods— kings, "our earthly Gods" (l. 230). In Granville's echoing words (perhaps most concretely in his participation in the talks that negotiated the peace) we see the word become action. His words help bring fate to fruition, in addition to making the fateful effects known. In this, he and the poet reenact the god-like creativity of the monarch who had decided to end the chaotic "Series of Intestine Wars" (l. 325):

> At length great ANNA said—Let Discord cease!
> She said, the World obey'd, and all was *Peace*!
> (ll. 327–28)

In Granville, himself a muse represented by a muse, the lines of force of "earthly Gods" and "God-like Poets" (l. 270) are brought together. Through him the implicit promise of the poem's opening couplet—to relocate in Windsor's green retreats the monarch's near the muse's seats—can be fulfilled:

> 'Tis yours, my Lord, to bless our soft Retreats,
> And call the Muses to their ancient Seats.
>
> (ll. 283–84)

In Granville we find compacted an avatar of the poet-statesman-king.

The methods of subrogation that make all this possible are themselves modulations of a larger principle of displacement which receives more extensive application in the poem's theme of violence sublimated. In Pope's ultimate vision of the Golden Age, we recall, there is no Edenic immunity to discord. Dangerous energies are only imprisoned and directed to higher ends:

> The shady Empire shall retain no Trace
> Of War or Blood, but in the Sylvan Chace,
> The Trumpets sleep, while chearful Horns are blown,
> And Arms employ'd on Birds and Beasts alone.
>
> . . . .
>
> Behold! *Augusta*'s glitt'ring Spires increase,
> And Temples rise, the beauteous Works of Peace.
>
> (ll. 371–78)

> In Brazen Bonds shall barb'rous *Discord* dwell:
> Gigantick *Pride*, pale *Terror*, gloomy *Care*,
> And mad *Ambition*, shall attend her there.
>
> . . . .
>
> There *Faction* roar, *Rebellion* bite her Chain,
> And gasping Furies thirst for Blood in vain.
>
> (ll. 414–22)

This is how Albion's Golden Days are ushered in. The principle of displacement, writ little and writ large, controls and explains a good deal that is happening in *Windsor-Forest*, and it may ultimately help us to reach the unlocked spring or deepest meaning of the poem.

The oaks of Windsor Forest, for example, serve in the poem as a vehicle of removal and, at the same time, absorption, of poetical trans-portation. Early on we hear,

> Let *India* boast her Plants, nor envy we
> The weeping Amber or the balmy Tree,
> While by our Oaks the precious Loads are born,
> And Realms commanded which those Trees adorn.
>
> (ll. 29–32)

And later, Father Thames informs the forest that it is only by being themselves displaced that her oaks are fulfill their charge:

> Thy Trees, fair *Windsor*! now shall leave their Woods,
> And half thy Forests rush into my Floods,
> Bear *Britain's* Thunder, and her Cross display,
> To the bright Regions of the rising Day;
>
> . . . .
>
> For me the Balm shall bleed, and Amber flow,
> The Coral redden, and the Ruby glow.
>
> (ll. 385–94)

It is no small mark of Pope's intensely decorous art that the image of the oaks here elaborated is itself borrowed, or, more precisely, displaced, from a Golden Age vision—that of Virgil's *Pollio*, now revisited—which Pope had come to regard as overstated. The "stubborn oak shall distil dewy honey," Virgil prophesied, and "every land shall bear all fruits." As Aubrey Williams has noted, now Pope was only willing to imagine a Golden Age in which, after the manner of the *Georgics*, peace and perfection are joined to industry and toil, and in which Mantua is to be planted with Palestinian palms.[3] One can, perhaps, never fix with confidence the limits of Pope's allusions, but here we know that we are not merely playing with words when we say that the displacement capacity of Pope's oaks is comprised, to a considerable extent, of the displacement, with Virgil's aid, of sanctified Virgilian mythic materials.

Similarly, Pope's vision of a time to come,

> when free as Seas or Wind
> Unbounded *Thames* shall flow for all Mankind,
> Whole Nations enter with each swelling Tyde,
> And Seas but joint the Regions they divide;
> Earth's distant Ends our Glory shall behold,
> And the new World launch forth to seek the Old,
>
> (ll. 397–402)

is itself, as Maynard Mack has noted, a version, "with a difference," of Isaiah's prophesied exaltation of Jerusalem:[4]

> the Gentiles shall come to thy light, and kings to the brightness of thy rising. . . . Then thou shalt see, and flow together, and thine heart shall fear, and be enlarged; because the abundance of the sea shall be converted unto thee, the forces of the Gentiles shall come unto thee. . . . Therefore thy gates shall be open continually.
>
> Isa. 60: 3–11

The difference consists in a redefinition of "the Gentiles" and in the redirection of the converting sea. In our terms, it represents a displacement of the old Jerusalem by the new and, indeed, of God's Old Testament by his New.

One more example will, I hope, round off our brief survey of the poem's localized displacement procedures and, at the same time, lead us back to our discussion of its broader movements. Here I would like to try to extend, in another direction, Professor Mack's admirable defense of the following much-maligned couplet:[5]

> See *Pan* with Flocks, with Fruits *Pomona* crown'd,
> Here blushing *Flora* paints th'enamel'd Ground.
> (ll. 37–38)

The lines qualify for substantial appreciation along the lines of our present argument. One detractor, we may recall, sneered that "Pope would probably have defended these lines by remarking that every word in them of any significance . . . is to be found in descriptive passages of Milton. To which the answer would be: Precisely so; they are Milton's words and you have done nothing to make them your own."[6] It is not unlikely that part of Pope's defense (had he cared to make one) would have been very similar to the words hypothesized for him. *Windsor-Forest*, after all, virtually begins with sighing admiration for Milton's *Paradise Lost*:

> The Groves of *Eden*, vanish'd now so long,
> Live in Description, and look green in Song:
> *These*, were my Breast inspir'd with equal Flame,
> Like them in Beauty, should be like in Fame.
> (ll. 7–10)

Pope was not trying to keep his emulation a secret. But before we decide that Pope has done nothing to make, say, Pan and Pomona his own, we should consider carefully what Pope (or any other writer going to *Paradise Lost* for literary models) would have observed when he went to see how Milton made Pan and Pomona *his* own.

We are not surprised to find that these two figures, at least, appear in *Paradise Lost* as prime examples of Milton's own displacement techniques. The image of Adam and Eve's abode is lodged in our minds by the devaluation of a pagan mythological one:

> In shadier Bower
> More sacred and sequester'd, though but feign'd,
> *Pan* . . . never slept. . . .
> (4.705–07)

> to the Silvan Lodge
> They came, that like *Pomona's* Arbor smil'd
> With flow'rets deck't and fragrant smells; but *Eve*
> Undeckt, save with herself more lovely fair
> Than Wood-Nymph, or the fairest Goddess feign'd.
> (5.378–81)

In the same connection Pope would probably not have failed to notice that Milton compares Eve to Flora only once—as she appears to Adam after Satan has infused his dream into her (5.16)—and that the only other time she is compared to Pomona (to be degraded to terms of equality with her) occurs at the climactic moment when Eve, much against Adam's premonition, withdraws her hand from his "like a Wood-Nymph light" (9.386):

> To *Pales*, or *Pomona*, thus adorn'd,
> Likest she seem'd, *Pomona* when she fled
> *Vertumnus*, or to *Ceres* in her Prime,
> Yet Virgin of *Prosperpina* from Jove.
> (9.393–96)

In *Paradise Lost*, as we see here and as we have seen before, Milton makes his pagan deities his own by disposing his pantheon in a very special light. Olympus itself became for Milton a mere fiber in the fabric of displacement, one more exemplifying image of degenerated mythic truth and power: when "Jove usurping reign'd," the displaced gods on "cold Olympus rul'd the middle Air / Their highest Heav'n" (1.514–17); the poet's muse is "Nor of the Muses nine, nor on the top / Of old Olympus . . . but Heav'nly born" (7.6–7); "wide / Encroaching *Eve*," some fable, "had first the rule / Of high Olympus, thence by Saturn driv'n" (10.580–83). In all this, Olympus is an image or suggestion of power gained by, and yielded to, displacement. So it is in *Windsor-Forest*, where Olympus and the goddesses are made Pope's own in much the same way, but with a very different result. When we read the passage in which our maligned couplet occurs, we must not forget that the controlling word is *not*:

> Not proud *Olympus* yields a nobler Sight,
> Tho' Gods assembled grace his tow'ring Height,
> Than what more humble Mountains offer here,
> Where, in their Blessings, all those Gods appear.
> See *Pan* with Flocks, with Fruits *Pomona* crown'd,
> Here blushing *Flora* paints th' enamel'd Ground,
> Here *Ceres*' Gifts in waving Prospect stand,
> And nodding tempt the joyful Reaper's Hand,
> Rich Industry sits smiling on the Plains,
> And Peace and Plenty tell, a STUART reigns.
> (ll. 33–42)

Paradoxically, Olympus is made to *yield* to our imagination what she cannot offer our sight. Olympus gives place to more humble but greater mountains.

> *Jove*, subdu'd by mortal Passion still,
> Might change *Olympus* for a nobler Hill,
> (ll. 233–34)

just as the vainglorious mountains of ancients and idolaters are displaced by the holy mountains of *Paradise Lost*. The Stuart monarch assimilates the dislocated mythic substance of Pan and Pomona, Flora and Ceres. Queen Anne is replete with power, they are an emptied dream.

It may be that we reach an essential point of understanding about *Windsor-Forest* when we realize that, though Anne is here presented as analogous to Eve, she also bears something of the same relation to her as she does to the pagan deities: the comparison of Anne with Eve is inevitable and even implicit in the use of the Miltonic language. But Pope's image of a controlling, reigning sovereign, who oversees toilsome industry and far-flung commerce, who must carefully manage her nation's stores so that plenty can be preserved, and who harmonizes the forces of discord into a loud chord of "Peace!" is not the image of an Eve home on her hill in Eden. The peace of *Windsor-Forest* is only (to use Clausewitz's term) *Waffenstillstand*. Windsor-Forest / England cannot be Eden, Pope tells us. To say that it can, or should be, is to distort reality and to constrict the potentialities of the future. This is a subtle but crucial part of the poem's Tory reflection on the Whiggish naïveté that obscures the massive truth embedded in *Paradise Lost*.[7]

It is the effort to return to this encased vision that is reflected by the syntax of polite rejection and declination, which in turn shapes the poet's invocation of *Paradise Lost*: "These, were my Breast inspir'd with equal Flame, / Like them in Beauty, should be like in Fame" (ll. 9–10). Taken in the context of the poet's obvious abilities in the idyllic strain, the lines are in many ways comparable to Horace's paradoxical recusatio to identify himself totally with an accepted epos: magnificent epic description must somehow be joined to "si quantum cuperem possem quoque" (*Ep*.2.1.257). In much the same way as, in the pantheon passage, the word *not* controls and qualifies the series of mythological allusions that follow it, the poet's rhetorical hedge forces us to discriminate the non-Edenic features of a description that might otherwise seem a veritable snapshot of paradise before Satan's first visit:

> Here Hills and Vales, the Woodland and the Plain,
> Here Earth and Water seem to strive again,
> Not *Chaos*-like together crush'd and bruis'd,
> But as the World, harmoniously confus'd:
> Where Order in Variety we see,
> And where, tho' all things differ, all agree.

> Here waving Groves a checquer'd Scene display,
> And part admit and part exclude the Day;
> As some coy Nymph her Lover's warm Address
> Nor quite indulges, nor can quite repress.
>
> (ll. 11–20)

In spite of the invocation of the model of *Paradise Lost*, and in spite of the fact that Windsor Forest and Eden are both contrasted to Chaos, the poet insists on the continuity of his vision with the postlapsarian condition of the world. He cannot wish away the universal evidences of strife, confusion, dissension, sexual coyness, and sexual repression which, even if they are constrained to a *concordia discors*, are signs of an essential difference between man within and without the Eastern Gate.

The poet of *Windsor-Forest* calls upon *Paradise Lost* because it contains the English, Christian version of the massive myth he wishes to make new. It is a myth which, like the one retold in Plato's *Politicus*, not only describes a creative, ordered condition of human existence, but also intimates the successor myths of reversal and displacement and, ultimately, of reenstatement by inspired, just men—ideal preacher-*politici*. All this, Pope invokes and reenacts in his own mythic structure. A version of the Edenic age gives way to a version of Milton's age of Nimrod, a perversion of man's heroic impulses:

> Proud *Nimrod* first the bloody Chace began,
> A mighty Hunter, and his Prey was Man.
>
> (ll. 61–62)

This, in turn, is converted into peace by the talisman of poet-Granville-Anne. But, as we saw earlier, it is a distinctly sublimated state, a half-illuminated "shady Empire" where war and blood are still to be seen in "the Sylvan Chace" (ll. 371–72) and where rebellion is chained but not extinguished (cf. l. 421).

The vision of perfectibility presented in *Windsor-Forest* is, in fact, a reversal of the terms of regeneration envisioned in *Paradise Lost*: now man is encouraged to cultivate and exploit his materialistic nature rather than to alter it; the trajectory of man's expulsion from Eden becomes the route to a demiparadise of controlled commercialism. This is Milton's vision displaced, his Paradise removed. It is this mythopoeic transportation, symbolized by the genius of England's industry and shipping, which is perhaps suggested in the "secret Transport" which "touch'd the conscious Swain": "Fair *Liberty*, *Britannia*'s Goddess rears / Her chearful Head, and leads the golden Years" (ll. 90–92). This is how Pope unlocks the massive, secret spring of Christian liberty Milton had recreated. This is the poet's act of demythological recovery: "Of ancient Writ [he] unlocks the learned Store, / Consults the Dead, and lives past Ages o'er" (ll. 247–48). Britannia's goddess Liberty is also "Britannia's Standard" of liberation (l. 110):

> Oh stretch thy Reign, fair *Peace*! from Shore to Shore,
> Till Conquest cease, and Slav'ry be no more:
> Till the freed *Indians* in their native Groves
> Reap their own Fruits, and woo their Sable Loves.
>
> (ll. 407–10)

It is in the process of opening all the "Shades" of Windsor/England (cf. l. 4), of insisting on the moral realism involved in imagining and creating his "shady Empire" as distinct from an unattainable Eden, that the poet has made available once more the unaltered source of Liberty (with all its attendant promises and dreams) enshrined in *Paradise Lost*.

In Milton's poem, we recall, the last vestige of paradise is dislodged by the great flood:

> then shall this Mount
> Of Paradise by might of Waves be mov'd
> Out of his place, push'd by the horned flood,
> With all his verdure spoil'd, and Trees adrift
> Down the great River to the op'ning Gulf,
> And there take root an Island salt and bare.
>
> (ll. 829–34)

It was in this locus of displacement that Milton, we suggested, may have found his own prophetic hill on his own real or figurative island. In *Windsor-Forest* the outflowing and displacement of demi-Eden are assigned a reversed meaning. In language remarkably similar to Milton's, postlapsarian man is here called upon to abandon the ideal of an insular paragon and to channel his fallen impulses into the pursuit of a sublimated postlapsarian ideal. Great River Thames, with his "shining Horns" (l. 332), looks forward to a golden age of transport:

> Thy Trees, fair *Windsor*! . . . shall leave their Woods,
> And half they Forests rush into my Floods,
>   Bear *Britain's* Thunder, and her Cross display,
> To the bright Regions of the rising Day;
>
> . . . .
>
> For me the Balm shall bleed, and Amber flow,
> The Coral redden, and the Ruby glow.
>
> (ll. 385–94)

Here we must extend our appreciation of Pope's imperial allusiveness by recalling that Milton sets his own trees adrift from Eden's "Groves whose rich Trees wept odorous Gums and Balm" (*P.L.*, 4.248). Pope's importation of "The weeping Amber or the balmy Tree" (l. 30) is itself one part of his emulation of Milton's displacement procedures. The emulation itself, a statement of displacement, gives rise to a significantly different Golden Age from that imagined by the poet of *Paradise Lost*. It is a vision of straitened, middle-state man, ambitious only of that to which postdeluvian creatures can realistically attain:

> My humble Muse, in unambitious Strains,
> Paints the green Forests and the flow'ry Plains,
> Where Peace descending bids her Olives spring,
> And scatters Blessings from her Dove-like Wing.
> (ll. 427–30)

In the last four lines of the poem, Pope's editors have observed, he followed the model of Virgil in returning to his own beginnings.[8] As Virgil ended the *Georgics* with the opening of the *Eclogues*, so Pope's closing couplets echo the first lines of *Spring*:

> First in these Fields I try the Sylvan Strains,
> Nor blush to sport on *Windsor*'s blissful Plains:
> Fair *Thames* flow gently from thy sacred Spring,
> While on thy Banks *Sicilian* Muses sing.
> (ll. 1–4)

In the close of *Windsor-Forest*, we should add, the Virgilian convention is observed, even while the genius of the place is no longer Sicilian or Roman, but English:

> Ev'n I more sweetly pass my careless Days,
> Pleas'd in the silent Shade with empty Praise;
> Enough for me, that to the listening Swains
> First in these Fields I sung the Sylvan Strains.
> (ll. 431–34)

The poet subtly asserts his own poetic liberty, his own self-sufficiency and independence, in his own return to beginnings. His beginning fields, his poetic locus, we come to recognize, are a version of Milton's removed island, of Eden displaced or redisplaced.

THE "THRONE USURPED"

But we may suspect that even in 1713 Pope's faith in the myth of English monarchical power as a cause sufficient for an Augustan utopia was far less than complete. In the very next year, in *The Rape of the Lock*, canto 3, he was exploding the dignity of Queen Anne:

> Here Thou, Great *Anna!* whom three Realms obey,
> Dost sometimes Counsel take—and sometimes *Tea*.
>
> (ll. 7–8)

Instead of the Queen's mythical power to create order with a word, we are treated to Belinda's horrific bandying of the divine Logos: *"Let Spades be Trumps!* she said, and Trumps they were" (l. 46). As the era of the Georges lengthened out its dull tenure, Pope despaired more and more of basing the authority of his public voice on a mutual dependency of throne and poet. As Maynard Mack has said,

> The time was past when any serious writer could find his place to stand beside the throne. Dryden had managed this, and in his finest poems speaks as if the establishment, with the monarchy its center, spoke through him—the last principle of order in a disintegrating world. But for Pope, after the death of Anne, the throne as center of the dream of the civilized community has become absurd. What he gives us instead, in various versions, is intimations of a throne usurped, or a throne occupied by shadows. . . .
>
> Dryden's angle of vision was no longer available to a serious poet, but there was a possible alternative. . . . Though the throne is empty, there remains an alternative center, and a power of a different kind: the poet-king-philosopher in his grotto, midway between the garden and the river.[9]

Pope's innovative imitation of the First Epistle of the Second Book of Horace, *To Augustus*, creates a tone of cynicism toward the king that is striking in its bitterness, especially on the score of George's neglect of the poet-king relationship and, therefore, of the heraldic office:

> Yet think great Sir! (so many Virtues shown)
> Ah think, what Poet best may make them known?
>
>   . . . .
>
> How barb'rous rage subsided at your word,
> And Nations wonder'd while they dropp'd the sword!
> How, when you nodded, o'er the land and deep,
> Peace stole her wing, and wrapt the world in sleep;
>
>   . . . .
>
> But Verse alas! your Majesty disdains;
> And I'm not used to Panegyric strains:
>
>   . . . .
>
> "Praise undeserv'd is scandal in disguise:"
> Well may he blush, who gives it, or receives;
> And when I flatter, let my dirty leaves
> (Like Journals, Odes, and such forgotten things

> As Eusden, Philips, Settle, writ of Kings)
> Cloath spice, line trunks, or flutt'ring in a row,
> Belfringe the rails of Bedlam and Sohoe.
>
> (ll. 376–419)

Brower has remarked that the "Augustan twilight"—"the failure of the Tories, the disappointments of Pope and his friends, the death of the men who had created the brief illusion of a new literature and a new culture"—becomes, in Pope's later poetry, "a timeless image of decline and fall."[10] But we must emphasize that the authority of Pope's later voice, proclaiming, in straightforward or inverted terms, the order of a regenerate society, does not partake of that decline. Pope did not give up. His poetry is the drama of a private man in search of a public authority: George II, Pope implies, derives his kingly image from the likes of Settle; as a result, the supposed king and the supposed poet confirm each other in their lack of true office. In the process of demolishing the myth of George's Augustanism, Pope makes available the convertible bricks and beams of a new myth of poetic authority; he becomes the spokesman for a higher secular power. This process and authority are implied in *To Augustus*. They become explicit in the two coordinated dialogues that make up the *Epilogue to the Satires* (1738).[11]

The central question of the *Epilogue* is raised early in the first dialogue:

> 'Who's the Man, so near
> His Prince, that writes in Verse, and has his Ear?'
>
> (l. 45–46)

Where, in other words, is the authorized herald of England's cultural integrity? The *Epilogue* opens with a suggestion from the imaginary interlocutor to the poet: your poetry plagiarizes Horace anyway; why don't you adopt his moderation, please the crown, and thereby win the place that Horace enjoyed?

> 'Tis all from *Horace*: *Horace* long before ye
> Said, "Tories call'd him Whig, and Whigs a Tory."
> . . . .
>   But *Horace*, Sir, was delicate, was nice;
> *Bubo* observes, he lash'd no sort of *Vice*:
> . . . .
> His sly, polite, insinuating stile
> Could please at Court, and make AUGUSTUS smile.
>
> (1. 7–20)

The poet rejects this suggestion, and in doing so he also rejects the Augustan solution to the problem of the poet's public authority. The established power of a corrupt Augustus cannot distribute the heraldic office. To delude himself on this point would be to default on his vision of the poet's highest responsibility. Sarcastically, therefore, he apologizes for his adolescent constancy to the ideal:

> Dear Sir, forgive the Prejudice of Youth:
> Adieu Distinction, Satire, Warmth, and Truth!
> (1. 63–64)

If he could accept the position of George's herald, all his problems would be solved:

> Then might I sing without the least Offence,
> And all I sung should be the *Nation's Sense*:
> Or teach the melancholy Muse to mourn,
> Hang the sad Verse on CAROLINA's Urn,
> And hail her passage to the Realms of Rest,
> All Parts perform'd, and *all* her Children blest!
> (1. 77–82)

But this cannot be. In the final analysis, the moral authority the king confers on the poet derives from virtue, and

> *Virtue* may chuse the high or low Degree,
> . . . .
> Dwell in a Monk, or light upon a King.
> (1. 137–39)

The poet suggests that the king, in the present situation, does not have this authority. Pope does not wish to destroy the office of the herald, but he does want to change the source of its power. The king is dead; as the first dialogue ends, we find that he has given his substance to the false herald of the powers of vice:

> hers the Gospel is, and hers the Laws:
> . . . .
> Lo! at the Wheels of her Triumphal Car,
> Old *England*'s Genius, rough with many a Scar.
> . . . .
> Hear her black Trumpet thro' the Land proclaim,
> That "Not to be corrupted is the Shame."
> (1. 148–60)

In the second dialogue of the *Epilogue* the black myth is razed by the poet himself and "Old England's Genius" (which is akin, perhaps, to what Dryden called Juvenal's "commonwealth genius") is explicitly restored.

Pope solves his problem by asserting his heraldic relation to a legitimate power, established by virtue, which has been displaced by the court of the degenerate Augustus. He will be the poet of a shadow authority that is pristinely Roman and Greek. He wil create its empire, or "court," in *his words*:

> . . . does the Court a worthy Man remove?
> That instant, I declare, he has my Love:
> I shun his Zenith, court his mild Decline;
> Thus SOMMERS once, and HALIFAX were mine.
> . . . .
> How can I PULT'NEY, CHESTERFIELD forget,
> While *Roman* Spirit charms, and *Attic* Wit:
> . . . .
> Or WYNDHAM, just to Freedom and the Throne,
> The Master of our Passions, and his own.
> (2. 74–89)

It is these men, and the power they represent, whom Pope serves as anointing poet. He will not perform his offices for anyone less. The rabble, it follows,

> may be hang'd, but not be crown'd.
> Enough for half the Greatest of these days
> To 'scape my Censure, not expect my Praise:
> Are they not rich? what more can they pretend?
> Dare they to hope a Poet for their Friend?
> What RICHELIEU wanted, LOUIS scarce could gain,
> And what young AMMON wish'd, but wish'd in vain.
> (2. 111–17)

Through his relationship to men like "All-accomplish'd St. JOHN" (2. 139), he shows himself a "Friend to ev'ry worthy mind" and can therefore speak as collective Man, who feels "for all mankind" (2. 203–04). Nor should we doubt, the poet proudly informs us, that proclamation thus derived has ample power:

> Yes, I am proud; I must be proud to see
> Men are not afraid of God, afraid of me:
> Safe from the Bar, the Pulpit, and the Throne,
> Yet touch'd and sham'd by *Ridicule* alone.
> (2. 208–11)

The poet's ridicule is the weapon that demolishes the false proclamation of the false king's false heralds:

> Ye tinsel Insects! whom a Court maintains,
> That counts your Beauties only by your Stains,

> Spin all your Cobwebs o'er the Eye of Day!
> The Muse's wing shall brush you all away:
> All his Grace preaches, all his Lordship sings,
> All that makes Saints of Queens, and Gods of Kings.
> . . . .
> Not *Waller*'s Wreath can hide the Nation's Scar,
> Nor *Boileau* turn the Feather to a Star.
>
> (2. 220–31)

Pope declares the dignity and efficacy of his public voice in terms of the full mythic glory of the prophet-herald:

> O sacred Weapon! left for Truth's defence,
> Sole Dread of Folly, Vice, and Insolence!
> To all but Heav'n-directed hands deny'd,
> The Muse may give thee, but the Gods must guide.
> Rev'rent I touch thee! but with honest zeal;
> To rowze the Watchmen of the Publick Weal.
>
> (2. 212–17)

His office does not rely on dead mythologies of kingship, though it derives "divine right" from its constituent myths. Chaining the monster results in an immense harnessing of cultural energy:

> Let Envy howl while Heav'n's whole Chorus sings,
> And bark at Honour not confer'd by Kings;
> . . . .
> Truth guards the Poet, sanctifies the line,
> And makes Immortal, Verse as mean as mine.
>
> (2. 242–17)

As we have seen in other examples of this mythopoetic mode, the herald's claim to authority is one with his kerygma. In his voice the mythic essence of English power and virtue is finally restored, though the restoration has tragic overtones. We must be careful not to mistake tragedy for despair.

Notes

1. Citations from Pope's works are to *The Twickenham Edition of the Poems of Alexander Pope*, ed. John Butt et al. (New Haven, 1939–69), hereafter referred to as *TE*. The "Advertisement" first appeared in 1717.

2. In *The Garden and the City: Retirement and Politics in the Later Poetry of Pope, 1731–1743* (Toronto, 1969), Maynard Mack has explained how the Pope of the 1730s "drew about him publicly [the] almost seamless garment formed of ancient Rome and Twickenham and seventeenth-century retirement precedents, which signalized the posture of the honest satirist

protesting a corrupt society" (p. 193). My discussion throughout this chapter is heavily indebted to Mack's study.

3. See Aubrey Williams, *TE*, 1: 137 and Mack, *The Garden and the City*, p. 39.

4. "On Reading Pope," *College English* 7 (1946): 268.

5. Ibid., pp. 264 ff. For Mack's most recent comments on these lines, see *The Garden and the City*, pp. 94–95.

6. Bernard Groom's comment ("Some Kinds of Poetic Diction," *Essays and Studies by Members of the English Association*, 15 [1929]: 149), cited and answered by Mack, "On Reading Pope," pp. 264 ff. Don Cameron Allen, *Mysteriously Meant: The Rediscovery of Pagan Symbolism and Allegorical Interpretation in the Renaissance* (Baltimore, 1970), pp. 292 ff., discusses Milton's allusions to Pomona.

7. For a discussion of Pope's effort "to turn the tables" on "the traditional Whiggish hatred of the Normans," see Earl R. Wasserman, *The Subtler Language: Critical Readings of Neoclassic and Romantic Poems* (Baltimore, 1959), pp. 114 ff.

8. See *TE*, 1: 194.

9. *The Garden and the City*, pp. 234–36.

10. *Alexander Pope: The Poetry of Allusion* (Oxford, 1959), p. 318.

11. The reader is referred to Mack, *The Garden and the City*, pp. 120 ff., for a description of the political and topical referents of the dialogues.

[from "The Self-Regarding 'I' and the Egotistical Sublime"]

WALLACE JACKSON

Subjectivism seems to originate as a reaction to institutions no longer doing their job. This explanation has been frequently offered to account for the emergence of what was at one time called "preromanticism." And we have seen Pope's poetry warn over and again of the consequences when the sacred is displaced in favor of the merely visionary, a function of the expansionist ego, the sublimity of the "I," as Pope rightly recognized. Such is the essence of the Satanic temptation, the promised promotion of the self in the scheme of things. But what happens when Pope comes to regard himself, when he occupies the center of his own stage, and becomes his own subject? This is the question that interests me here, and it requires some extended attention to three poems commonly defined as Horatian imitations. Most scholars concerned with *Horace, Imitated* have noticed that the various poems offer "a much more central concern with the role of the poet and a clear sense of the poet in *propria persona.*" Yet their incipience is not uncharacteristically referred to a *jeu d'esprit,* a "relaxation from the greater moral seriousness demanded by the *opus magnum.*"[1]

Are we to give credence to the idea that these works arise from Boling-broke's hint to Pope, or would we be better advised to look for their importance in relation to concerns already defined in these pages? Insofar as the *First Satire of the Second Book,* the *Epistle to Arbuthnot,* and the *First Epistle of the First Book* turn Pope's vision upon himself—and the poetic act itself—they set before the reader a definition of the poet and the man. They seem, that is, to be the glass in which Pope regards himself in a manner appropriate both to his personal identity and to his vocation as poet. And as this is so, his poetry moves within concentric circles almost simultaneously constructed. The *Essay on Man* is an exploration of generic identity; the *Epistles to Several Persons* inquires into the behavior of particular men and women in the world; and the *Imitations* serve to permit the satirist to observe himself. Nowhere in Pope's work is the social function of the satirist's role better or even as well set forth. If we think of his poetry in the terms I have just been suggesting, we see that the *Imitations* complete a process in the observation of humankind extending from man's relation to the divine to one man's special notice of himself. These poems seem to leap from his pen in the early and middle years of the 1730s, the most sustainedly productive years of his life, and the types of the *vir bonus*, Bolingbroke, Bathurst, Oxford, the Man of Ross, yield now to Pope himself.

The three poems in particular that I have specified clarify Pope as poet and as man, incorporating him therefore within a context of other lives and other performances. Obviously, the *Imitations* provided him with various opportunities: for political and social commentary, for a direct engagement with contemporary life. The *Imitations* offer something more, noted by Griffin as the possibility of seeing the self "more fully . . . in the presence of the antiself."[2] And Griffin plausibly poses Hervey and Walpole as Pope's anti-selves, even as Timon is the opposite of Burlington, Martha the antithesis to Atossa, and Cibber the contrary to Bolingbroke. Such a setting up of self and antiself is a characteristic Popeian strategy, and there is little reason to deny its continuity within the *Imitations*. But my more immediate interest is to suggest the relation between a historical and a personal identity. However flawed Alexander Pope may have been—and have known himself to be—the historical identity of the poet, and his public vocation, are what saved him from himself. These remarks merely signify that I am coming round on my argument from another perspective, and that the *Imitations* offer another justification for the familiar Popeian recourse to the historical context. Over and again, identity has been the complex issue. Who is Belinda or Eloisa and what is the nature of their self-betrayals? What saves us, or does not save us, from ourselves? I find these concerns central to the *Imitations*, to the effort to locate once again the humanist context, the reclaiming historical identity that is a stay against personal misadventure.

To Arbuthnot is therefore a key document, for it is uniquely a poem about Pope and about the vulnerabilities of the man himself. Against this document play the *First Satire of the Second Book* and the *First Epistle of the First Book*; self-preservingly they define the man emergent in his historical role. They imply the immediate practical bearing of the ruling passion as it directs and determines a life, and they demonstrate the historical validity and contextual utility of the satirist's calling. In this regard, Griffin's optimism exceeds my own. He remarks that "the private and public selves may only appear to be antitheti-cal."[3] I think, rather, that we approach a crisis here in Pope's vision of the human estate, and that the nature of this crisis extends beyond the oppositions apparent within one man to embrace the universe of type and antithesis. A Cibber does oppose a Bolingbroke, and the abiding question bears on which of the two will prevail. Because this issue is so central to Pope's imagination, it dictated the creation of both the *Essay on Man* and the *Dunciad*. And, because it is equally vital to his sense of himself, it required another and different forum that the *Imitations* provided. There is consequently a certain heroism evident in these poems, an effort to bring the greater subject down, as it were, to Pope himself, and to leave the issue, as I believe he leaves it, in doubt. Perhaps this is finally why one cannot speak convincingly of Pope's humanist optimism or pessimism. There is too much evidence on both sides of the question, too much historical reality informing that knowing intelligence. And from this line of reasoning I gather further support for the urgencies informing Pope's mythopoeic imagination: the haunting and persistent reality of the Fall not merely as a present condition with which man lives, but as a threat portending another and more disastrous fall.

To preserve the residue of grace that makes the middle kingdom habitable or to lose it entirely are the large-scale polarities of Pope's greater subject. If in the *Imitations* he comes round on himself, it is only to drive the question home. Yet it had been there from the beginning: in Pope's own ambitious candidacy for celebrity evident in the *Temple of Fame*, and in the personal wisdom that leaves him attendant upon the one greater man of the *Essay on Man*. Now, however, the topic shifts slightly, and it is not a question of the divine pattern but of historical patent, of an intelligence seeking to verify its chosen role and assessing the obligations that pertain to it. That this should be his intention here is consistent with Pope's earlier efforts. From the small center of himself that he gives us in *To Arbuthnot* we move outward to the enlarged identity of the guardian poet, the man who merges with his role to be more than he would otherwise be. This effort, I take it, springs from a fundamental habit of mind, which tests the various impulses of the self against its derived ideals, and in turn provides the only legitimacy the self may claim.

What will emerge here is not new to our reading of Pope; it merely refocuses our attentions upon a context compatible with other contexts we have so far explored. Pope's imagination seems never to take eccentric passages, seems never to be deceived by subjects irrelevant to his main design. Because this is so, we should be more wary of the notion currently growing in our scholarship that Pope's chief poetic pattern was in some way broken or aborted. Whatever the fate of the projected *opus magnum*, there is another and larger design within his work that does not suffer the frustrations of intention or execution that supposedly vitiated that program. There is little sense of a radical incompleteness as, say, with Coleridge, equally little evidence that his sources of power fell away, as with Wordsworth. There is, rather, the evidence of steady progression of the sort we now associate with Milton or Blake, but yet seem to deny Pope. In the 1730s, Horace offered him what others had offered him earlier: models for fulfilling the larger design. And if we reflect that he is one of the most assimilative of English poets, there is no question of an alteration of purpose or direction in these works of his last full decade. For Pope, it was always a matter of taking what he needed from a widely diversified literary past to further coherent and complexly compatible goals, to compose his perceptions into the unity that is the very substance of imagination's figure.

The *First Satire of the Second Book* was published in February 1733; it identifies Pope as both guardian of the realm and good friend at Twickenham to those who, like himself, have performed serviceable acts within the state. The satirist's classic complaint is that his verses are received as "too bold," not "complaisant enough," "too rough," or "weak" (2–5). Beat about by various charges, he seeks "Council learned in the Law" (8). Fortescue advises flattery or at least discretion, but the particular terms of Pope's response, following Horace, suggest that satire is both a pleasure and a self-revelation: "In me what Spots (for Spots I have) appear, / Will prove at least the Medium must be clear" (55–56). Thus it is an "impartial Glass" (57), an instrument in which "my Muse intends / Fair to expose myself, my Foes, my Friends" (57–58). Satire is set over and against the law, a reflecting eye that without bias detects folly, an honest judicial medium ensnaring those like Mary Howard, Lady Mary, Walter, and Chartres, rogues normally exempt from effective legal retribution. Under the governance of the muse, satire is a divine gift, the satirist's vocation a dedication, a ruling passion. Horace serves as bardic prototype for Pope, even as Boileau and Dryden figure forth the satirist within kingdoms that respect and protect his role.

Pope's attacks on the various antitheses of the satirist, the libelers Delia and Sappho, the cheats Walter and Chartres, bring forth the clarified form of the poet. Blackmore and Budgell, the unhappy contemporary equivalents of Virgil and Pindar, are rejected as poetic models. Maresca notes that Pope's "lines about Dryden and Boileau (111–14) are based upon Persius's description of the satire of Horace and Lucilius. . . . And shortly before this, in lines 105–6, Pope has echoed Dryden's translation of Juvenal's appeal to the precedent of Lucilius."[4] It is apparent that Pope locates himself within a context of classical and modern satirists in order to elucidate a bardic identity and the tradition to which he now elects to belong. In the *Temple of Fame* he had found four poets in the "Centre of the hallow'd Quire." If in his commitment to the epic tradition he had previously found his model in Homer, he here discovers it in Horace, in those "grave *Epistles*, bringing Vice to light" (151), which are not to be confused with "*Libels* and *Satires!* lawless Things indeed!" (150). The guardian of the realm is thus an exponent and champion of "Virtue" (105), a defender of "Her Cause" (109), and entitled to the protection of church and law. And Pope's obligatory performance is directed against those who "'scape the Laws" (118). Within the misapprehensions that beset his identity and confuse his purpose, he derives a historical weapon superior to the uncertain and tenuous retribution of the law. Fortescue's good-natured exoneration of "grave *Epistles*" is a concession to the lawfulness of satire, but the mockery and ridicule it provokes are above legal jurisdiction ("My Lords the Judges laugh, and you're dismiss'd" [156]).

The devolution of Pope's identity from its public into its private form, in which as retired poet he offers retreat to Bolingbroke and Peterborough, is an expression of the *contemptus mundi* animating the benevolent man. Bolingbroke's restorative "Feast of Reason and . . . Flow of Soul" (128) and Peterborough's orderings of Pope's garden define the self harmonized within its own acts of peace. Guardians of the realm and custodians of the garden, Pope and his friends cultivate an order within the self, a temporary georgic repudiation of strife that is itself an education of communality superior to what the world can offer. Much more emphatically than Horace, Pope turns from the present moment to clarify the resources of the self and to discover its patent in the historical community of satirists and in the contemporary fellowship of men greatly good. The poet poses himself between the world and retirement from it and contemplates the uncertain justice of the former. It is clear that the *type* of the satirist wins his case: in common judgment he may be flatterer or libeler, a discordant creature within the body social; but the long perspective of history vindicates him even beyond what the *adversarius* can grant. The accordant selves, private and public, define him as enlisted in the impartial service of the muse. His satiric performance is thus a persistent manifestation of justice or virtue, his "Glory" a "Moderation" (67) of partisan callings, his identity an "honest Mean" (66), momentarily returning us to the ethical formulas of the *Moral Essays*. The poet as scourge of virtue, bringing vice to light, is yet the occasion for the laughter of good men.

This is the burden of the *First Satire*. The succession of satirists is a grace within time, a visionary profession that mocks human institutions ("Hard Words or Hanging, if your Judge be *Page*"[82]), and speaks in defiance of the poet's particular fate. Pope's poem is of course coupled to its model, but it moves well beyond the limited Horatian context to define a justification of the satirist more personal and more convincing than any other similar statement by him. The poet seeks his freedom and dedication within the urgencies of history, and, obedient to the necessities that have summoned him, he confirms and enacts the prototypical performance. In the final analysis, the antidote to the poisons and corruptions of Delia and Sappho, Walter and Chartres, is the bardic vision of virtue that the presence of evil makes necessary. Pope's argument is a variation of the *Essay*'s derivation of good from ill, an exploration consistent with the bases of his thought, but here employed to explain the urgencies compelling the poet. At the beginning of the satire he asks "Advice" (10) of Fortescue; what he gives in return is an insight into the persistently emergent form of the poet as satirist.

As the satirist's patent is derived historically, his act is a guarantee of historical veracity. Pope does more than glance at this idea in his reference to George II: "And justly Caesar scorns the Poet's Lays, / It is to *History* he trusts for Praise" (35–36). But the satirist's judgment informs history, and the issue focuses on Pope's ironic deployment of "justly." The justice "Caesar" expects is one in which he will be disappointed, for a justice that he scorns is being prepared as decisive. Brower notices that "there is a degree of personal seriousness in Horace that Pope rarely ever reaches in his *Imitations*."[5] Pope's special performance drives the personal into the general and plays off two articulations of justice within time and society. Fortescue's advice ("Better be *Cibber*" [37]) is another bad suggestion, prudent perhaps, but irrelevant to what is the burden of the poem, the emergent identity of the satirist. Pope's immediate response is to cite his ruling passion ("Each Mortal has his Pleasure" [45]), but it is subsequently quite clear that such pleasure involves the correspondent risk of self-revelation: "In me what Spots (for Spots I have) appear." The point is of course that "the Medium must be clear," and again one revelatory medium (satire) is posed against another (law). Satire is thus a grave charge ("Satire's my Weapon, but I'm too discreet / To run a Muck and tilt at all I meet" [67–70]). This is precisely what he will do in the *Epistle to Arbuthnot*, but that poem reverses the terms of the *First Satire* and moves toward a "personal seriousness" exploited by Pope as a personal comedy.

The legitimate power of scribal succession is designed to resolve the discontinuity between the word and the world addressed in the *Temple of Fame*, and thus to constitute a historical continuum acting under the conjoined aegis of church and state. If in the *Essay on Man* nature is the window through which man looks upward to God, satire is the glass in which man looks backward into history, which means, in effect, upon his own image. As in the *Essay*, satire is "Wit's false mirror," now held up not to nature's light, but to history's. In the *Rape of the Lock*, "A heav'nly Image in the Glass appears" (I, 125). In the *First Satire*, satire is an "impartial Glass." Belinda's glass is the instrument by which the "other" is appropriated, animistically embodying those powers she desires and reflectively confirming them. That Belinda "bends" (126) to the glass suggests that her sovereign is the power she has assumed. Pope's glass is impartial; that is, the appropriation of its power carries with it the correspondent risk of self-revelation: "In me what Spots. . . ." This peculiar kind of priesthood confirms the (literally) visionary profession, but entails equally the risk of self-knowledge, meaning that the text in which one reads history is also the text in which one is read. Pope's image forces a reconsideration of the price of power and knowledge exacted by the quasi-divine instrument he employs. His allusive contact with his own earlier poem displaces the meaning of knowledge from its mythic context into the texture of history, transposing (metamorphosing) forbidden knowledge into the revealed truth that legitimizes a high cultural enterprise. The single metaphor of *glass* brings the *Rape* and the *First Satire* into proximity, offering alternative commentary on the relation between illusion and revelation as each is alternately served by the medium in which each appears.

The self that appears to Belinda is a variation of the *Essay*'s "you," now appropriated by the self as constitutive of its "I." The self that appears within the envisioning glass of Pope's *First Satire* enforces recognitions inconsistent with "Cosmetic Pow'rs" (*Rape*, I, 124), providing thereby a variation on the motif of disguise or dissemblance. Sappho "at her toilet's greazy task" is inconsistently Sappho "fragrant at an ev'ning Mask" (*Epistle to a Lady*, 25–26). The absurd disjunction between one identity and another indicates the distance between artifice and art, between false and true naming (libels, for example, and satire), analogous to that between the ludicrous and despicable "Temple of Infamy" and the *Temple of Fame*. The made *thing* that is Sappho is sister to Belinda conjured under the rubric of "Cosmetic Powers." And this correspondence admits the introduction of another between Eloisa and the "other" she invokes, the sainted sister and vestal virgin enjoined to save her from herself, to metamorphose her identity from the "you" she has become into the "I" she desires to be. Obviously, this is a strategy susceptible to substantial variation, to be played now one way and now another. In the *First Satire*, the made *thing* is not the self, but the potentially self-betraying instrumentality wielded by the poet. Only by these means can satire be justified, for only in this way can it be secured against effective appropriation by the selfhood, the internally subversive and power-seeking "other." On the contrary, it is the component reality of the "other" that satire reveals, the "other" that eludes the punitive retribution of the law.

As a poem about art and history, the *First Satire* gathers the shadowy identities of the *Essay on Man*, reconstituting the interior drama of that poem into one of contemporary personages disposed on the historical field. Simultaneously, the poem is an apologia for the purposiveness of the ruling passion, disposing its similar manifestations within the continuum of a bardic tradition. At this late stage it seems unnecessary to emphasize again an allusive mode that sustains complex relations to an unfolding body of poetry, Pope's own. The *First Satire* does not violate Pope's design; it merely transposes its elements from one plane to another, another act of metamorphosis that may be equally characterological or formal, a principal of behavior or genre. This fluency bespeaks the coherence of an imagination that posits the totality of its meanings as a function of a complex symbolism, organizing its various structural principles so as to drive his poems into various contexts, and thus to break them down and recreate them again. It is a continual process of reformulation, analogous perhaps to the making of a long poem by combining its discrete parts into one entity. But reformulation itself posits process, disintegration and reintegration, mythologizing and demythologizing, and posits the terms in which categorical absolutes (nature, history, etc.) are validly recomposed as we move from one dimension of meaning to another, from one poem or set of poems to another. The object of this method is to guarantee veracity; crudely put it is an intellectual *system*. More nicely, it is the result of an "inner logical discipline" that creates the genuine "language of allegory."[6]

And it is within this general context that the self-exposingly ironic comedy of *To Arbuthnot* takes its meaning, demanding from us a recognition of Pope's identity transposed, from the poet to the man, and requiring our acknowledgment of the self-revelatory veracity of the medium itself. The relation between the *First Satire* and *To Arbuthnot* is that between a public and a private self, between history and autobiography, between poetry as a social institution and the poet as a man. As such the relation tends to confirm Pope's habit of dialectic, of playing off against each other two opposing perspectives that, taken together, constitute a new and larger entity. This is the method of the *Essay on Man* and the *Dunciad*, of *To Burlington* and *To Bathurst*, of *To a Lady* and *To Cobham*, and even of the *Rape* and *Eloisa*. It would be an overstatement to insist upon this kind of activity as a perfectly consistent methodological principle governing Pope's poetry, but it is not, I think, unreasonable to propose such a procedure as a function of an imagination that conceives in terms of thesis and antithesis, and builds its larger structures on the basis of elaborately designed tensions between opposing principles.

On the other hand, as I have suggested, Pope defines his concepts within related dramatic contexts, so that the exploration of *nature* within the *Essay on Man* is leagued to the variant inquiry of *To Burlington*, and both poems are linked to a comparable study of the same term in *Eloisa* and the *Rape*. As a poetic method it makes critical control over any single work nearly impossible, for it requires the reader to continually re-encounter Pope's poetry as an accretive and cumulative text, and not merely as a documentary index to moral or conceptual values, the method, by and large, of nineteenth-century Pope criticism. The priority of *nature* (with its particular associations) in the *Rape* blends with the meanings of *nature* in *Eloisa*. No meaning assumes any special priority independent of its context, and each context qualifies the other in relation to such contingent values as devotion, love, and sexuality. We tend, that is, to discover that what we may wish to take as absolutes are always slipping into the status of relative propositions, and that the dramatic situation retains thereby its priority. I propose this argument only as a rather belated rejoinder to the Arnoldian critique, which was rhetorical rather than Aristotelian. A truly dramatic criticism applied to Pope would, I trust, reach some of the same conclusions about him that I have reached in this study.

The *Epistle to Arbuthnot* is not, strictly speaking, one of the Imitations, though Butt refers to its "easy Horatian talk."[7] Pope was busily writing it in 1734, while Arbuthnot was dying, and its employment of Arbuthnot as interlocutor differs significantly, say, from the use of Fortescue in the *First Satire*.[8] Moreover, *To Arbuthnot* answers the other work in a very specific way: the poet as heir to the past yields to the poet as man besieged and confounded by the present. In the one poem the poet's passions are lawful, historically justified by the satirist's traditional role; in the other his passions are comedic, tumultuous, justified by nothing more than his own failure to control the fools and knaves who rush upon him. If, then, the *First Satire* moves toward the delineation of the ordered and pellucid poet, *To Arbuthnot* rushes toward picturing the disorder and confusion of man trapped in the moment, a victim of those seeking fame and himself a victim of his own. Following the bardic vision of the *First Satire*, *To Arbuthnot* is the comedy of the performing self of the poet.

Aden remarks that "a case can be made for Warburton's procedure in giving some of the speeches to Arbuthnot in the 1751 edition of the *Works*."[9] I believe so too. There is no need to review the evidence for the poem as verse dialogue. Aden sums it up briefly, noticing among other things Butt's hedging on the subject: "The change from epistle to dialogue may be the work of Pope."[10] Our evidence can be derived internally, from the nature of the speaker and the dramatic situation Pope presents. Knoepflmacher comments on the "speaker's brilliant self-definition of his role as satirist."[11] It is a good place to begin, for it immediately poses *To Arbuthnot* against the *First Satire* and raises questions as to the differences of self-definition evident in each poem. Initially, Pope is a reasonable man besieged by fools: "All *Bedlam*, or *Parnassus*, is let out" (4), and his complaint about the reality from which he has fled is that it is random and inconsistent. Beyond this objection, the argument suggests that he is without a principle by which to discourage, or a desire by which to accommodate, the demands made upon him. In the putative *real*—the poem's fictive situation—the poet cannot function as a poet. He must, that is, behave as a man, and it is in this way that he is most vulnerable. From the outset the poem dramatizes the inadequacies of the speaker to control a situation that will not submit to his defensive stratagems. He does therefore what all men do in comparable circumstances—falls back upon his virtues and offers them as the cause of his misfortunes.

The long apologia beginning with line 125 and continuing until the Sporus portrait (305) is both autobiography and self-justification. Its bathetic self-dramatizations are equally rhetorical poses and self-revelations, insofar as the poem plays out the comedy of the performing "I" at its center. Ehrenpreis attacks the rhetorical analysis of persona in *To Arbuthnot* as it separates speaker from author, observing that once "this split is accomplished, the connection of the poem with history is destroyed."[12] But we are spared this conclusion by returning to the fictive situation. The poem is about Alexander Pope, but it is also by Pope. We need not destroy the autobiographical accuracy of the text to remark on the context within which the autobiography exists, that of verse dialogue. By anybody's account, an interlocutor speaks at least five times in the poem, although the 1751 edition also gives the last two lines to Arbuthnot. On each occasion except the fifth, he counsels prudence, advises restraint. His last interjection, at line 390, is the briefest of all: "What Fortune, pray?" It occurs while the speaker is in full career celebrating his parents' virtue, and if Pope cannot be silenced he may be encouraged in the harmless random discourse honoring father and mother. And if he cannot be checked, he can be mocked. Pope's *adversarius* here is not a Fortescue, and Pope is not a satirist *in the poem*. He is a man irritated by attack and demand, and although speaker (Pope) and author (Pope) are the same person, they are different figures at different times and in different roles. In other words, *To Arbuthnot* is a poem about Pope; its autobiographical veracity need not deflect us from the bathos informing the poem. That we should not be so deflected indicates Arbuthnot's purpose here. The poem provides sensible evidence of the dissociation of besieged speaker from author, and sufficient confirmation of that control exercised by the poet behind the poem, yet unavailable to the principal actor within the poem.

To avoid this conclusion we must argue, with Ehrenpreis, that the work's intention, grounded in fact, is "pseudo-rhetorical," a "conventional means of giving life to the speaker-poet's expression of his own views."[13] The other alternative is to suggest that the bathetic self-dramatizations are masks of the poet's own devising, personae chosen by him. Ehrenpreis's essay is directed against this latter position. But neither argument contends with the role of Arbuthnot, with an *adversarius* who is honored (and with good reason) far more than Fortescue. And it is through Arbuthnot that Pope, as author, communicates his distance from his speaking self. On this evidence we can build a case for a sustained complexity: the poem is poetic autobiography of a peculiarly witty sort, a structure of self-revelations in which speaker can be distinguished from author, though both are ultimately one. We shall shortly need to ask why Pope would want to write such a poem, but for the moment it is enough to notice that a complex authorial consciousness carries on relevant levels of awareness, self-justifying and self-mocking, and in the process pays tribute to Arbuthnot. If we then bring this work into relation with the larger context, it is evident that Pope is again constructing a performance of the self who is self-victimized, and the satirist self-satirized merely rings a variation on a pervasive theme.[14]

If the *First Satire* defines the emergent identity of the poet as satirist, and appeals to history to legitimize that role, *To Arbuthnot* focuses not on history but on man in the present moment, and man enmeshed in the moment is the world's victim and his own. It is a fine Popeian thrust, and *To Arbuthnot* brings it neatly home. The two works enforce Pope's characteristic act of coming round on his subject again. They illustrate an ironist's state of mind, a skepticism that compels the linking of radical alternatives to which a subject is made to submit. *To Arbuthnot* looks back upon the *First Satire* and qualifies our expectations of the poet who is also a man. Satire is an "impartial Glass," Pope warned, in which "what Spots (for Spots I have) appear." *To Arbuthnot* demonstrates this truth while admonishing the ego militant in its claims against the world.

Through Arbuthnot, Pope mediates the element of *play* in the *Epistle*. Pope is and is not the one who knows, is and is not his own subject. In another play, Arbuthnot is the glass in which the reader reads Pope, even though Pope, in the poem, refuses to read himself in the same glass. Yet at the same time the poem is a glass through which we look back to the securely self-justified author, now withdrawn and leaving us with his "other," while enjoying the play he has initiated. It is another sort of god-role, though obviously one with sufficient mind, and it allows Pope to objectify the "other" and thus to undemonize himself. The poem reveals Pope's "Spots," as the *First Satire* told us it must, but such a ritual revelation (the act of writing satire) again establishes the poet as knowing the price of knowledge and being willing to pay it. Nothing is more dunciadic than paying the wrong price for the wrong knowledge, and it is this mock that echoes within the *Rape*. In *To Arbuthnot*, self-knowledge is antithetical to the mere factuality of the autobiographical mode. Pope's speaker knows everything there is to know about himself, yet the play of the poem is to withhold from him the redemptive self-knowledge held within the poem's glass. It is into this glass that he refuses to look. Here again a single metaphorical principle sustains a protracted meditation on *knowing* and doubles back on the excoriations of the *Essay*'s "you," the *mon semblable* of the poem's "I."

In *To Arbuthnot*, Pope is himself a variation of the hidden god whose simulacrum within the world's body is all that can ever be directly declared or apprehended, and whose presence is behind those texts that are themselves manifestations of his knowing. One may guess at how such a recognition served the interests of a poet whose constant revision of his private self, in the letters, was a major occupation. All of this suggests a very perverse play on the sociality of self-love, which, it would seem, is inconsistently committed to public declaration, if only because such declaration must be mediated by various acts (texts) which simultaneously reveal and conceal, unhappily inviting and necessitating misreadings. And obviously it raises questions about the incoherence of the self and about the artistry that preserves the representations of the self and passes on an identity to posterity. Clearly, however, such reflections bear on Pope's occasional georgic temptations, to leave the world that is a diminished thing to the diminished things who act within it, to cultivate, for example, a single determinate meaning such as Twickenham, a text and a context of another kind.

The ironic mode of the speaker's vauntings thereby balances us between kinds of knowing. Pope, we say, is speaking the truth about himself, but truth has assumed the status of an idealized image of the poet and of the self who fulfills it. In other words, the poem details a vexatious relation between the selfhood and self-love, between the poet's investment in the pride of self and that true recognition of his function that is the legitimate purpose of his calling. Because of the ironic mode we recognize a distance between, say, Pope and the Sensibility poets. Weiskel observes how these later poets are tempted "back into the safer, regressive precincts of narcissism, the renunciation of the gloomy egoist devoted to Solitude, Contemplation, or Melancholy."[15] Such dark deities of the narcissistic sublime are courted by the poet seeking new sources of power and vision. Pope's own dark divinity in *To Arbuthnot* is pity (self-pity), the inversion of pride and thus another adjunct to the selfhood. In terms of the psychological myth informing the *Essay*, Pope's self-pity is an attempt to justify what he would have his auditor understand as a proper self-love. But if we are reading the poem as I suggest, that definition is one Arbuthnot refuses to accept.

It is also true that what the Horatian poems offered Pope was a historical analog to his own role as satirist, and Horace functions as another source of authority for a poet vitally interested in such sources. The "Advertisement" to the *Imitations* makes this clear:

> The Occasion of publishing these Imitations was the Clamour raised on some of my Epistles. An Answer from Horace was both more full, and of more Dignity, than any I cou'd have made in my own person; and the Example of much greater Freedom in so eminent a Divine as Dr. Donne, seem'd a proof with what Indignation and Contempt a Christian may treat Vice or Folly, in ever so low, or ever so high, a Station. Both these Authors were acceptable to the Princes and Ministers under whom they lived.[16]

If the *Imitations* provide Pope with a center of personal authority, they also permit him, sheltered under this authority, to speak of his own anxieties both as poet and as man. The poems define another contest of alternative *voices* (*First Epistle*) similar to the alternative identities that in the *Essay* contend for mastery and dominance. In sum, the dialectical principle that poses the *Essay on Man* against the *Dunciad* (and self-love and selfhood in the *Essay*) is sustained within the *Imitations*. Clearly, the contest between Montaigne, Locke, Aristippus, and St. Paul, on the one side, and the dark powers represented by London and the voice that whispers "Be but Great" (101), on the other, is the humanist contest between authoritative history and the self that seeks its authority in itself (confirmed by the voice of London). These dark powers are the equivalent to mid-century solitude, contemplation, or melancholy, the voices solicited by the self in isolation, the voices of the gothic mode. What happens at mid-century amounts almost to a reversal of the humanist position: the dark powers are invoked as sources of energy, a kind of Faustian courtship of the demonic for the sake of appropriating (or realizing) proscribed powers (proscribed in the special sense of being antisocial). This line of inquiry allows us to glimpse the prophetic tone in Pope's poetry, and to understand how lucidly the conflict between alternative powers is set forth. The poets of mid-century who have escaped the containing formulations of Pope's *nature* and *history* seek for the source of their visions in those feelings that the greater writers before them (Spenser, Shakespeare, Milton) felt. The mid-century transmutes these early writers into the context of primitivism. When Weiskel discusses Collins's *Ode on the Poetical Character* he notes that "Milton represents a poetic potentiality prior to the alienation of the divine and the natural, but this possibility is just now closing for the aspiring poet."[17] Exactly, but the observation points to the essential difference between Collins and Pope, and virtually defines the premise on which the *Essay* is written.

For Pope, closure is a function of the will to power; to recognize this truth is the burden of the *Rape*, even as the relation between desire and closure animates Eloisa's despair in her poem. There the problem is focused on the relation between physical and spiritual love. Later the subject becomes self-love and social love. When we approach Pope in these terms we get the right sense of an extended subject, which, in the *Dunciad*, is metamorphosed into various corruptions of sexuality, including the lingering and abiding oedipal fantasy that distinguishes the relation between Cibber and his "mighty Mother." Much of the *Dunciad*'s comedy is invested in the farcical behavior of the body: the dunces are forever losing their footing, falling, slipping, diving, etc., as though they are in a crazy-house of their own making (which in fact is precisely where they are). And this crazy-house of nature incorporates and requires a perverse sexuality as the inevitable antithesis to the relation between man and nature specified in *To Burlington*. Pope is highly consistent in exploring the varieties of love, throughout his poetry, though we seldom think of him in these terms. What kinds of love are yet possible in the fallen world? And what kind of self-love, to come back to *To Arbuthnot*, is a form of self-betrayal? *To Arbuthnot* addresses this question, and in doing so its comedy borders the far darker comedy of the *Dunciad*. But another problem also arises, and this bears on the extent to which the poet may be tempted to ally himself with his own selfhood, to take himself, in other words, at his selfhood's evaluation. Arbuthnot is in the poem to prevent this occurrence, to permit Pope to explore his own susceptibility to self-pity without running the risk of being ensnared by it. If we think again of the *Dunciad* we may recognize that to some large extent it is simply a story of the kingdom of antipoetry that Cibber brings into being, the tale of the poet who chooses and is chosen by that kingdom in despair of the true realm of poetic vision.

Differently from the *Essay on Man*, but in a way that bears comparision, the *First Epistle* dissolves an illusory idea of priorities. The excitement of the work arises as we conceive of Pope listening to the various voices of the poem. To be kept from himself (41) suggests a discord in search of a principle of concord. And those who best release him to be himself are the spiritual doctors, Montaigne and Locke, Aristippus and St. Paul. To be oneself is to be free ("Sworn to no Master, of no Sect am I" [24]), yet such freedom is qualified by "Life's instant business" (42). If the "blood rebel[s] . . . / With wretched Av'rice, or as wretched Love," there are "Words, and Spells, which can control / (Between the Fits) this Fever of the soul" (55–58). Such words are spoken by virtue, wisdom, and philosophy. They are opposed by "London's voice" (79) and one "who whispers, 'Be but Great' " (101). Yet the court and the people are enthralled: "a King's a Lion" and the "People are a many-headed beast" (120–121). To be under a spell is to be subject to "some whimzy, or that Dev'l within / Which guides all those who know not what they mean" (143–44). And the dark night of the mind is signified by "Proteus, Merlin, any Witch" (152). Rich and poor, king and people, eunuch (literally) and Sir Job are transformed beings, and such transformations are the fevers of the soul, the self enmeshed in its own desires. The drama of contraries embraces spiritual doctors and witch doctors, and the *First Epistle* is an allegory of the material world envisioned as enchanter,[18] the world realized as Circean transformer of man into beast. Not to know what one means is an abuse of the ruling passion, a failure of self-knowledge, a denial of God's datum.

The *First Epistle* is thus concerned with an exploration of those duplicities inhabiting self-consciousness, and though not exactly a psychomachia it leagues with both the *Essay on Man* and the *Dunciad* as it is attentive to the emergent powers within the self that usurp purpose and distort coherence. This is the fate of all those "who know not what they mean" or discover for themselves "how ill I with myself agree" (175). The determining ideas of the *Essay* are re-examined and re-applied to the special case of the poet. The myth of the concordant being self-orchestrating his ruling passion breaks down. He is a "Demi-god" except when clouded by a "Fit of Vapours" (188). Both glory and jest, he recapitulates the indeterminateness of human nature, and the imagination becomes the instrument for creating fictions of identity. Horace says: "*Quo teneam vultus mutantem Protea nodo?*" (With what knot can I hold this face-changing Proteus?). Pope says that no knot can hold him (or Merlin, any witch), for these magicians are not eccentric to us but exist within, and if they are to be bound, it is with "Words, and Spells."

It is a question of who binds whom. To "lock up all the Functions of my soul" (40) is to transform the radiant center of human identity into a prison-house. To resist the demon within, however, is to enclose him within incantations that spring from the poetic word and its informing humanist wisdom. The *New Dunciad* is anticipated on the level of personal violation, and the poet's quest is for a lost but native nobility that the one greater man, Bolingbroke, is again petitioned to provide: "my Guide, Philosopher, and Friend" (177). Pope's tale here is of the self lost within itself ("That keep me from Myself" [41]); its ruling passion controverted by the devil within, a latent self-duplicity to be opposed by the evocation of the clarified self: "That Man divine whom Wisdom calls her own" (180). The struggle for the soul of man is what the poem is all about, and as it is so the conflict shifts from the *Essay's* generic inquiry into a more immediately personal drama. Yet the psychomachian elements of the *Epistle* require that we view Pope as a figure assisted in his struggle against evil on earth and in his own mind, and thus as a variation of the pilgrim-knight as poet, aided by the chevalier Bolingbroke, himself a variation of the grace-lending Christ.[19]

Earlier I noted how a unit like *glass* functions to keep some texts in proximity to one another. *Whispering* is another element of the same kind, reducible to a particular mode of address that keeps the larger mythic context before the reader. In Belinda's "Morning-Dream" a "glitt'ring" youth "Seem'd to her Ear his winning Lips to lay, / And thus in Whispers said, or seem'd to say" (I, 25–26). At the close of the *Temple of Fame* "One came, me-thought, and whisper'd in my Ear" (498). Here, in the *First Epistle*, "A Voice there is that whispers in my ear" (11). What do we make of this whispering if not a sensibility alert to its own intuitions, and yet at least on one occasion equally alert to the psychic subversions that such intuitions may signify. G. K. Hunter makes the interesting remark that Pope "believed that the Frame of Order should not be accepted passively; it requires its martyrs and witnesses to demonstrate against any betrayal of standards . . . , and for Pope the basis of this witness must always be the individual sensibility of the poet, which gives him access to truths which are concealed from others by the disorders of real life."[19] But surely the matter is not so simple, for what happens to the poet when he becomes involved, as in *To Arbuthnot*, with the disorders of real life? And, moreover, what happens to anybody, Belinda included, who becomes so involved? How does one then bear true witness, maintain a cause, attack an enemy, judge between a truth and a falsity *whispered* in the ear?

To my mind such queries point toward the problem inherent in self-knowledge, the basis of true speaking and true hearing, and return us to *To Arbuthnot*, wherein true speaking simply cannot be heard for what it is. I believe this situation always has within it what Tuve signifies when she says that "the large literature of virtues battling with vices, which we are accustomed to think of solely as a great tableau of the psychomachia we call the moral struggle, had running through it another kind of image as well—the spirit's quest for a lost but native noblesse."[21] On the one hand, this quest seems always on the brink of giving up the world, abandoning it to its own ineradicable subversions, and thus permitting the self's orientation towards its own acts of soul-making and soul-saving. On the other hand, self-love *is* social. I find these separate topics subject to endless re-orchestration in Pope. They seem always to invoke a variation of the same quest for significant data, the evidential basis of action, which again must remind us of the word opened to the alternatives it conceals, of the self opened also to the possibilities inherent within it. Thus the ruling passion is a "direction," instinct another datum, sense an intuition. The "Frame of Order" may require its martyrs, but it may also indifferently accept the sacrifices of its fools. How does one finally arbitrate the difference? Pope's quest seems remarkably innocent of an itinerary: "As drives the storms, at any door I knock, / And house with Montagne now, or now with Lock" (24–25). Very good, but on the principle of any port in a storm, what then? "Back to my native Moderation slide, / And win my way by yielding to the tyde" (33–34). Is moderation experientially derived, or is it what it seems to be: "native" and thus another datum? The poem keeps positing the possible coalescence of a "me" and a "Myself," now subversively kept apart, that requires what for its unity: a *Nichomachean* mean, a *concordia discors*? The incompanionable reality of a "me" and a "Myself" restates the internal betrayals of the *Essay*, the subversion of a "me" akin to that which threatens reason. If the defilement of the "I" is at the heart of things, no wonder then the self's anxiety about who speaks the privileged and whispered word.

In the fifth book of *Paradise Lost*, Eve wakes to tell her Satan-inspired dream to Adam:

> Close at mine ear one call'd me forth to walk
> With gentle voice, I thought it thine; it said,
> Why sleep'st thou *Eve*? now is the pleasant time,
> The cool, the silent, save where silence yields
> To the night-warbling Bird, that now awake. . . .
>
> (35–40)

Just previously, Adam, "her hand soft touching, whisper'd thus. Awake" (17). And again: "Such whispering wak'd her" (26). The voice close at her ear and Adam's voice seemed to her one voice, having the same purpose, to "wake" her from sleep. In Pope's text, *whispering* is the unit that recapitulates or, more exactly, summons division, the normal state of the Popeian hero.

If it is to the resolution of division that the *First Epistle* is addressed, we might expect the poem to continue to play upon the issue by inquiring into causality. Thus the question: "Say, does thy blood rebel, thy bosom move / With wretched Av'rice, or as wretched, Love?" (55–57). "Like rebel nature of *Eloisa*, rebel blood is a unit in the figuration of the myth and an occasion of division. Pope's text (not Horace's) continues to elaborate just what division involves, and it involves the separation of the self into its warring components, a conversion under the aegis of an internal voice that whispers its subversive doctrine. Wretched avarice is a lust, as, I presume, is "as wretched" love. These passions are unhappily companionable in a misreading of the divine datum or a willful perversion of it. We might want to say that love is as wretched because it has fallen to the condition of avarice, and thus suffers a dislocation, that each is overly fond of its object and, being obsessed by the object, can be said to lust after it. For such reasons the lines draw in their wake the un-Horatian reference: "Slave to a Wife, or Vassal to a Punk" (62). I am reading this line as further explication of "as wretched Love," of the consequence of uxoriousness, and I wish just narrowly to resist re-allegorizing avarice and love as the fallen companions in the fallen garden.

I am not quite sure what the text licenses at this juncture, though it is obvious that the poet who knows the redemptive word ("Know, there are Words, and Spells, which can controll / [Between the Fits] this Fever of the soul") is about to speak (whisper?) it: "All that we ask is but a patient Ear" (64). The poetic vocation is listening to the word and speaking of it. Surely, Pope's text is here playing upon the Edenic myth, recapitulating it, as it were, yet within the Horatian frame, an overwriting placed upon the Horatian text correspondent to the loosely formulated eighteenth-century notion of "imitation." We fall through Horace's text into Pope's more profound text, and the sort of action I am describing here correlates with the transposition of the *Rape* into the Horatian mode of *To a Lady*. In this regard, much of Pope's writing is actually a re-writing of other texts, either his or, as here, Horace's (the Latin poet's *Epistle* into Pope's *Epistle*). This sort of imaginative enterprise tends to provide, within Pope's canon, a body of homologous texts.

When Barthes explores the Racinian hero he asks the primary question: "Who is this Other from whom the hero cannot detach himself? First of all—that is, most explicitly—it is the Father. . . . The Father is the Past."[22] In Pope's texts we have seen various versions of the "other." In the *Essay*, the "other" is the resident "you," the dark primordial interloper and seducer whose purpose is to estrange reason from self-love, and to displace the latter by an*other*. Yet the "other" is equally the father figured as "Guide, Philosopher, and Friend." Hence Bolingbroke, whose admonitory presence in the text is first seen as an intrusion: "St. John, whose love indulg'd my labours past / Matures my present, and shall bound my last! / Why will you break the Sabbath of my days?" (1–3). The question is designed to remind us of the unwelcome presence of the "other" as the self prepares to elude judgment and thus escape its eye: "ah let me hide my Age!" (5). It is not the voice of this "other" that Pope wishes to hear, for he knows that it will urge upon him the relentless duty to which he has responded over and again in the past, but from which he now wishes to claim the right of surcease, to inhabit "Life's cool evening satiate of applause" (9). Thus, in the Barthesian sense, the father is the past, but what is equally the past is the original divisiveness from the father that continues to inhabit the present. And what is being asked for is the freedom to serve no master: "Sworn to no Master, of no Sect am I" (24). So that the father is imaged exactly as he appears to the poet: a task*master* who binds the son to his authority. This is to re-imagine the master–slave relation of *Eloisa*, the difference being that Eloisa's master is a tyrant to whom she willingly enslaves herself, whereas Pope's is the father he would deceive. Thus Pope's claim to arbitrate his own duality, to distinguish the identities of his voices, is another claim to freedom consequent upon self-knowledge.

He must therefore in his own text demonstrate the talismanic power of the word he wields, which is his ultimate claim to authority. Yet it would seem that the word can only recapitulate the antitheses inherent within it: "'Tis the first Virtue, Vices to abhor; / And the first Wisdom, to be Fool no more" (65–66). True enough, but how does one avoid washing one's hands with Pilate? I take it that in the *First Epistle* self-knowledge continues to be the issue, a knowledge that derives its authority from the divine design of the *Essay on Man* now displaced onto the *Epistle*. To break faith with that design is to be invaded by "some whimzy, or that Dev'l within / Which guides all those who know not what they mean" (143–44). To know not what you mean is to re-create the internal subversions of the *Rape* or *To Bathurst* or the *Essay*, for self-knowledge compels the figuration that Pope transposes from text to text. This activity by the poet seems the only way to posit its inexhaustible vitality, its endless pertinence. A coherence invades the text that will not let language slide into the mere relevance of moral admonition, or lodge final authority in the individual sensibility of the poet. Thus, in one sense, the *First Epistle* is an act whereby the poet self-consciously dispossesses himself of his power, claims almost to have no power, and calls upon Bolingbroke to lend his grace to end the ceaseless cycle of ascendant and descendant voices, imaged in the poem as yet another variation of the darksome round: "I plant, root up, I build, and then confound, / Turn round to square, and square again to round" (169–70). And he solicits the power of a "Guide, Philosopher, and Friend" who is himself a *maker*: "Who ought to make me . . . / That Man divine" (179–80). Finally, Pope's imperative ("ought") is justified by the knowledge (self-knowledge) of an abiding duality resolved only in the grace-lending charity of his initiation-master.

What does this say, then, about the "individual sensibility of the poet"? As I read the three Horatian imitations, they express a very substantial dubiety about that sensibility, show how at any moment it may be betrayed by the very principle of subjectivity on which it resides. Thus Atossa, for example, or Villiers and Timon. Hence the appeal to a heraldic tradition, or to an authority outside the self that must come to discipline that sensibility to an order not of its own making. Perhaps this very authority principle is what the Wartons sensed as a diminishment of what they also sensed as their own humanity, a pre-Blakeian "hardening" of the laws governing human nature. Yet one of the crucial questions is why Pope should return to the *Dunciad* years after its three-book form had been completed. It seems to me that the return is made mandatory by the very betrayals to which a sensibility is subject and despite the various data (sense, taste, ruling passion, etc.) that Pope summons. If Pope reads Satan as a fable of that sensibility possessed, as I am inclined to believe he does, then it is precisely what cannot be constrained by the wisdom (the *voices*) immanent in history. Satan, in sum, is not a good listener; in Bloom's terms he is too strong to be schooled. This awareness necessitates Pope's strategy in the *Essay on Man*, a kind of bullying of the "you" by an elaborate rhetorical attack upon it. But the *First Epistle*'s ironic concession is that "Words, and Spells . . . can controll / (*Between the Fits*) this Fever of the soul" (my italics). Clearly, "Fever" signifies the irrationality of the sublime moment, and "Words" a forcible restraint, the white magic of spiritual doctoring. Pope's image is of Satan as the powerful sick man of the self, whose sickness is his greatness, fevered by the conviction that what is offered as the law is merely a trick by which power perpetuates itself, sustains its authority, compels submission. This was, after all, Eloisa's view of things. Pope seems never for a moment to have doubted his understanding of Satan, but he may very well have come to feel that he had never rationalized it within a suitable vision, and hence the return at the end of his life to the *Dunciad*.

Yet a not incidental purpose of the *Epistle* is to set the satirist in relation to the man, an act of soul-making, a dedication to spiritual doctoring that takes its inception from Pope's reference to the "Sabbath of my days." The sabbath is at once a respite and a dedication, a turning from the world to return to the world. *To Arbuthnot* bespeaks the sentimental language of the besieged poet; the *First Epistle* bespeaks an encounter with the "Functions of my soul," and continues thereby to orchestrate a relation between the private and the public man. There is surely something to Hunter's idea that the *Imitations* "involve primarily a substitution of the order of the individual mind for the Order of the external world . . . as a basis for belief and action, a substitution of subjective evaluation for the traditional acceptance of received values, objectively justified."[23] Yet there is only *something* to it, for Pope's spiritual doctors are themselves the voices of a sustaining wisdom, one that looks from the world's body to the human soul. The man who hears the voice of the selfhood (" 'Be but Great' ") is abandoned to his own subjectivity, to a center that turns out once again to be a trap in another variation of the prevailing metaphor of center and circumference. The obligatory task here is that of focusing attention inward, of listening with the unsectarian ear, and "Late as it is," of "put[ting] my self to school" (47).

I earlier cited Angus Fletcher on the subject of demonological possession and referred his remarks to the *Epistle to a Lady*. The Horatian *First Epistle* brings us round again to the demonic voices that are themselves the disguised agencies of the selfhood and thus to the delusions that arise from subjectivity. Following this reflection, we can return to the ambiguous valuation of *blood* in *Windsor-Forest*, and to the working out of the addiction to blood-letting that the poem dramatizes. It seems equally necessary to recognize that Pope's obsessive or addictive being is what the sublimity of self comes to: in effect, the closed circle of being, a kind of hell, which in turn determines another fall and another imprisonment. When the self falls, it thinks it has risen, and this misperception determines its blindness to the inverted reality that has come into being. The head is now the foot, the bottom become the top. The world turns upside down and hell is heaven. Pope signifies as much in the *Dunciad* by a kind of comedy of the body referred to earlier. Within the crazy-house of nature we "reason downward, till we doubt of God" (IV, 472) because the mind is deluded and its normal actions are inverted. When this happens, everything else is predictable: "Virtue [is] local, all Relation scorn" (IV, 479). Pride, confederate with erring reason, is now enthroned, and man's imperial faculty, will, is literally mystified: "Of nought so certain as our Reason still, / Of nought so doubtful as of Soul and Will" (IV, 48–82).

The relation between body and soul is equivalent to that between nature and grace and informs the *Epistle to Burlington*. The good gardener is there instructed to "treat the Goddess like a modest fair, / Nor over-dress, nor leave her wholly bare." The care of the body is extended into the treatment of the specific place, wherein the good gardener "varies shades from shades," etc., and is advised to "Still follow Sense, of ev'ry Art the Soul." From the relation between soul and body is born those "Idea's" that distinguish Burlington.

And we may further trace this conception into the *Essay on Man*: "All are but parts of one stupendous whole, / Whose body Nature is, and God the soul" (I, 267–68). Similarly, Pope employs the idea of the displaced or usurped body in the *Epilogue to the Satires, Dialogue I*, where "pale Virtue [is] carted in . . . [Vice's] stead!" (150). The fallen body that is virtue intrudes within the anarchic disorder of England. Beyond such substitution, the body is vulgarized by being "all liv'ry'd o'er with foreign Gold" (155). This sort of action is figured in the *Rape of the Lock*, and Belinda's excessive adornment of body is a reflection of the corruption of soul it signifies. In itself the idea has a long history of which Fletcher reminds us by commenting on Hugh of St. Victor's *Soliloquy on the Earnest Money of the Soul*: "The whole Christian life-pattern is set forth here in cosmetic terms, even to the mirror (the *speculum*) in which the lady examines her adorned self."[24] And by this route we may return to the *First Satire*, to Pope's description of satire as a "Medium" or "impartial Glass" in which the "Soul stood forth."

Beyond this immediate context, Pope's dualism bears on the critical precepts of the *Essay on Criticism*. There it is said that

> *Art* from that Fund [of Nature] each *just Supply* provides,
> Works *without* Show, and *without Pomp* presides:
> In some fair Body thus th' informing Soul
> With Spirits feeds, with Vigour fills the whole,
> Each Motion guides, and ev'ry Nerve sustains;
> *It self unseen*, but in th' *Effects*, remains.
>
> (74–79)

The art of critical explication is the reduction of the body to its informing principle, the revelation of an irreducible and determining "Spirit" that permeates the text and makes it what it is. Pope's metaphors of body and soul, surface and essence, extend to include the distinction between "Expression" and *"Thought"* (*Essay on Criticism*, 318) and compel a sense of his own poetic. For what is contained within the texture of language, its enveloping network, is the mind at the center. Translated within the terms of my own argument, Pope's text is the expressive form for the subject at its center, for the protean reality of the myth which demands its various embodiments, yielding finally to a holistic imagination. The Popeian virtuosity is, then, a product of a lifetime's assessment of the body of literature, its treasury of historically recoverable forms that fulfill variously the complex ideational reality of the myth. Body and soul thus dance within the multiple harmonics of form and idea, and as that dance unfolds before us, we witness the myth disposed into the various generic patterns that now invoke Milton or Homer and again Horace or Ovid. It is difficult to imagine a more complex poetic enterprise or one that more greatly tests the resources of a literary imagination. It should give us, however, some extended sense of what history and nature mean to

Pope and of how his texts assume that burden. And because all of this is true, the *Dunciad* could never be trifling of any sort, could never be merely *satiric* in the limitedly topical application that word occasionally assumes.[25] However sprightly the *Dunciad* may be, it is the most tragic utterance of which the eighteenth century was capable, the final frightening creation of a body without a soul, a god without a mind.

Notes

1. Leranbaum, *Pope's* "Opus Magnum," pp. 129, 130.
2. Griffin, *Poet in the Poems*, p. 188.
3. *Ibid.*, p. 192.
4. Thomas Maresca, *Pope's Horatian Poems* (Columbus: Ohio State University Press, 1966), p. 50.
5. Brower, *Poetry of Allusion*, p. 290.
6. Frye, *Fearful Symmetry*, p. 11.
7. TE, 4:xxx.
8. Fortescue was added to the *First Satire* in 1751 by Warburton. Howard Weinbrot discusses both the *First Satire* and the *Epistle to Arbuthnot* at substantial length in his new book, *Alexander Pope and the Traditions of Formal Verse Satire* (Princeton, N.J.: Princeton University Press, 1982). I regret not being able to consult his work before my manuscript had gone to press.
9. John Aden, *Something like Horace* (Nashville, Tenn.: Vanderbilt University Press, 1969), p. 14.
10. TE, 4:94.
11. U.C Knoeplfmacher, "The Poet as Physician: Pope's *Epistle to Dr. Arbuthnot*," MLQ, 31 (1970): 440.
12. Irvin Ehrenpreis, "Personae," *Restoration and Eighteenth-Century Literature*, ed. Carroll Camden (Chicago: University of Chicago Press, 1963), p. 32.
13. *Ibid*, p. 33.
14. Received opinion on the subject of *To Arbuthnot* is well represented by Lilian Feder. She remarks that the "emphasis on his humanity and his high moral standards becomes an essential and consistent feature of Pope's Horatian *persona*; he continues to emphasize these qualities in his portrait of himself in the *Imitations of Horace, An Epistle to Dr. Arbuthnot*, and *The Epilogue to the Satires*." See "Sermo or Satire: Pope's Definition of His Art," *Studies in Criticism and Aesthetics, 1660–1800*, ed. Howard Anderson and John S. Shea (Minneapolis: University of Minnesota Press, 1967), p. 147.
15. Weiskel, p. 120.
16. "Advertisement" to the *Imitations*, TE, 4:3.
17. Weiskel, *Romantic Sublime. p. 130.*
18. Cf. Maresca, p. 186.
19. See Rosemond Tuve, *Allegorical Imagery: Some Mediaeval Books and Their Posterity* (Princeton, N.J.: Princeton University Press, 1966), especially pp. 40–47.
20. G. K. Hunter, "The 'Romanticism' of Pope's Horace," *Essays in Criticism*, 10 (1960):404.
21. Tuve, p. 44.
22. Barthes, *On Racine*, p. 38. See also Anthony Wilden, "Lacan and the Discourse of the Other," in Jacques Lacan, *The Language of the Self* (Baltimore: The Johns Hopkins University

Press, 1968): "what the subject must seek is what Lacan calls the symbolic identification with the father—that is to say, he must take over the *function* of the father through the normalization of the Oedipus complex. This is an identification with a father who is neither Imaginary nor real: what Lacan calls the Symbolic father, the figure of the Law" (p. 165). This remark bears on my discussion here and elsewhere in the text of the relation between Pope and Bolingbroke in the *Essay on Man*, and on that between the jealous god and God ("the figure of the Law") in *Eloisa to Abelard*. Cf. Wilden's essay as it develops the relation between knowledge and recognition, and issues in a discussion of " 'ontological insecurity' " ("to be an object for the other is to have lost one's being as a person," [p. 166]).

23. Hunter, p. 391.
24. Fletcher, *Allegory: Theory of a Symbolic Mode*, p. 133 n.
25. Ralph Rader, "The Concept of Genre and Eighteenth-Century Studies," *New Approaches to Eighteenth-Century Literature* (New York: Columbia University Press, 1974), pp. 79–117. See especially Rader's comments on the *Rape of the Lock*, p. 104.

Art and Integrity: Concepts of Self in Alexander Pope and Edward Young

Douglas Lane Patey

In 1759 Edward Young published his celebrated *Conjectures on Original Composition*, a puzzling work that challenges readers to find the connection between its long initial discussion of literary matters and its final pages, a meditation on Young's lifelong obsession: death. Modern anthologies usually reprint only the first part, on artistic imitation, genius, rules, and the use of rhyme; but the essay really reaches its rhetorical climax as Young turns his attention to the sickroom to recall Joseph Addison's final words, "See in what peace a Christian can die!" Using all the terms of his previous discussion—Addison's carefully staged death is a "triumph" displaying a "genius for eternals," a "monument" deserving our "applause" and "emulation"—Young challenges us to connect literature with life by reading his essay aright: "This [Addison's death scene] you will think a long digression; and justly: if that may be called a digression, which was my chief inducement for writing at all."[1]

In fact, Young has been planting hints all along. He advises poets to study great models: "Imitate; but imitate not the composition, but the man." He borrows his chief "rules of art" from ethics ("Know thyself," "Reverence thyself"), promising "to repay ethics in a future letter, by two rules from rhetoric for its service" (no doubt the rules of decorum and of the need to join pleasure with instruction in an exemplary work). Most of all, he says of Addison's climactic scene: "His compositions are but a noble preface; the grand work is his death: that is a work which is read in heaven." What is remarkable in all this, from a modern viewpoint, is the ease with which life and art unite to form a single oeuvre. Formally identical, the arts of poetry and of living (and dying, the *ars moriendi* of which churchmen wrote so much)[2] use the same means ("rules") to achieve the same exemplary ends. Nor perhaps can we find a poet in whom the arts of writing and of living more conspire to such designed wholeness than Alexander Pope.

Our most ordinary assumptions about life and art hide Pope's integrity from us. We have lost that vision of life's wholeness that motivated Solon's

Douglas Lane Patey, "Art and Integrity: Concepts of Self in Alexander Pope and Edward Young." Reprinted from *Modern Philology* vol. 83, No. 4 (May 1986) by permission. Published by the University of Chicago.

maxim, "Call no man happy till he is dead"—of life as given shape by the effort to realize its proper shape, according to the hierarchy of ends that classical and Christian philosophy once provided. Alasdair MacIntyre writes in his great recent account of the passing of this vision, *After Virtue*:

> The social obstacles [to seeing life whole] derive from the way in which modernity partitions each human life into a variety of segments, each with its own norms and modes of behavior. So work is divided from leisure, private life from public, the corporate from the personal. So both childhood and old age have been wrenched away from the rest of human life and made over into distinct realms. And all these separations have been achieved so that it is the distinctiveness of each and not the unity of the life of the individual who passes through those parts in terms of which we are taught to think and to feel.[3]

To MacIntyre's list must be added another fateful separation that originated in Pope's own age, the century that invented both the name and concept of "aesthetics": that between art and the rest of life.[4] "Learn then what MORALS Criticks ought to show" exhorts the *Essay on Criticism*, but no longer can we accept Pope's effortless identification of literary–critical with moral skills—of critical acumen with "good nature," "good breeding," and "generosity," as against bad readers' "pride" and "faction"—nor, having separated off the realm of the aesthetic, can we any longer make intelligible his claim that in all the departments of life, "Nature's chief Master-piece is writing well."[5]

Pope's life, as much as his art, elides what we would sever. Sure of his vocation from the start, Pope seems to have reached maturity by a direct route, never detouring through ordinary childhood or adolescence (if we are to believe historians such as J. H. Van den Berg, adolescence was only just being invented).[6] The Victorians bequeathed to us a division between the private world of home and family (guided by a feminine moral intelligence) and the outer world of work, where different norms apply; but Pope and most of his closest friends were leisured bachelors, who conducted their work at home or in one another's houses. Of these very houses, practitioners of the new social history of architecture, such as Mark Girouard, report that only in the late seventeenth century were spaces commonly set aside for use solely as bedrooms—the result of a new concern for personal privacy—though for the often invalid Pope, sickroom, workroom, and drawing room could never fully be distinguished, either at Twickenham or at the many houses where he visited, wrote, and took physic.[7] Pope wrote most of *An Essay on Man* during a long convalescence at Lord Bolingbroke's Dawley Farm; many of his house parties suggest a condition of permanent *levée*. As such reflections suggest, we do Pope a disservice in one-sidedly labelling him a "public poet": he did not understand the "public" and the "private" as do we.[8] The same poet who condemned public men for their private lives—who found, even in a single, seemingly detached "private" vices a synecdoche for the whole moral and intellectual life of dunce, peer, or politician—made sure as had no poet before him that the public knew the details of his own life, so that Pope himself could stand surety to his poetic pronouncements. Thus the *Epistle to Arbuthnot*, Pope's defense of his career as a satirist, climaxes by referring his audience to the evidence—directly relevant from his point of view, dubiously so from ours—of his enduring friendships and exemplary-filial piety.

For this poet who "thought a Lye in Verse or Prose the same," private and public life form an ethical continuity, while art and life conjoin to make a satire a mode of political action. Aristotle had taught that politics is the perfection of ethics; for Pope, during his last years chief poetic spokesman for the Opposition to Walpole, all political reform is finally not institutional but moral (in effect, doing one's duty). Isaac Kramnick and, more recently, Brean Hammond have shown us that it was more than anyone else his lifelong friend Henry St. John, Viscount Bolingbroke—through his periodical *The Craftsman*, the chief prose voice of Opposition—from whom Pope learned the terms in which to sing.[9] Bolingbroke wrote in *The Idea of a Patriot King*: "Let not princes flatter themselves. They will be examined closely, in private as well as in public life: and those, who cannot pierce further, will judge of them by the appearances they give in both. To obtain true popularity, that which is founded in esteem and affection, they must, therefore, maintain their characters in both; and to that end neglect appearances in neither, but observe the decorum necessary to preserve the esteem, whilst they win the affections, of mankind. Kings, they must never forget that they are men: men, they must never forget that they are kings."[10] The evidence is overwhelming that it was Bolingbroke who taught Pope to understand the polity as the embodiment of an "ancient constitution," a Polybian balance of three estates (king, peers, and commons). As in any moral teleology, the ideal form of the state may be more or less completely realized: freedom and stability are the products of each member's actively fulfilling his role; tyranny and "corruption"—a word never far, at this period, from its Latin sense of division into parts—of failure to enact one's role.[11] Thus, according to Bolingbroke, "Depravation of manners exposed the constitution to ruin; reformation [of manners] will secure it" (3:75). So much did Pope identify political with moral rectitude—doing one's duty—that he could write in *An Essay on Man* with a jab at Walpole's administration: "For Forms of Government let fools contest; / Whate'er is best administered is best" (3.303–4).

We should recognize in this political model a structure of thought that informs the whole universe of the *Essay on Man*, where, "reasoning but from what we know," Pope identifies all the levels in the chain of nature as "ranks," "callings," "stations," and "estates." (As the Marxists remind us, there is no better way to mask an ideology than to make it appear "natural.") The notion of a calling—what Martin Luther called *Berufung*—comes heavily freighted with religious overtones (it is a "vocation"), so we should not be surprised to discover that just as the natural universe is providentially ordered, so is the hierarchy of stations in society: Bolingbroke himself says that under the rule of a Patriot King, "the orders and forms of the constitution" will be "restored to their primitive integrity, and become what they were intended to be" (75). Right moral (and political) action, because it is action in accordance with the role given one by God, may therefore be understood in terms drawn from the arts, and in particular in the language of decorum: Pope writes in the *Essay on Man*, "Act well your part, there all the honor lies" (4.194), and Bolingbroke speaks of evildoing as "depravation of *manners*." Here, finally, we may find a clue to unlock one of the deepest paradoxes running through the *Essay on Man*: although Pope understands the virtuous life to be one of active pursuit, he persistently describes it in terms that suggest stasis: "rest" and "standing still." "The only point where human bliss stands still," he tells us, is virtue; "here we can rest."[12] Right doing takes on the aspect of passivity (and immobility) because it consists finally in submission to role: thereby the self realizes its proper end, so that in virtuous *doing* the self is *being* what most truly it is.

As this account suggests, Pope's vision of the integrity of moral and political life, of the public and private realms, and indeed of art and life, rests on an understanding of the self fundamentally at odds with more modern notions of human identity. A number of recent writers have attempted to define a shift in concepts of the self that seems to have occurred in the later eighteenth century; we know that Pope and the Scriblerians spilled much ink to controvert Locke's doctrine of human identity (as continuity of consciousness, but not identity of substance), yet it remains to be explained what was their own understanding of what in the *Conjectures* Edward Young called "the stranger within thee."[13] Because the eighteenth-century shift in concepts of self is at the heart of the modern impasse in ethical theory, MacIntyre's *After Virtue* is once again of help. Dryden's Almanzor, crying before he takes up the duties of kingship, "I am myself alone," might stand as a type of the modern self (better examples are villains such as Milton's Satan, whose protestations of his independence from God sound curiously like Sartre's account of the ego). This self exists antecedently to the roles in which it may happen to find itself and so is defined by none of them; constituted not from without but only from within, it is responsible only to itself, to the rules it itself makes (hence the predicament of modern ethics). The Popean self, on the other hand, is defined from without (by providence): it is essentially constituted by its roles, and so by the moral ends (in the broadest sense of "moral") that those roles embody. MacIntyre writes of this older self:

> In many pre-modern, traditional societies it is through his or her membership in a variety of social groups that the individual identifies himself or herself and is identified by others. I am brother, cousin, and grandson, member of this household, that village, this tribe. These are not characteristics that belong to human beings accidentally, to be stripped away in order to discover "the real

me." They are part of my substance, defining partially at least and sometimes wholly my obligations and my duties. Individuals inherit a particular space within an interlocking set of social relationships; lacking that space, they are nobody, or at best a stranger or an outcast.[14]

Pope explains his major premise in epistle 3 of *An Essay on Man* ("Of the Nature and State of Man with respect to Society"): "*Nothing made wholly for* itself, *nor yet made wholly for* another" (Argument). They are dunces who

> Find Virtue local, all Relation scorn,
> See all in *Self*, and but for self be born;

Dulness triumphs as her wizard extends a cup

> which whoso tastes, forgets his former friends,
> Sire, Ancestors, Himself

—the roles that constitute their very nature, and the aspects under which Pope celebrates himself in the *Epistle to Arbuthnot* (*Dunciad*, 4.479–80; 518–19). The completest dunce is the modern self (the Rousseau of the *Confessions*, perhaps); he is like Atossa in the *Epistle to a Lady*, who is "scarce once herself," and so whose ironic reward for such feigned existential independence is to grow "sick of herself thro' very selfishness" (lines 116, 146).

The Popean self is simultaneously responsible to all the roles it inhabits ("Kings, they must never forget that they are men; men, they must never forget that they are kings"); hence its integrity across all those departments of life that we would sever. Moreover, because the realization of these ends is not a single act but a *process* that must unfold over time, the virtuous life has not only wholeness but shape—a narrative shape comprised of and comprehending beginning, middle, and end.[15] Hence Pope's persistent analogizing of a well-lived life to a well-constructed work of art (especially a drama), most clearly visible in his "Epistle to Miss Blount, with the Works of Voiture" (1712). Clarissa echoes this poem when, in the speech Pope added to the final canto of *The Rape of the Lock*, she counsels Belinda to enact a role—marriage—more likely than that of the character she has been personating to lend meaning and shape to the whole of her life (and death). The narrative of such a life is marked by continuity through all its stages: in both poems about women, it is the virtue of "good humor," the artful rendering of and acquiescence in role, that enables such continuity. For Miss Blount in the "Epistle,"

> *Good Humour* only teaches Charms to last.
> Still makes new Conquests, and maintains the past,
> (Lines 61–62)

as in the *Epistle to a Lady* it is her "Temper" that "can make to morrow chearful as to day" (lines 257–58). Pope again calls upon the telling rhyme of *past* with *last*, implying continuity and fulfillment, at the end of the *Epistle to Cobham*:

> And you! Brave COBHAM, to the latest breath
> Shall feel your ruling passion strong in death:
> Such in those moments as in all the past,
> "Oh, save my Country, Heav'n!" shall be your last.
> (Lines 262–65)[6]

Addison's death scene, as Young understands it, perfects the drama of his life—as in another way did Pope's own, attended by the deist Bolingbroke, parson (not yet Bishop) Warburton, and the Catholic priest Pope requested to administer the last sacrament.

Art and life, the public and the private, the corporate and the personal are continuous for the Popean self because the roles in which each is embodied—poet and gentleman, moralist and friend, citizen and son—form a hierarchy of ends. These, in turn, are harmonized in the hierarchic structure of the (providentially ordered) polity, so that the narrative enactments not only of individual lives but also of groups—marriage, we recall, is a social state—join to form the larger narrative of social life:

> Heav'n forming each on other to depend,
> A master, or a servant, or a friend,
> Bids each on other for assistance call,
> 'Till one Man's weakness grows the strength of all.
> Wants, frailties, passions, closer still ally
> The common int'rest, or endear the tie.
> —*An Essay on Man*, 2.249–59

But it is at this point in Pope's argument, perhaps, that common sense begins to rebel: whatever the merits of Pope's teleological account of the narratives of individual lives, we may say, his notions of the way these are harmonized in larger social wholes do not describe the world as we know it. Yet we should understand that our complaint has its place in the history of the ethical theory Pope has outlined. It was the very understanding of duties as resident in roles and of virtues as the narrative enactment of these roles, that later in the eighteenth century, as visions of the nature of the social order changed, was to fragment the realms Pope was able to join—and in the process to give birth to the modern, autonomous self.

"Every individual is distinguished by his calling," writes Adam Ferguson, "and has a place to which he is fitted"; but Ferguson writes not of those social (and socializing) callings that Pope had understood to comprise the fundamental divisions of the polity, but in a chapter of his *Essay on the History of Civil Society* (1767) entitled "Of the Separation of Arts and Professions."[17] For Pope, our callings are harmonized within a hierarchy of roles whose fundamental unity is (in the broadest sense) political:

> 'Twas then, the studious head or gen'rous mind,
> Follow'r of God or friend of human-kind,
> Poet or Patriot, rose but to restore
> The Faith and Moral, Nature gave before;
> . . . .
> Taught Pow'r's due use to People and to Kings,
> . . . .
> 'Till jarring int'rests of themselves create
> Th'according music of a well-mix'd State.
> Such is the World's great harmony.
> —*An Essay on Man*, 3.283–95

Meanwhile, however, social theorists from Mandeville onward had become increasingly aware of the extraordinary proliferation of specialized occupations by which the nation's work was done. In the opening chapter of *The Wealth of Nations* (1776), just after his famous account of "the important business of making a pin," Adam Smith writes eloquently of other trades, closer to the heart of the nation:

> How many different trades are employed in each branch of the linen and woollen manufactures, from the growers of the flax to the bleachers and smoothers of the linen, or to the dyers and dressers of the cloth! . . . (The woollen coat, for example, which covers the day-labourer, as coarse and rough as it may appear, is the produce of the joint labour of a great multitude of workmen. The shepherd, the sorter of the wool, the woolcomber or carder, the dyer, the scribbler, the spinner, the weaver, the fuller, the dresser, with many others, must all join their different arts in order to complete even his homely production.[18]

(Even "thinking itself, in this age of separations, may become a peculiar craft," notes Ferguson in a passage that heralds the nineteenth-century invention of the "intellectual.")[19] It was becoming apparent that the fundamental divisions of society were less the traditional estates than the division of labor, resulting in a shift, as John Barrell has recently shown in detail, from a political to a fundamentally economic conception of the "well-mix't State."[20]

The blow to traditional accounts of duty and of the self was devastating. The spinner, the weaver, and the fuller rarely see beyond their own occupations to the economic whole of which they are parts: the hand that guides commerce is, as Smith put it, invisible. Where labor is not yet divided, Smith claims, "Every man . . . is in some measure a statesman, and can form a tolerable judgment concerning the interest of society, and the conduct of those who govern it"; but, as Ferguson warns, "under the *distinction* of callings . . . society is made to consist of parts, of which none is animated with the spirit of society itself"; "men cease to be citizens."[21] In other words, occupations such as spinning, weaving, and fulling have become primary roles, but these roles (and the ends they embody) do not form a hierarchy that is intelligible to the agents themselves. Nor, indeed, is it possible to extract any very comprehensive notion of duty from such roles: certainly none whose narrative enactment can give shape and meaning to the whole of a life. Barrell cites Hazlitt's criticism of a social model that conceives economic roles as primary in an essay on "The New School of Reform" (1826): "This is their *idea of a perfect commonwealth*: where each member performs his part in the machine, taking care of himself, and no more concerned about his neighbours, than the iron and wood-work, the pegs and nails in a spinning-jenny. Good screw! good wedge! good ten-penny nail!"[22]

Occupational roles cannot connect the world of work with the worlds of the personal or private, or with the larger world of the citizen: they do not define the whole self. Predictably—because, as MacIntyre puts it, "every philosophy presupposes a sociology"—the effects of defining such roles as primary can be felt in a broad sample of subsequent literature and life. It was because these roles left so much of life unguided that the late eighteenth and early nineteenth centuries labored so energetically (and so fruitlessly) to impose further moral education on "the worker." At the other end of the social scale, because it redefined managerial roles, the new theory of society entailed a crisis in concepts of moral leadership. Fiction yields up such revealing characters as that splendid embodiment of role detached from informing hierarchy, Josiah Bounderby of Coketown (from Charles Dickens' *Hard Times*). So thoroughly has Bounderby severed the corporate from the personal that he has falsified the story of his origins and upbringing; to solidify his identity as a "self-made man" (a modern self), he thus recreates Pope's dunce, who "forgets his former friends, / Sire, Ancestors, Himself." Even the virtuous Charles Darnay of *A Tale of Two Cities*, when he enters the larger world of affairs, preserves calm in the privacy of his family by repeatedly lying to his wife—and she, we are told, subscribing to the same discontinuity of roles, does not resent but is grateful for such sequestration. It would be difficult to imagine the mistress of Pemberley accepting Lucie Manette's fragmented role, and we might contrast Dickens' perennial suspicion—even more widespread today—that there is no moral way to get rich with the ideal of magnanimous leadership Pope instances in Arthur Browne and Ralph Allen of Bath (whether the latter is described as "low-born" or "humble").[23] Those areas of life that Pope had found continuous have begun to come apart, and the (modern) self to be sought beneath or beyond them—often precisely by becoming "a stranger or an outcast," like John Harmon in *Our Mutual Friend*, or like Arnold's scholar-gypsy.

Finally, however, even the recognition that we come to Pope encumbered by beliefs about self and society different from his cannot lay to rest our earlier suspicion that his picture of the "well-mix't State" is altogether too cheerful. There is ample evidence that Pope himself shared this suspicion. I do not mean merely to point out the (important) fact that the same poet who sang, "Whatever is, IS RIGHT," spent most of his career battling perceived wrongs. Rather, I would argue that it is only when he is writing most programmatically, and especially, as in the *Essay on Man*, when under the influence of "the greatest man in the world" (Lord Bolingbroke), that Pope's vision of the polity becomes utopian.[24]

The Craftsman taught Pope and other Opposition writers of the 1720s and 1730s that where the form of the ancient constitution is realized, there can be no "faction," for political parties exist only to represent divergent interests, and all interests are harmonized in the hierarchic structure of the ideal state. Bolingbroke believed that the differences that spawned Whig and Tory had long since played themselves out (been harmonized), so that the real division that remained was between a corrupt court—Walpole's administration, countenanced by the king—and the country party, the true English interest; the Opposition platform, therefore, was somehow to oust Walpole in favor of "disinterested" public leaders (i.e., a government of their own party). Not only, then, is the problem of political reform not institutional but moral; it also reduces to the problem of moral leadership. Once exemplary moral leaders come to power, all else will follow. As Pope read in Bolingbroke's longest reform tract, *The Idea of a Patriot King* (a work he valued so highly as secretly to have printed, at his own expense),

> As soon as corruption cease to be an expedient of government, and it will cease to be such as soon as a Patriot King is raised to the throne, the panacea is applied; the spirit of the constitution revives of course; and, as fast as it revives, the orders and forms of the constitution are restored to their primitive integrity, and become what they were intended to be . . . . Under him [the people] will not only cease to do evil, but learn to do well; for by rendering public virtue and real capacity the sole means of acquiring any degree of power or profit in the state, he will set the passions of their hearts on the side of liberty and good government. A Patriot King is the most powerful of all reformers.
>
> —Bolingbroke, 3:75

Such views are utopian in that they ignore the real problems of getting and keeping power. They ignore the realities of wielding power even for good in a world of tragic moral choices, choices that must necessarily be sometimes between evils. (It is surely no accident that so many of Pope's—and Swift's— ideal statesmen were either retired or out of office.) Bolingbroke's Patriot King cuts through all these difficulties by the sheer force of his moral example: "The sure effects of his appearance will be admiration and love in every honest breast, confusion and terror to every guilty conscience, but submission and resignation in all. A new people will seem to arise with a new king. Innumerable metamorphoses, like those which poets feign, will happen in very deed: and while men are conscious that they are the same individuals, the difference of their sentiments will almost persuade them that they are changed into different beings" (Bolingbroke, 3:75). Rarely has the language of politics risen so close to that of religious conversion—"statecraft as soulcraft," in George Will's phrase. It is this strain in Bolingbroke, and in Pope at his most programmatic— the belief in an organic society and in the infinite perfectibility of human nature—that has so endeared them to recent Marxist students of the period, such as Kramnick, Raymond Williams, and E. P. Thompson. (It was said of an earlier generation of critics that they succumbed to the Tory ideology of the writers they studied; the observation now applies better to critics from the left than from the right.) But we should not suppose that anything like Bolingbroke's extreme views constitute Pope's ordinary stance: the *Dunciad* alone teaches us otherwise. When Swift sought the ideal polity, he looked not to Europe but to imaginary lands peopled by giants or horses; Pope, at the center of Opposition efforts for political reform, looked to England but shared all Swift's distrust of human princes. Torn between programmatic ideals and recalcitrant facts, Pope chose to accept both—resulting, as Irvin Ehrenpreis has shown, in a recurrent tension in his poems between high-minded precepts and subversive examples.[25] This poetry calls for the combined intellectual and moral efforts of active readers, that they may first understand, then seek to bridge such gaps.

Having been warned against too ready an assimilation of a Tory vision of society, we must not then simply turn about and become Whigs: both the history of ethical thought and the posture of subsequent poets such as Edward Young suggest that there is no way but Pope's to integrate political fact with moral principle, the private with the public, art with life. Explicit political content, as has often been recognized, is strikingly absent from most of the major poetry produced in the generation after Pope's death. John Sitter has written of such poets as Akenside, the Wartons, and Young: "For what begins to replace the opposition literary contract is a new agreement with the reader in which poetry will be opposed not to a particular politics but (ostensibly) to all politics. Such a shift dramatically restricts the province of poetry while at the same time severely limiting the legitimacy of political or economic activity as a theater for any sort of ambition on the part of the intellectual or artist." (He wisely adds, however, that "the very calls to depoliticize poetry and to lift it 'above' the conflicts of modern history constitute a new politicization of poetry"; Young's way of divorcing politics from poetry corresponds in important respects with the assumptions of the new economic model of the polity.)[26] Both in the *Conjectures on Original Composition* and in his poetic reply to Pope's *Essay on Man, Night Thoughts* ("Man, too, he sung; *immortal* man I sing"), Young advances a program of escape: escape not only from politics, but also from all the entanglements of the self with its worldly roles—from all those realms in which Pope had sought continuity, and so, from Pope's point of view, from the self itself.[27] And just as Pope had posited a reader active in recognizing discontinuity and in seeking to achieve an integrity of self with role, Young's ideal reader, whose aim is fundamentally a state of self-forgetfulness, is essentially passive. In the *Conjectures* Young contrasts the effects of epic, whose learned thoughtfulness returns us to ourselves, with those of the higher genre of tragedy: "Let epic poets think; the tragedian's point is rather to feel. . . . As what comes from the writer's heart reaches ours; so what comes from his head sets our brains at work, and our hearts at ease. It makes a circle of thoughtful critics, not of distressed patients; and a passive audience is what tragedy requires" (Young, 2: 574–75).[28] Half a century later, when Wordsworth argued for a more active conception of the reader's role, it was this view of literary response, not Pope's, to which he was objecting.[29]

Young in fact envisions two modes of self-forgetfulness, corresponding to what for him are the two major divisions of poetry: "original" and "moral" poetry. The distinction may be traced to Joseph Warton's between the didactic poetry of wit (including satire) and the "pure" poetry of nature (and finally, indeed, to Pope's own report in the *Epistle to Arbuthnot*, "That not in Fancy's Maze he wander'd long, / But stoop'd to Truth, and moraliz'd his song").[30] The *Conjectures on Original Composition*, as its title implies, concerns itself mainly with the former; Young announces at the start: "You may remember that your worthy patron, and our common friend, put some questions on the serious drama, at the same time that he desired our sentiments on original and on moral composition. . . . I begin with original composition" (Young, 2:549). Even Addison's own compositions (with the possible exception of his death) qualify not as original but moral, as Young promises to explain in a further letter (never written): "P.S. How far Addison is an original, you will see in my next; where I descend from this consecrated ground into his sublunary praise: and great is the descent, though in to heights of intellectual power" (2:584). The primary function of original composition is escape: "To men of letters and leisure, it is not only a noble amusement, but a sweet refuge; . . . it opens a back-door out of the bustle of this busy and idle world, into a delicious garden" (2:550). Its tools are "liveliness" and, of course, "novelty,"[31] both of which "capture" and "engross the attention," a faculty of judgment whose otherwise unimpeded operation, as Young and his contemporaries conceived it, arrests the train of imagination, waking the mind from poetic "reverie" or "ideal presence."[32] Together, these means detach us from our ordinary "interests," inducing instead a state of self-forgetfulness:

> We read imitation with somewhat of his languor who listens to a twice-told tale: our spirits rouse at an original: that is a perfect stranger, and all throng to learn what news from a foreign land: and though it comes, like an Indian prince, adorned with feathers only, having little of weight, yet of our attention it will rob the more solid, if not equally new. . . . If an original, by being as

excellent as new, adds admiration to surprise, then we are at the writer's mercy; on the strong wing of his imagination we are snatched from Britain to Italy, from climate to climate, from pleasure to pleasure; we have no home, no thought, of our own, till the magician drops his pen; and then, falling down into ourselves, we awake to flat realities, lamenting the change, like the beggar who dreamt himself a prince.

—Young, 2:552

(Original composition comes as "a perfect stranger" because in writing it, the author has consulted his truest self, "the stranger within.") Young's theory of our response to original composition, then, is a step on the way to the consolidation of that bulwark of the separation of art from life, the concept of "aesthetic disinterestedness,"[33] and so also toward the theory of art as an escape from Schopenhauerian will.

Young has little to say in the *Conjectures* (except negatively) about "moral" composition, but guided by his admission there that his own poems are of this kind, we may look to his earlier *Night Thoughts* (1741–46) for some account of moral composition's assumptions and intended effects. What we find is a variant of the previous account, a theory of literature as the vehicle of a specifically Christian escapism. Here the soul is deliberately led to look inward, in order to disentangle itself from all merely worldly (and hence false) roles, and so to uncover its true self, whose home is in eternity. (In moral composition, the dreaming beggar really is a prince.)

Night 1 is explicitly modeled on the georgic or "survey" procedure of the *Essay on Man*, but Young posits such a radical discontinuity between the temporal and the spiritual, the world without and the truth within, that all Pope's sources of vision are obstructed. We live, "prisoners of earth," in "an opaque of Nature and of soul," a fractured world of unintelligible changes whose recalcitrant parts frustrate all efforts to find wholeness. In a brilliant variant of the common Augustan conflation of the categories of space and time, Young conveys this sense of fragmentation by describing the temporal realm as broken into discrete, atomic "moments": "Time is dealt out by particles"; "Each Moment has its sickle, emulous / Of Time's enormous scythe"; we are each "moment's prey," awaiting a time when "momentary ages are no more."[34] Such atomized experience yields nothing to Popean survey:

> How dim our eye!
> The present moment terminates our sight;
> Clouds, thick as those on doomsday, drown the next;
> We penetrate, we prophesy in vain.
>
> (Lines 363–66)

"All, all on earth is shadow, all beyond / Is substance," and no georgic can connect the two, or lead us to knowledge of that realm of wholeness "where change shall be no more" (lines 120–22). The solution is to look not to nature or to history, but directly at divine substance—that is, to look within. The poet exhorts Lorenzo in *Night* 9:

> Look inward, and look deep, and deeper still;
> Unfathomably deep our treasure runs
> In golden veins through all eternity!
> (Lines 425–27)

Night 1 opens with an apostrophe to Sleep and a discussion of dreams, dreams that, as Young recounts them, sound very much like the lyric "original compositions" of his Miltonizing contemporaries:

> While o'er my limbs Sleep's soft dominion spread,
> What though my soul fantastic measures trod
> O'er fairy fields; or mourn'd along the gloom
> Of pathless woods; or, down the craggy steep
> Hurl'd headlong, swam with pain the mantled pool;
> Or scaled the cliff; or danced on hollow winds,
> With antic shapes, wild natives of the brain?
> (Lines 92–98)

Original compositions abet escape; here, in the form of dreams, they are an earnest of the soul's escape from its fragmented worldly self to its true otherworldly wholeness. The dreaming mind's

> Ceaseless flight, though devious, speaks her nature
> Of subtler essence than the trodden clod;
> Active, aerial, towering, unconfined,
> Unfetter'd with her gross companion's fall.
> (Lines 99–102)[35]

"Dull sleep instructs, nor sport vain dreams in vain"; the obvious reversal follows: if "all on earth is shadow," then the roles in which the worldly self is "confined" are mere dream; "*Night* visions may befriend," but "Our *waking* dreams are fatal" (lines 106, 163–64). In later books of the poem, as Young makes clearer his religious intentions, conversion takes the place of dream as the chief mode of Christian escape from the world to the true self. By day, the poet tells Lorenzo in *Night* 5, the world's "gaudy scenes . . . thrust between us and ourselves," but nocturnal meditation "strikes the thought inward; it drives back the soul / To settle on herself, our point supreme" (lines 311–12, 129–30). To the converted (whole) soul, and to it alone, is wholeness revealed. As a result, georgic survey is possible for Young, but it proceeds in a manner opposite to Pope's. Instead of "looking thro' Nature, up to Nature's God," Young argues that "Wisdom for parts is madness for the whole"; "To read

creation," we must "read its mighty plan / In the bare bosom of the Deity"—
we must, that is, first read ourselves.[36] In *Night* 9 the poet has reached a
spiritual state wherein finally he can achieve the georgic that earlier eluded
him. Dismissing that fallen vision that "makes a universe an orrery," "no
meet apartment for the DEITY"—dismissing, that is, the methods of Popean
survey—Young proceeds to his own rapturous inventory of universal harmon-
ies: "new-awaked, I lift / A more enlighten'd eye, and read the stars."[37]

The difference between Young's survey and Pope's is perhaps best described as one of degree: of the degree to which each poet supposes God's
ordering will to be immanent in nature and society, the spiritual in the
temporal.[38] For Young, the two realms are so discontinuous that only by
renouncing the temporal can their connection be seen: one must lose the world
in order to find it, and so too of the self. (Thus his rather trite repertory of
Pauline paradoxes, such as "Revere thyself,—and yet thyself despise" 6.128).
Moral knowledge comes in the sudden illumination that is conversion. But
such knowledge brings with it no implications for political behavior: Young
comes no closer to politics in *Night Thoughts* than to say that conversion teaches
us "to know how much need not be known" (5.738) and that "Religion,
public order, both exact / External homage, and a supple knee" (6.293–94).
As in the economic model of the polity, the issue of citizenship does not arise.
But for Pope, on the other hand, the spiritual is immanently present just
beneath the surface of ordinary life, and so, just as natural philosophy finds
its perfection in physico-theology, the moral agent finds his true self in
society—not beyond but within his worldly roles. The hierarchic order of
society is thus for Pope a repository of moral value, a hierarchy of ends that
we must realize in ourselves if we are to actualize our proper narratives.

As such language suggests, we compose our narratives—our selves—
through moral *art*: by learning to adapt means to ends. In this way *decorum*
becomes for Pope the name for all those rules of conduct that govern us in
the moral as in the aesthetic realm. Decorums are "rules" in the sense explained
in the *Essay on Criticism*, specifications of means useful in achieving given ends.
In both life and art, "Just *Precepts* [are] from great *Examples* giv'n," and in
both realms, because of the continuity of the temporal with the spiritual, we
draw from such "great *Examples* . . . what they deriv'd from *Heav'n*" (lines
98–99). Learning, in Pope's view, comes not by sudden illumination but
through the slow accretion of partial insights, and literature itself contributes
to our moral education in part by telling and showing (in its didactic and
narrative modes, respectively) what adaptations of means to ends are available
to us.[39] And in both art and life, finally, our learning proceeds by imitation.
Young's concept of imitation, uprooted from those systems of belief (like
Pope's) that gave it meaning, is hopelessly impoverished: it is really no
more than a name for aspiration. His advice that writers "imitate not the
composition, but the man" gives no hint, no rules about how this is to be
done, just as Bolingbroke's account of political reformation as a kind of

conversion leaves us ignorant of how the feat is to be accomplished. For Pope, however, imitation is nothing less than, in David Morris's words, "a mode of learning—a source of knowledge."[40] It is the process by which we learn to realize ourselves as well as our works, that by which integrity is made possible both in life and in death. "Oh let me die his death!" cries the bewildered soul in *Night* 5 (lines 367–68), awed by the last moments of the "good man"; to which Young replies: "Then live his life."

Notes

1. Edward Young, *The Complete Works, Poetry and Prose* (London, 1834), 2:583. All quotations from Young are from this edition.
2. See Nancy Lee Beaty, *The Craft of Dying: The Literary Tradition of the "Ars Moriendi" in England* (New Haven, Conn., 1970).
3. Alasdair MacIntyre, *After Virtue: A Study in Moral Theory* (Notre Dame, Ind., 1981), p. 191.
4. The word "aesthetics" was coined by Alexander Baumgarten in 1735. The best account of the emergence in the seventeenth and eighteenth centuries of the aesthetic as a new category of thought remains Paul O. Kristeller, "The Modern System of the Arts," in *Renaissance Thought II: Papers on Humanism and the Arts* (New York, 1965), pp. 163–227.
5. Alexander Pope, *An Essay on Criticism*, lines 560, 724. All quotations from Pope are taken from *The Poems of Alexander Pope*, ed. John Butt et al. (New Haven, Conn., 1963).
6. See J.H. van den Berg, *The Changing Nature of Man: Introduction to a Historical Psychology* (New York, 1961). Pope writes in *An Essay on Man* (4.175): "The Boy and Man an Individual Makes, while according to Keats in the preface to *Endymion*, "The imagination of the boy is healthy; but there is a space of life between, in which the soul is in a ferment, the character undecided."
7. See Mark Girouard, *Life in the English Country House: A Social and Architectural History* (New Haven, Conn., 1978), chap. 5; and Peter Thornton, *Seventeenth-Century Interior Decoration in England, France, and Holland* (New Haven, Conn., 1978), chap. 7.
8. On the history of distinctions between public and private realms, see Alan F. Westin, "Privacy in Western History: From the Age of Pericles to the American Republic" (Ph.D. diss., Harvard University, 1965); and Barrington Moore, Jr., *Privacy: Studies in Social and Cultural History* (New York, 1984). According to Moore, "With us the concept of private life denotes an existence apart from and to some extent in opposition to current political and social concerns, a sphere of personal autonomy," whereas, for instance, "the [ancient] Athenians did not believe in this kind of bracketing-off of certain aspects of private behavior," their "words for private conveying some hint of the antisocial" (pp. 117, 154, 275).
9. See Isaac Kramnick, *Bolingbroke and His Circle: The Politics of Nostalgia in the Age of Walpole* (Cambridge, Mass., 1968); and Brean S. Hammond, *Pope and Bolingbroke: A Study of Friendship and Influence* (Columbia, Mo., 1984).
10. In *The Works of the Late Right Honourable Henry St. John, Lord Viscount Bolingbroke* (Dublin, 1794), 3:120. All quotations from Bolingbroke are from this work.
11. Hammond gives a detailed account of the meaning of "corruption" in Bolingbroke's political vocabulary (pp. 129–36); for the larger meaning and conceptual context of the term, see my *Probability and Literary Form: Philosophic Theory and Literary Practice in the Augustan Age* (Cambridge, 1984), pp. 114, 308.
12. Pope, *An Essay on Man*, 4.311; 3.1; see also 4.42, 166.

13. Young (n. 1 above), 2:564. The most notable contributions to this growing literature include Patricia Spacks, *Imagining a Self* (Cambridge, Mass., 1976); John O. Lyons, *The Invention of the Self* (Carbondale, Ill., 1978); Stephen D. Cox, *"The Stranger within Thee": Concepts of the Self in Late-Eighteenth-Century Literature* (Pittsburgh, 1980); Christopher Fox, "Locke and the Scriblerians: The Discussion of Identity in Early Eighteenth Century England," *Eighteenth-Century Studies* 16 (1982): 1–25; and, most recently, two studies whose conclusions parallel my own, Ann Hartle, *The Modern Self in Rousseau's "Confessions": A Reply to St. Augustine* (Notre Dame, Ind., 1984), and Geoffrey Thurley, *The Romantic Predicament* (New York, 1984), chap. 5.

14. MacIntyre, p. 32.

15. If the identity of the self is essentially narrative, then particular states of the soul will yield recognizable narrative patterns in ordinary life. I have examined several versions of one such pattern in " 'Love Deny'd': Pope and the Allegory of Despair," forthcoming this year in *Eighteenth-Century Studies*.

16. In the *Epistle to Arbuthnot*, using the same rhyme, Pope makes clear that it is virtuous action that enables such continuity and fulfillment: "Welcome for thee, fair Virtue! all the past! / For thee, fair Virtue! welcome ev'n the *last*!" (lines 358–59).

17. Adam Ferguson, *An Essay on the History of Civil Society*, ed. Louis Schneider (London, 1980), p. 181.

18. Adam Smith, *The Wealth of Nations*, ed. R. H. Campbell, A. S. Skinner, and W. B. Todd (Oxford, 1976), p. 181.

19. Ferguson, p. 183; for the nineteenth century, see most recently T. W. Heyck, *The Transformation of Intellectual Life in Victorian Britain* (New York, 1982).

20. See John Barrell, *English Literature in History 1730–80: An Equal, Wide Survey* (New York, 1984), chap. 1, whose argument I follow closely here.

21. Smith, p. 783; Ferguson, p. 218.

22. Quoted in Barrell, p. 31.

23. Pope is perhaps the last great English poet in whom we find "the unabashed celebration of wealth—not just spiritual wealth, but material" (Aristotle's "magnificence"), as Geoffrey Thurley (n. 13 above) suggests, pp. 96–97.

24. "I have lately seen some writings of Lord B's, since he went to France," Pope writes to Swift on March 25, 1736; "Nothing can depress his Genius: Whatever befals him, he will still be the greatest man in the world, either in his own time, or with posterity" (*The Correspondence of Alexander Pope*, ed. George Sherburn [Oxford, 1956], 4:6; cf. Pope to Jonathan Richardson, 3:326). Brean Hammond mounts a strong case, based on both external and internal evidence, for the now unfashionable view that the *Essay on Man* began as a versification of Bolingbroke's philosophy (n. 9 above), chap. 5.

25. See Irvin Ehrenpreis, "Pope: Bipolar Implication," in *Acts of Implication: Suggestion and Covert Meaning in the Works of Dryden, Swift, Pope, and Austen* (Berkeley and Los Angeles, 1981), chap. 3.

26. John Sitter, *Literary Loneliness in Mid-Eighteenth-Century England* (Ithaca, N.Y., 1982), pp. 108, 107.

27. For a different view of *Night Thoughts* as a reply to Pope, see Daniel W. Odell, "Young's *Night Thoughts* as an Answer to Pope's *Essay on Man*," *Studies in English Literature* 12 (1972): 481–501.

28. Young's theory of the passive audience is also partly the result of contemporary Theories of the passions, which were understood in Cartesian fashion to be states in which the mind is not active but acted upon; see, e.g., George Taylor, " 'The Just Delineation of the Passions': Theories of Acting in the Age of Garrick," in *The Eighteenth-Century Stage*, ed. K. Richards and P. Thomson (London, 1972), pp. 51–72.

29. For a sensitive account of Wordsworth's attempt to "renegotiate the contract between writer and reader," though one that muddies the historical background of that effort,

see Clifford Siskin, "Wordsworth's Attentive Reader" (Ph.D. diss., University of Virginia, 1978).

30.   Joseph Warton, *An Essay on the Genius and Writings of Pope* (London, 1756), dedication; Pope, *Epistle to Arbuthnot*, lines 339–40.

31.   "Novelty" is one of course the chief ingredient of "originality" itself, but readers of the *Conjectures* have not been careful to ascertain precisely what this term means in the essay. By "originality" itself—as opposed to the capacity for it, original *genius*—Young means simply finding new material to put in old forms, and he explicitly disavows any "burden of the past" resulting from so many materials having become already the subjects of verse: "Why are originals so few? Not because the writer's harvest is over, the great reapers of antiquity having left nothing to be gleaned after them." Thus he advises, "Let us build our compositions with the spirit, and in the taste, of the ancients; but not with their materials" (2:553, 555). Progress, in Young's view, in poetry as in science, is the bringing of new materials into established forms. Thus, although not yet fully possessed of the modern distinction between the arts and the sciences (itself a product of the dispute between the ancients and the moderns), Young believes that the "arts mechanic are in perpetual progress and increase, [while] the liberal are in retrogradation and decay" because the former (like "broadening rivers") continue to conquer new territory ("fresh untrodden ground"), while the latter remain satisfied to walk only in familiar paths (2:561). Like so many other Augustan critics, Young will therefore recommend that poets turn for original material to the discoveries of science: "Consider, my friend, knowledge physical, mathematical, moral, and Divine, increases; all arts and sciences are making considerable advance . . . and these are new food to the genius of the polite writer" (2:571); compare this, for example, with John Aikin, *An Essay on the Application of Natural History to Poetry* (London, 1777).

32.   This is a reversal of earlier Augustan theories of the role of attention in reading and should be understood in connection with Young's account of the passive audience; for an extreme statement of Young's position, see Archibald Alison, *Essays on the Nature and Principles of Taste* (Edinburgh, 1790), pp. 8–14.

33.   On the development of this concept in the eighteenth century, see Jerome Stolnitz, "On the Origins of Aesthetic Disinterestedness," *Journal of Aesthetics and Art Criticism* 20 (1961): 131–43. This is of course a concept that Pope would not have understood (or would have consigned, with other duncical divisions, to Dulness); for its classic modern refutation, see George Dickie, "The Myth of the Aesthetic Attitude," *American Philosophical Quarterly* 1 (1964): 56–65.

34.   *Night Thoughts*, 1.367, 193–95, 359, 144. (*Night Thoughts* is quoted by book and line number.) For the background of this procedure, see Ralph Cohen, "The Augustan Mode in English Poetry," *Eighteenth-Century Studies* 1 (1967): 3–32; and Louis T. Milic, "The Metaphor of Time as Space," in *Probability, Time and Space in Eighteenth-Century Literature*, ed. Paula Backscheider (New York, 1979), pp. 249–58.

35.   Compare Young's argument in *Night* 5: "By day the soul is passive, all her thoughts / Imposed, precarious, broken, ere mature. / By night, from objects free, from passions cool, / Thoughts uncontroll'd and unimpress'd, the births / Of pure election, arbitrary range" (lines 118–22).

36.   Pope, *Essay on Man*, 4.322; Young, *Night Thoughts*, 6.385, 96–97.

37.   *Night Thoughts*, 9.789, 785, 1303–4.

38.   See Mary Poovey's comparison, on the same grounds, of the novelistic worlds of Fielding and Richardson: "Journeys from This World to the Next: The Providential Promise in *Clarissa* and *Tom Jones*," *ELH* 43 (1976): 300–315.

39.   Modern philosophers have returned to Pope's view of literature's instructive function; see, e.g. MacIntyre (n. 3 above), p. 201, and Hilary Putnam, "Literature, Science, and Reflection," in *Meaning and the Moral Sciences* (London, 1978), pp. 83–94.

40.   David Morris, *Alexander Pope: The Genius of Sense* (Cambridge, Mass., 1984), p. 6.

Index

♦